Britain's Medieval Episcopal Thrones

Britain's Medieval Episcopal Thrones

History, Archaeology and Conservation

Charles Tracy

with a chapter by
Andrew Budge

and contributions by
Hugh Harrison, Peter Ferguson, Paul Woodfield,
Eddie Sinclair, Christopher Paterson and John Allan

Oxbow Books
Oxford & Philadelphia

Published in the United Kingdom in 2015 by
OXBOW BOOKS
10 Hythe Bridge Street, Oxford OX1 2EW

and in the United States by
OXBOW BOOKS
908 Darby Road, Havertown, PA 19083

Hardcover Edition: ISBN 978-1-78297-782-7
Digital Edition: ISBN 978-1-78297-783-4

A CIP record for this book is available from the British Library

Library of Congress Cataloging-in-Publication Data

Tracy, Charles, 1938-
 Britain's medieval episcopal thrones : history, archaeology and conservation / Charles Tracy ; with a chapter by Andrew Budge and contributions by Hugh Harrison [and 5 others].
   pages cm
 Includes bibliographical references and index.
  ISBN 978-1-78297-782-7 (hatdcover edition) -- ISBN 978-1-78297-783-4 (digital edition) 1. Christian antiquities--Great Britain. 2. Chairs (Cathedra)--Great Britain. 3. Thrones--Great Britain. 4. Great Britain--Antiquities. 5. Great Britain--Church history. I. Budge, Andrew. II. Title.
  BR133.G61T73 2015
  274.2'03--dc23
                         2014044978

Printed and bound in the United Kingdom by Short Run Press, Exeter

For a complete list of Oxbow titles, please contact:

UNITED KINGDOM
Oxbow Books
Telephone (01865) 241249, Fax (01865) 794449
Email: oxbow@oxbowbooks.com
www.oxbowbooks.com

UNITED STATES OF AMERICA
Oxbow Books
Telephone (800) 791-9354, Fax (610) 853-9146
Email: queries@casemateacademic.com
www.casemateacademic.com/oxbow

Oxbow Books is part of the Casemate Group

MARC FITCH FUND

Front cover: Exeter Cathedral bishop's throne from north-east. G. Young
Back cover: St Davids Cathedral bishop's throne from north-west. A. Budge

Contents

Acknowledgements

Above all, I owe a debt of thanks to my fellow contributors, who have added so much value to the project. The essence was distilled at Exeter, and nurtured by John Allan, the cathedral consultant archaeologist, and Conrad Donaldson, chairman of the Friends, who funded a forensic study of their throne, unquestionably the finest in Europe. At the same time, the dean and chapter at St Davids Cathedral lent their support for a similar appraisal of their own remarkable monument. At Wells, prebendary Elsa van der Zee and the Friends of the cathedral funded the photogrammetric ground survey by The Downland Partnership Ltd. Such a positive response from these institutions was encouraging. All of the participating cathedrals, including Hereford, Lincoln and Durham, have put themselves out to facilitate our work, and generously agreeing to waive any photography fees. The publishers, Franco Cosimo Panini Editore, kindly sanctioned the copying of two figures from the recent monograph on the church of S. Francesco, Assisi. Finally, I would like to acknowledge the invaluable assistance received from Adrian James, the Assistant Librarian at the Society of Antiquaries.

We have greatly benefitted from the specialist knowledge of many colleagues, and independent experts, including Kevin Blockley, Anne Crawford (Archivist at Wells), John Crook, Ffiona Eaves, Wyn Evans, Liv Gibbs, Catherine Hassall, Robert Higham, Rachel Howells, Simon Jervis, Ellie Jones, John Kenyon, John McNeill, Michael A. Michael, Richard Morris, Zoë Opačić, Christian Opitz, Nona Rees (Librarian and Archivist, St Davids), Warwick Rodwell, Gervase Rosser, Jerry Sampson, Diane A. Walker, Christopher Wilson, Brett Wright and, last, but by means least, has been the expert photographic contributions, particularly of Hugh Harrison, Gary Young, Martin Heider and Samuel Mather. Jane Read prepared the meticulous ground plans.

Finally, I am indebted to the Marc Fitch Fund who funded the extra photographs.

Preface

Whereas most people will probably be aware of the early-13th-century stone throne at Christ Church, Canterbury, if only from its prominent position on the cathedral chancel steps, it may come as a surprise that in Britain's medieval cathedral churches of the 14th century there survive as many as six episcopal thrones. Yet, of course, six from the 36 medieval cathedrals in England, Scotland and Wales is a lamentably low number, and, as in all medieval studies, this statistic alerts us to the dangers of over-generalisation.[1] Four of them are in oak and two in stone. They can be found at Exeter, Wells, St Davids, Hereford, Lincoln, and Durham. Apart from the chair at Lincoln, they are otherwise of monumental scale, easily exceeding the dimensions of the Italian Early-Christian bishop's chairs and the other survivals from the 1st millennium on the continent of Europe. Curiously there are no surviving British thrones from the 15th century, although a unique component of the lost *cathedra* at Llandaff will be highlighted.

Apart from the summary treatment on British medieval thrones by Francis Bond in his 1910 publication on English choir-stalls, Britain's 14th-century episcopal thrones in timber and stone have never been published as a single body of material. This contrasts with the generally greater level of bibliographical attention paid to the subject in France, Germany and Italy. The Canterbury throne, recently the subject of a painstaking historical analysis, is not featured in any great detail in this book. Its intriguing wood-panel-like sides, and its presumed relationship to contemporary medieval carpentry must remain, for the time being, an open question. With regard to the astonishing 14th-century British timber thrones studied here, at Exeter, St Davids and Hereford, the insights revealed bring these extraordinary monuments into the light for the first time.

By the turn of the 19th century, ancient episcopal thrones were much neglected and in need of repair and restoration. The Victorian architect, George Gilbert Scott (1811–1878), who was called in at different times to all three cathedrals to undertake both conservation and restoration work, is discussed in some detail. Regrettably, his impressive conservation credentials failed to carry the day with the Exeter cathedral chapter, over the proposed removal of the painted panels on the pulpitum. Otherwise he was given a more or less free hand over a sensitive restoration of the throne. On arrival at Hereford, Scott inherited a poisoned chalice from his predecessor, the architect Lewis Cottingham. In spite of Scott's well documented reservations to the pre-ordained but disastrous reordering of the choir, he had no choice but to make the most of a bad job. In the process he did his best to mitigate, as far as possible, the resulting inevitable damage to the choir-stalls. Scott's policy on conservation always showed a respect for the original design, any new work strictly building on what had been there before. Apart from his restoration work, superbly exemplified on these three great monuments, Scott's respect for the Gothic style produced a creditable record in designing neo-Gothic church furniture, notably the choir-stalls at Exeter, Salisbury and Rochester.

Given that there were no precedents, for anything architecturally comparable at this date and on this scale, either in Britain or the continent of Europe, the tiered and spiring architecture of these three massive 14th-century British timber thrones, particularly the earliest of them at Exeter, constantly begs the question with regard to the sources of both concept and design. One can only conclude that the availability of good quality oak in parts of Britain, and in the case of St Davids by sea from Ireland and even the Baltic, encouraged all three architects to take risks and experiment. This process had only recently been demonstrated on the ground-breaking choir-stalls at Winchester Cathedral, resulting in an unprecedented multi-tiered monument of considerable delicacy. Exeter's ciboriuim-like design is sometimes compared to the many fine medieval font covers found in English parish churches. Whereas they equally demonstrate the multiple design potential of the medium's tensile propensities, these 15th- and 16th-century inventions are far too late for comparative purposes. On the other hand, one could reasonably cite the mighty timber octagon at Ely, which was envisioned as little as a decade or so later, as a stylistic ancestor.

The little-known stone thrones at Wells and Durham also play their part in this line-up of distinguished British medieval church furniture. The Wells monument emerged relatively unscathed from the attentions of Anthony Salvin's restoration in the 1840s. But the efficient scraping of his workmen and the extent to which the throne was an integral part of the 14th-century redesign of the choir and presbytery ensure that the bishop's seat now melds into its surroundings. It has none of the swagger of its West-Country cousin at Exeter, nor the ebullient qualities of Edward II's tomb at Gloucester, nor yet the overwhelming profusion of the Percy monument at Beverley. The attentions of the visitor to Wells are drawn elsewhere, to the vaults, to the evocative entrance to the chapter house or to the awe-inspiring scissor-brace arches of the crossing. By contrast, the boldness of the conception of the throne at Durham is not in doubt. All bishops since Bishop Hatfield have had to climb the steps above that bishop's gaudy tomb to a seat perched high above the choir. Yet even with such hubristic intent the monument is overshadowed by the grandeur of the cathedral itself and, in terms of late 14th-century finesse, by the Neville altar screen to the east. It too remains under-explored.

For all their differences, the designs of these two stone thrones distil a raft of contemporaneous ideas, the Wells throne being a particularly confident demonstration of the motifs of the second quarter of the 14th century. They are more than mere exercises in formal ambition, their designs, if not dimensions, being closely related to those of reliquaries. Their construction and location alludes to objectives beyond the glorification of God. Together with their oak counterparts these episcopal thrones provide rich material for the examination of the competitiveness of cathedral chapters in the 14th century, of the veneration with which bishops (or at least the roles they performed) were held, of the motivations of the bishops themselves, and of the way in which architecture could be used for both political and spiritual ends.

Charles Tracy
Andrew Budge

Note
1   It is regretful that no medieval Scottish thrones survive.

CHAPTER 1

EPISCOPAL THRONES IN THE EARLY-CHRISTIAN CHURCH

1

Episcopal thrones in the Early-Christian church

For a better understanding of the origins, symbolism and functions of the episcopal throne, known as *thronus, cathedra* or *sedes episcopalis* in medieval texts,[1] here is attempted an historical, contextual, liturgical and typological rehearsal of the monument's development between *c.* 300 and *c.* 1300 AD. This introductory chapter attempts to set the scene for a discussion of the much later surviving British thrones, in wood and stone, erected at Exeter, Wells, St Davids, Hereford, Lincoln and Durham cathedrals in the High Middle Ages.

Since early times, Christ, as the incarnate Word, was shown seated on a throne and teaching his apostles. St Peter inherited Christ's mantle, and was considered to be a universal saint, the door-keeper of heaven and patron of the church and the papacy. As such he is often seen vested as pope or bishop, with or without tiara or mitre. A broad-brush account of the role of bishops in the Early-Christian diocesan administration and church liturgy – the physical context of their basilicas, and some idea of the construction and design of their thrones will follow.

Several thrones are to be found in the Roman catacombs, directly carved out of the tufa, some of which were believed to have been associated with St Peter.[2] The saint's punning name evoked the undisputed solidity of both his throne and see – thus Christ says:

> *"Tu es Petrus, et super hanc petram aedificabo Ecclesiam meam; et portae inferi non praevalebunt adversum eam"*. ("Thou are Peter and upon this rock I shall build my church, and the gates of hell shall not prevail against it").[3]

These rough stone chairs which displayed the chi-rho symbol, were in constant use in the catacombs before the Peace of the Church, for the instruction of catechumens and for officiating at the sacrament of baptism, which came later to be conducted only at Easter and Pentecost.

The tradition of synthronons

The term "synthronon" describes the seating arrangement for the clergy in Early-Christian and later-Roman basilican-style churches with apsidal east ends. It consists of two or more integral stone benches arranged on either side of a bishop's throne at its centre. St Augustine (354–430) stressed the need for a bishop's chair to be set above his clergy: "Bishops sit higher than the other priests so that they may act as the 'look-out' to keep watch over their flock".[4] This raising-up of a bishop's chair is echoed in a 4th-century frescoed and carved low-relief depiction of Christ preaching to the disciples in the catacombs (Fig. 1.2). The word *thronus* was adopted from Roman imperial usage. It can be compared to the position of a Roman judge, or president, when in session in his courthouse, with clerks and assessors on either side.[5]

The so-called Peace of the Church is reckoned from the promulgation of the Edict of Milan in 313 AD.[6] It is not until the 5th century that the general adoption of the synthronon is confirmed in a chapter of the 5th-century manuscript, the *Testamentum Domini nostri Jesu Christi*, "How to build a

Fig. 1.2 Fresco of Christ and the apostles. Cemetery of S. Hermes, Rome. Before 337. After J. Wilpert, Roma Sotteranea. Le Pitture della catacombe romane illustrate da Giuseppe Wilpert (Rome 1903), pl. 152.

Fig. 1.3 St Peter and St Paul, Gerasa, now Jarash (Syria). 6th century. View of sanctuary. By permission Royal Archaeological Institute. G. Young.

The earliest-surviving examples, excavated in the 1930s, are best preserved in Syria, for instance, at the 6th-century church of St Peter and St Paul, Gerasa. A view of the east end of this church shows the footprint of the semi-circular double-tier of raised benching, with the *cathedra* placed higher than the altar (Fig. 1.3).[10] The vestigial presbytery furnishings at Gerasa, and their former positioning, can be recognised from the stone bases and sockets in the pavement. "… immediately in front (of the *cathedra*) is a reliquary formed of a square block fixed to the floor … On its north face is a fragment of marble revetment, but there is no trace of the altar, which probably stood west of the reliquary, where the stone paving is interrupted".[11]

Another depiction of the synthronon in use can be found in the 4th-century chapel of S. Aquilino at S. Lorenzo, Milan (Fig. 1.4). As at S. Hermes, Christ is seen teaching the Apostles in the manner of an ancient orator (Fig. 1.2). Whilst in that place the apostles are accorded their individual thrones of a basic un-ornamented design, at Milan the style is impressionistic. The plain gold of the background contrasts with the naturalistic style of the seated figures, who are clearly set within a building. "The scene is modelled on the bishop and his clergy during the service, more particularly at the moment during the synaxis when the Bishop was delivering his sermon".[12] Whenever present, the latter would have been the celebrant at Mass. After the Peace of the Church, the early dioceses were much smaller than those during the second half of the millennium, and bishops often circulated around the diocese to satisfy the needs of their satellite churches and *familiae*.[13] His *cathedra* was

church", which exists only in a Syriac version.[7] It provides a graphic description of the synthronon's function:

> "And let there be the Throne towards the east; to the right and to the left places of the presbyters, so that on the right those who are more exalted and more honoured may be seated, and those who toil in the word, but those of moderate stature on the left side. And let this place of the Throne be raised three steps up for the Altar ought also to be there".[8]

The tenets of the earlier 3rd-century manuscript, *Didascalia Apostolorum*, which survives in both Syriac and western versions, confirms that, in most of the Roman churches, the use of a synthronon was probably commonplace even before the Peace of the Church.[9]

Fig. 1.4 S. Lorenzo, Milan. Chapel of S. Aquilino. Late 4th-century apse mosaic. Wikimedia Commons. Giovanni Dall'Orto.

the symbol of his teaching office and the place from which he delivered the liturgical sermon.[14]

In Early-Christian times, episcopal thrones were, usually, high-backed armed chairs of stone, which would have been draped with textiles. A variety of materials was used, such as alabaster, wood and bronze. The Roman seats of authority were associated with persons of status, rhetoricians, philosophers, magistrates and government administrators. Some thrones, such as those of St Mark at Alexandria, St James at Jerusalem, and St Peter at Antioch and, later, at Rome, were considered so venerable, that they achieved a quasi-relic status.

In the basilican churches the synthronon played a central role, irrespective of whoever was conducting the liturgy. In this, and in many other aspects of the Early Church, the insights of the respected 20th-century liturgist, Gregory Dix, are enlightening. He saw the synthronon as:

> "clearly reflected in the symbolism of the heavenly 'assembly' of the church triumphant … in the visions of the Revelation of St John … In this book everything centres upon 'the golden altar' which is

before the throne of God and the Lamb. Before it stands the multitude, … of the redeemed. And the four and twenty elders of heaven have their seats in a semi-circle around the 'great white throne of God and the Lamb', as the earthly presbyters have their seats around the white-clothed throne of the bishop".[15]

As already noted, the frescoed and mosaic semi-domes above the Early-Christian *cathedrae* usually showed a figure of Christ and the apostles. At the same time, the distinctive apocalyptic influence, referred to above, is generally recognisable, such as the images of the sacrificial Lamb of God, the Holy Spirit, and the sun and the moon. Unusually, the 9th-century apse mosaic at S. Cecilia-in-Trastevere, Rome, shows Christ blessing according to the Greek rite, between SS Peter, Valerian and Cecilia on his left and SS. Paul, Agatha and Paschal (with the square nimbus) on his right (Fig. 1.5). On this occasion the 12 Apostles are depicted as the "flock of the Faithful" underneath.

There were two distinctive types of liturgy in the Early-Christian basilicas, the synaxis, and the eucharist. The former "consisted

Fig. 1.5 S. Cecilia-in-Trastevere, Rome. Interior view with late-13th-century high altar ciborium by Arnolfo di Cambio, and 9th-century apse mosaic. Wikimedia Commons. Mari 27454.

The form and style of bishops' thrones in the East from the 4th to the 9th century

It is worth trying to distinguish between the thrones of the eastern church, inspired, ultimately, by models in Constantinople, with those in the west, which took their design from Rome.

For political reasons, some of the former are found on the mainland of Italy. The survivors are rare, but the eastern apse in the cathedral of S. Maria Assunta, Torcello, for instance, dates back to the church's foundation in 639 by the Byzantine exarch Isaac of Ravenna. Its brick synthronon, with a lofty marble bishop's *cathedra* in the centre may have survived from this period (Fig. 1.6) In fact, the Northern Adriatic is characterised by a group of these elevated episcopal thrones from as early as the late-4th century. In the northern basilica, within the excavated historic religious quarter at Concordia Sagittaria, Chromazio, near Venice, the archbishop of Aquileia consecrated the first bishop on a throne of this type.[20]

At Poreč Cathedral, Croatia, across the Adriatic from Venice, erected by Bishop Eufrasius (bp 543–554), the *cathedra* is not especially elevated.[21] The synthronon is decorated with coloured intarsia marble panels, set with semi-precious stones (Figs 1.7 and 1.8). The panels immediately behind the throne display a fictive Calvary cross, flanked by candle stands. This spectacular late-6th-century furnishing scheme, also includes a cornice of stucco work and an inlaid classical frieze, and is a continuation of the overtly Apocalyptic mosaic iconographical scheme above. It surely must betray this bishop's guiding hand, a sentiment that was corroborated by the Byzantine specialist, Ann Terry, during her study of the presbytery. The buried lowest step of the synthronon and *cathedra* were discovered below the raised floor.[22] The *cathedra* itself may have been carefully sited above the shrine of St Maurus of Parentium, of noble Roman birth, who died *c.* 584. The shrine appears to have been moved into this new position from the earlier church. In any case, "a limestone slab found at the foot of the *cathedra*, speaks of a container (*Hoc Cubile*) which encloses the holy body of the confessor Maurus".[23]

Other surviving furnishings at Poreč, including the altar with a box for relics, now

of public readings from the scriptures, the singing of psalms, a sermon and a number of set prayers".[16] It was the Christian liturgy of the Word, and had at its heart the sermon. "Its delivery was as much the bishop's 'special liturgy' and proper function at the synaxis as the offering of the eucharistic prayer was his special liturgy at the Eucharist".[17] At his consecration a bishop received a "gift of grace", to equip him as a "prophetic teacher" of the church's doctrine.[18] He preached *sitting* upon his "teacher's chair" from the throne behind the altar, "as the representative of God revealing Himself to the world".[19]

of a *cathedra* decorated on both sides. As on the ivory throne at Ravenna, its iconography is much more complex and quite different from that found on western episcopal thrones. The dimensions are remarkably small at 4 ft 10in × 1ft 10 in × 1 ft 9 in (1473 × 559 × 533 mm), and its miniaturised proportions suggest that it was built for an adolescent, rather than a robed archbishop.

There are *cubiculae* within the *sinister* chair wing, and on the back *exterior* (Figs 1.9b and 1.10). The latter is asymmetrical and could be a later insertion, but today the openings are interconnecting, and lead to a large circular cavity. The throne is surmounted by a, possibly, secondary double-sided medallion, which was purported to contain the figures of Matthew, Mark, Luke and John supporting the Cross. The back *interior* displays a tree, against which is placed a ram (Fig. 1.9a). On the *sinister* chair

Fig. 1.6 (left) S. Maria Assunta, Torcello. Bishop's throne. Conway Library, The Courtauld Institute of Art, London.

Fig. 1.7 (below) Poreč Cathedral, Croatia. Interior of eastern apse. Wikimedia Commons. Peter D. Klaus.

in pieces, were also mentioned.[24] Of special interest are the discarded deeply-engraved dolphin panels, which were, originally, the *cathedra* wings. Three *comparanda* were adduced, firstly, a limestone Roman example in the Museo Civico, Concordia Sagittaria, displayed with objects from a necropolis and, probably, a funerary seat, secondly, two limestone sculpted components of two chair wings decorated with dolphins in the Museo Archeologico, Aquileia, and thirdly, dolphins carved on two synthronon ends at S. Apollinare in Classe, Ravenna.[25] Terry claimed that dolphin end panels were a commonly seen feature in the Upper Adriatic. At Ravenna one of the arms is inscribed with the name of Archbishop Damianus (bp 693–709). The dolphin had symbolic resonance for both pagans and Christians. They could represent the individual Christian, or might assist the transition of a pagan to the afterlife.

The apostles Peter, Mark and James were known as bishops of Rome, Alexandria and Jerusalem, respectively. The putative throne of St Mark, supposedly transported with the saint's relics from Alexandria, via Grado, to Venice in 828, can be seen in the treasury at St Mark's Cathedral (Figs 1.9a and b; 1.10; 1.11). It is included here as an example of a monument with distinctive near-Eastern characteristics. It was extensively analysed in 1954 by André Grabar.[26] It is a rare example

*Fig. 1.8 Poreč
Cathedral, Croatia.
Detail of cathedra and
synthronon. F. Eaves.*

wing is a figure dressed as an evangelist as a youthful robed and beardless young man (Fig. 1.10). Can this really be Matthew? He stands in front of a petalled mandorla, behind which is an arrangement of six wings. He holds a book in his right hand. There are nine stars between the wings, and the angels blow horns, one of them carrying a baton. At the base, and flanking the *cubiculum*, are two palm trees. For Grabar, the angels are heralding the resurrection of the dead, and he saw this panel as distinctly funerary.[27] The design on the *dexter* chair wing is similar, and the quadruped was identified as symbolising the evangelist, Luke (Fig. 1.11). The back *exterior* with the eagle and lion is again similar, and Grabar was in no doubt that it displayed the symbols of John and Mark (Fig. 1.9b). The *cubiculum* on this side is again flanked by palm trees and surmounted by another similar-looking tree. At the apex, there is a crescent moon.

Grabar offered a late-Byzantine interpretation of the chair's symbolism. It comprised both a funerary theme, as well as

Fig. 1.9 a and b. St Mark's Cathedral, Venice. St Mark's throne. Front and back views; Procuratoria of the Basilica of St Mark's, Venice. Detail below.

*Fig. 1.10 (left)
St Mark's Cathedral,
Venice. St Mark's
throne. Sinister chair
wing. Procuratoria of the
Basilica of St Mark's,
Venice.*

*Fig. 1.11 (right)
St Mark's Cathedral,
Venice. St Mark's
throne. Dexter chair
wing. Procuratoria
of the Basilica of St
Mark's, Venice.*

an evocation of Paradise, which embodies the Tree of Life, with the four rivers, representing the four Gospel books, flowing down from below the Cross (on the front) (Fig. 1.9a). This is also inscribed on the spherical disk above, and over the front of the seat. He and later authorities have also posited a similar funerary and reliquary function for the throne, on account of its physical miniaturisation and its provision of the generous *cubiculae*, recalling a "throne of the martyrs" of the apostolic period, and ultimately deriving from Roman burial practice. Although Grabar struggled with the dating question, he was insistent that the monument could not be later than the 6th century. In 1984, Gaborit-Chopin suggested that "it seemed possible to attribute the *Sedia* to a 6th-century workshop in the Eastern Mediterannean region, possibly in Alexandria".[28]

A hitherto unforeseen hypothesis for the origin and function of the throne has recently been published by Stephan Hüller.[29] He begins by anchoring the object to Egypt, by asserting that the alabaster comes from the plain of Tell el Armana, some 300 miles

(483 km) south of Alexandria. His thesis is thorough, informed, and greatly benefits from a profound knowledge of Jewish culture, useful in an examination of a monument with a "distinctly Semitic feel".[30] He questions Grabar's readings of some of the images. For instance, the latter's "Lamb of God" on the interior seat back has curved horns, which has to be a ram, recalling that in the story of Abraham and Isaac (Genesis 22: 1–14), which prefigured Christ's sacrifice. This leads to a wholly Old Testament interpretation of the iconography. He attempts to prove, from the secondary Hebrew "scribble" on the front of the throne, and certain details of the carved motifs, that the chair was made in 38 AD, not for St Mark, but for the new Messiah, Marcus Agrippa, then only a nine year old boy, which explains its miniaturised scale. The author's stimulating arguments will probably take decades to be ingested.

The extraordinary Byzantine "ivory" throne of Archbishop Maximian (bp 546–556) at Ravenna must be mentioned, if only to shed light on the political role of the Byzantine church in Italy under the eastern

others have done, as to whether the choice had anything to do with the throne's possible origin in Alexandria, where the Joseph story was particularly well known.

Additionally, on the seat front are the full-length figures of the four Evangelists and St John the Baptist.[36] Schapiro especially drew attention to:

> "the appointment of Joseph by Pharoah as his chief minister, with the ring, the robe, and the gold necklace, (being) like the ceremonial ordination of a bishop. For what does the ring placed on his finger mean, if not that the pontificate of faith has been awarded to him, so that he might himself designate others?"[37]

Von Simson stressed that the presence of John the Baptist and the evangelists demonstrates the function of the throne in the rite of baptism.[38]

He also argued that the monument must have been Maximian's own commission, created "in connection with the vast artistic programme which was to initiate and to proclaim the ecclesiastical role for which Ravenna had been selected by Justinian".[39]

Form and style of episcopal thrones in the West, *c.* 300–1300

During the 1st millennium of the Christian church, a bishop's throne was either in the form of an armchair with a straight, rounded or pedimented back, or in the style of the folding x-frame Roman *sella curulis*, the portable seats of Roman senators and magistrates. It seems that few of the stone thrones attempted to copy Roman models. During the Apostolic Period, in the catacombs there was little opportunity for fancy architecture, craftsmanship, materials or decoration, and, as already noted, chairs were literally rough-hewn into the rock. They were immoveable fixtures, as were most of the thrones forming part of a basilican synthronon.[40] Nonetheless, there had been a tradition that St Peter's possessed at least one portable throne, or chair, and there were probably many more for the use of bishops elsewhere. One can surmise that, for convenience, they would have been required when he officiated at one side of the high altar, and sometimes could have been used to carry a prelate in procession. There is a rare surviving example of a late 13th-century *sella curulis*, or faldstool, in bronze at Perugia Cathedral. A better known, but atypical, taxonomical relative is the stylistically composite throne of King Dagobert (*c.* 603–639), first

emperor Justinian (Fig. 1.1). According to the secular priest and scribe, Andreas Agnellus (805–845), Maximian was the first bishop of Ravenna to be called an archbishop.[31] The city, at that time, was part of the eastern empire, so the claim that the throne was the product of a Byzantine workshop, and probably made in Constantinople, is not surprising.[32] From its material alone, this episcopal chair is in marked contrast to the stone thrones in mainland Italy. It is round-backed and with no footstool, although it would, almost certainly, have been originally provided with one. Its visible surfaces are entirely of carved ivory, although, for structural strength, it was built on a wooden frame removed in the 19th-century restoration.[33] As such, it would have been both a highly sophisticated symbol of the archbishop, as well as a practical chair. Its ivory all-over embellishment was surely an overt reference to the Biblical throne of Solomon.[34]

Meyer Schapiro discussed the reasons for the prominent representation in the carved ivory panels on the chair sides of the story of Joseph, and investigated the standard interpretation of Joseph being betrayed by his brothers, but ultimately saving the Jews and the Gentiles i.e., that he was seen as an ante-type of Christ.[35] He pondered, as

King of the Franks. This was recorded in the mid-12th century by Abbot Suger at the abbey of St Denis, Paris (Fig. 1.12).[41] Whilst the seat and chair legs could conceivably be coeval with Dagobert, the gabled back is a modification by Abbot Suger, and the chair sides are redolent of the workshop of Charles the Bald. Lawrence Nees suggested that the triangular profile of this feature was inspired by the contemporary resurgence of interest in the Roman style, and, in particular, the *cathedra Petri*, to be discussed below.[42] Although few, if any, of the wooden Roman episcopal faldstools survive, there is a unique 14th-century painting of one, with a bishop *in situ*, in the parish church of St George at Pürgg, Styria (Figs 1.13a–b).[43] It is at the centre of a wall painting, which records the consecration of the chancel extension to an otherwise Romanesque church by Bishop Wocho of Passau in 1324. It is sited at the north-west end of this two-bay chancel, in close proximity to the medieval high altar. The sedilia for the clergy is on the adjacent south wall.[44]

However, to pass on, for the time being, from this discussion of a bishop's portable chair, a topic which will be reverted to in Chapters 2.1 and 3, we need to return to our present interest in the early permanent thrones. A more refined seat of the catacomb style is the mid-5th-century *cathedra* of Bishop Gaudiosus at S. Maria-della-Sanita, Naples, with its seat back surrounded by three strings of beading and, in the centre, a fictive architectural blind arcade with a version of the chi-rho symbol below (Fig. 1.14).[45] In the Roman necropolitan tradition, it probably stood in the crypt adjacent to the saint's tomb.

Although it is relatively difficult to recover the appearance of the synthronons erected in the basilicas occupied immediately following the Peace of the Church, it is particularly disappointing that no Roman thrones seem to have survived in anything approaching authentic condition from before the 12th century. Nees, who has made the study of Italian medieval episcopal thrones something of a speciality, observed that:

"... one thinks immediately of the ivory throne of Maximian in Ravenna, and the throne from Grado now in the treasury of S. Marco in Venice. Ancient thrones could survive, but in Rome they did not. Surely there were many episcopal thrones in Rome that were old, including that in the Lateran, with a claim to pre-eminence among them. The throne sitting today in the apse of the Lateran is mostly modern, but for its animal base. Its predecessor stands in fragments in the cloister of the church, but it is only as old as the thirteenth century. Evidently the genuine old thrones of the Roman churches failed an important test; they were old, but did not look old, did not bear in their style and iconography the signs of antiquity that lent them the authority of power. They could not compete with the richly decorated and highly signitive monuments appearing in France, elsewhere in Italy, indeed in Germany, and they were "restored" through the erection of thrones comprising *spolia*".[46]

As already mentioned, the profile of the throne back varied. St Ambrose's throne in Milan (4th century) is a straight-backed example, as is the probably 6th-century French throne at Nôtre Dame-de-Nazareth, Vaison (Vaucluse), with its steeply stepped-up elevation and classically-derived architecture (Figs 1.15 and 1.16). The latter could be a survival of the prosperous Gallo-Roman city, but we cannot be sure. The Byzantine throne, the evidence of which is extremely rare, may, as at Ravenna, have favoured the rounded back. By the mid-

Fig. 1.13
a. St George, Pürgg, Styria. Wall painting of Bishop Wocho of Passau consecrating the new chancel in 1324, with detail below;
b. Ground plan of 14th-century chancel. After Woisetschläger and Krenn 1982, 380. C. Opitz.

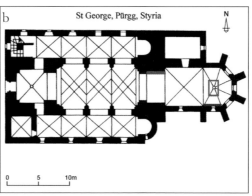

— Wall-painting

— Sedilia

☐ 18th century High Altar (presumably in roughly the same position as its medieval predecessor)

Fig. 1.14 S. Maria-della-Sanita, Naples. Throne of Bishop Gaudiosus. After de Fleury 1883–9, II, pl. 153. Society of Antiquaries of London.

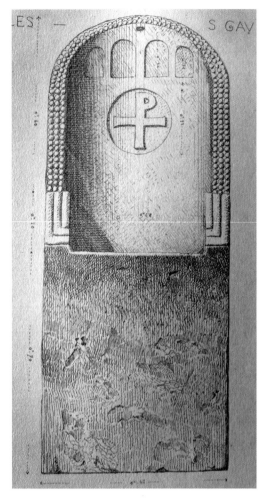

Fig. 1.15 (right) S. Ambrogio, Milan bishop's throne. J. Allen.

Fig. 1.16 Nôtre Dame, Vaison (Vaucluse). Bishop's throne. After H. Revoil, Architecture Romane du midi de la France, II (Paris 1873), pl. 23. Warburg Institute.

12th century in Italy, there was a noticeable change of design, with the introduction of a gabled seat back. The latter was typical of the southern-Italian group (see below).

Both the late-Roman and southern-Italian thrones betray a marked pretension to antiquity. The 13th-century thrones, at S. Maria-in-Cosmedin (Fig. 1.17), and SS. Nereo and Achilleo in Rome, employ prominent vigilant and protective lions, a footstool and, at the former, an inlaid decorated disk for the back panel, believed to be the work of the Cosmati family, who supplied the marble *schola cantorum*, and furnished the east end of that church.[47] Radford recorded in 1959 that the, apparently, lost seat front at S. Maria-in-Cosmedin was decorated with a slab of porphyry.[48] Mary Stoll emphasised that the red marble in the porphyry disk or nimbus with its starburst design, on the back of this papal throne represents royalty, and that Constantine had used this image.[49] S. Maria-in-Cosmedin was rebuilt in the early 12th century under Pope Calixtus. Stoll claimed that the reappearance of lions at the time of the reform of the papacy "purposefully associated these popes with old testament kings and Roman emperors", and that lions were already a plentiful symbol of both the city of Rome and the Roman Empire.[50]

The lower part of the throne at S. Lorenzo in Lucina, Rome (*c.* 1110), is made up of fragments of late-Roman sarcophagi, and the sides consist of Roman vine fruit and foliage decorative carving.[51] But hardly more conventional is the marble *cathedra* of St Gregory the Great (590–604), with its winged lion chair arms with, on the back, a fantastic

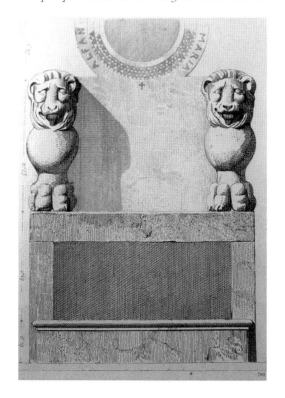

Fig. 1.17 (left) S. Maria-in-Cosmedin, Rome. Bishop's throne. Drawing after de Fleury 1883–89, II, pl. 152. Society of Antiquaries of London.

Fig. 1.18 S. Gregorio Magno, Rome. Pope Gregory VII's cathedra. a. Side view. Wikimedia Commons. Anthony M; b. Drawn detail of plan, back and side views. De Fleury (1883–89), II, pl. 149. Society of Antiquaries of London.

carved human figure and scrolling foliage in high relief (Figs 1.18a–b). The overwhelming choice in Italy of white marble as the suitable material for an episcopal throne was perhaps inevitable in a country well endowed with this prestigious material. Nonetheless, the Solomonic overtones would have played their part in the visual impact from these pristine white, and probably gilded, monuments.[52] The design and decoration of the Gregorian throne is essentially Roman. The pair of lions, incorporated into the front of the reconstructed throne at Salerno may be as early as the 3rd or 4th century (Fig. 1.19).[53] However, their heads seem to have been re-carved in the late-11th century, making them modified *spolium*.[54] Perhaps most striking of these Imperial-revival thrones is at S. Clemente, of the 1120s, where we find a rounded marble seat back with a secondary 12th-century inscription identifying this reconfigured monument as the work of Pope Anastasius (d. 1125) (Fig. 1.20). At a right-angle is the prominent inscription "Martyr" in large "Damascene" letters, thought to originate from the pontificate of Siricius (384–399). The host slab was discovered in the lower basilica, and must be Early-Christian *spolium*.[55] The lettering's conspicuous placing is intended to identify the monument with

the patron saint, who was St Peter's successor.

The vigorous group of 12th-century stone thrones in southern Italy, including Monte Sant' Angelo, Canosa, Calvi, Montevergine, and Bari, are *tours-de-force* of Arab-influenced decorative, figurative, and animal carving. They offer interesting examples of dedicatory and authorial inscriptions, some now thought to be forgeries. That at Monte Sant' Angelo, for

Fig. 1.19 Salerno Cathedral. Detail of bishop's throne. Conway Library, The Courtauld Institute of Art, London.

Fig. 1.20 S. Clemente, Rome. Bishop's throne, drawing after de Fleury (1883–89), II, pl. 166. Society of Antiquaries of London.

instance, was considered by André Grabar to be the precursor of the group, on the basis that its two inscriptions seemed to refer to a Bishop Leo, of Monte Sant' Angelo and Siponto after 1034.[56] This supposition upset the settled 12th-century dating, which took into account the tendency for some southern

Italian 10th-century patrons to pretend that their thrones were older than they really were.[57]

The elephant supporters of the Canosa throne are extraordinary enough (Fig. 1.21), but the better known Bari throne, with its Atlas figures supporting the seat on their shoulders, is sculpturally the most extraordinary cocktail of Roman and Arab influences. An anonymous chronicler recorded the enthronement of Archbishop Helia at S. Nicola, Bari in 1098.[58] The ceremony was attended by Pope Urban II and many archbishops and abbots at the time of a synod hurriedly called to organise the first Crusade. Again, Grabar relied on the date of the monument's inscription, as well as the written sources without question, although the likelihood of such an elaborate throne being prepared in so short a time has been adduced.[59] An early dating has also been challenged on art-historical grounds, as it is maintained that the monument's carving style is redolent of the mid-12th century.[60]

An interesting development in the design of an Italian episcopal throne is the late-13th-century Gothic architectural canopy of honour, or baldacchino. In the upper chapel of the friary church at Assisi, it encases the papal *cathedra* (Fig. 1.22).[61] The design is characteristic of late-13th-century Italian Gothic architecture and furniture, the latter enunciated in the high altar ciborium at S. Cecilia-in-Trastevere, Rome, although probably designed somewhat later by Arnolfo di Cambio (see Fig. 1.5). Giotto's fictive throne, in the *Ognissanti Madonna*, of *c.* 1310, painted for the Florentine Franciscan church in that city, seems to reflect the contemporary fashion for church furnishings.[62] At Assisi, the canopied marble *cathedra* stands above a flight of steps positioned in the eastern apse behind the high altar, with the late-15th-century marquetry timber clergy stalls flanking it on either side.[63] Originally, the synthronon would have been of stone. The throne is surmounted by a crocketted and pierced Classical pediment supported on red marble columns. The white marble chair with crocketted back, has two prominent lions as arm-rests. Under the footstool is sculpted a lion and a dragon at each end, with an adder and basilisk in the centre (Fig. 1.23). Beneath is the legend, "*Super aspidem et basiliscum ambulabis et conculcabis leonem et draconem*" ("Thou shalt tread upon the lion and the adder: the young lion and the dragon shalt thou trample under foot"), from Psalm 90: 13–15 in the Latin Vulgate. The text probably recalls the pope's extraordinary right of access to the friary. The frescoed *tondi* on the wall above contain the images of two early papal saints against a blue background. The decoration of the red painted back wall behind the chair is now unrecognisable.

The medieval Italian Gothic style was the product of the artistic patronage of the Neapolitan dynasty instigated by Charles I of Anjou. From 1266 to 1285, he invited artists from France and Italy to his court in Rome, employing executants such as Pietro Cavallini, author of the *Last Judgement at S. Cecilia-in-Trastevere*, and the Tuscan, Arnolfo di Cambio (*c.* 1240–1300), already mentioned as also working in this church. Cimabue was the chief muralist in the upper chapel at Assisi from 1277 to *c.* 1280 (he is documented as working in Rome a little earlier, *c.* 1272). In furniture this hybrid style stands in strong contrast to the general resistance in Italy, particularly in architecture, to the Western Gothic as a whole. The novel appearance of the canopied throne at Assisi, and the later painting of Giotto, as well as the treatment of Italian ciboria, suggests that the same architectural feature would have been employed in the late-13th century in France. Given the lacuna in our knowledge of French episcopal thrones, and other church furniture, at almost any time during the later Middle Ages, we can only speculate on the wholesale adoption of the style in the *cathedrae* of French Gothic cathedrals. The inspiration for the design of most of Britain's lost 14th-century canopied thrones is also, necessarily, a matter of conjecture. Otherwise, with the exception of Britain and Italy, one may judge that throughout northern Europe before the Council of Trent, canopies were rarely applied.[64]

Chairs of St Peter

Traditionally, there were two possible candidates for the "original" chair of St Peter in Rome, one at the basilica itself, which is now confined within Bernini's *cathedra Petri*, and the other, long since vanished, but mentioned by many authorities as existing in an oratory in the Ostrien cemetery of the catacombs, where "St Peter first sat, and baptised".[65] It

Fig. 1.21 Canosa Cathedral (Puglia). Bishop's throne. Detail. Conway Library, The Courtauld Institute of Art, London.

Fig. 1.22 S. Francesco, Assisi. Papal throne in upper chapel. From Bonsanti 2002, II, 1000, fig. 1915. Warburg Institute. Reproduced with kind permission, Franco Cosimo Panini Editore. F. C. Bottero, OFMConv.

Fig. 1.23 S. Francesco, Assisi. Upper chapel. Papal throne. Sculpted frieze under footstool. Detail. From Bonsanti 2002, II, p. 1000, fig. 1919. Warburg Institute. Reproduced with kind permission, Franco Cosimo Panini Editore. F. C. Bottero, OFMConv.

is said to have been greatly venerated, with perpetual lamps burning in front of it. A sample of their oil was, supposedly, sent by Pope Gregory to Theodolinda, _c._ 570–628, Queen of the Lombards.[66] This _cathedra_, which was considered to be of the Apostolic period, has never been identified.

Since the mid-17th century, the surviving putative chair of St Peter has been sheltered within Bernini's massive Baroque monument (Fig. 1.24). Scientific and scholarly 20th-century research has shown it to be a work of the late 9th century.[67] This is a large, formerly armed, oak chair with a gabled back, decorated on the front with ivory panels mostly illustrating the Labours of Hercules. From the early-7th-century carving style on the back of the "Hercules fighting the lion" plaque, the distinguished art-historian, Kurt Weitzmann, was able to date most of the ivories to the time of Charles the Bald.[68] From the type of the ivory portrait plaque and the style of the Heraclean images, he argued that the ivories were even commissioned by this Carolingian emperor.[69] Subsequently, Nees proposed that the chair was taken to Rome, because "after Charles the Bald had been forced out of Aachen by his older brother Louis the German in 870, the city was the only possible capital for a Roman emperor, and it would have been proper to have an impressive (and, indeed 'Romanizing') throne there" for use at his imperial coronation in 875.[70] Although it was never intended for use in the Vatican, it may have been stored there. In due course, on account of its suitably antique appearance, it seems to have been adopted for the promotion of the papacy.[71] The style of the chair, in terms of

its subsequent influence on the design of some thrones in Northern Europe, will be discussed later.

Having established that the chair is no older than the 9th century, it is worth recording the degree to which such a liturgical furnishing component, with no claims to authenticity, could have become invested for so long with the greatest possible aura of sanctity. As proof of this, one need look no further than the abraded state of the chair posts, which have suffered from the attentions of countless pilgrims, who liked to cut slivers from it to carry off as relics. This was also the fate of the Venerable Bede's Chair at Jarrow.

A fanciful legend had been woven around this chair, with attempts to establish its origins going back at least as far back as the 4th century. It was believed to have come from the church of the putative S. Prisca on the Aventine hill, which occupies the site of the house of Aquila and Prisca, who were traditionally thought to have sheltered St Peter.[72] It was the chair from that church, which Pope Damasus I (d. 384) was supposed to have transported to a new baptistery at St Peter's. The feast of the dedication of St Prisca's fell on 18 January, and can be found in at least 18 English monastic calendars.[73] The first of the two feasts of St Peter's Chair in the Roman calendar also fell on this date, although in England, only Abbotsbury, Dunster, Muchelney and St Augustine's, Canterbury made it a joint celebration of St Peter's Chair and St Prisca.[74]

The second feast was on 22 February, which was the commonly recognised date in England for the festival of St Peter's Chair. It was a celebration of the apostle's "enthronement" as bishop of Rome.[75] St Prisca's was a minor feast and St Peter's could be either major or minor.

The episcopal throne and the cult of relics

The practice of the cult of relics has already been discussed in relation to their accommodation at 4th-century Gerasa, 6th-century Poreč, and the *c.* 6th-century throne of St Mark. The practice can be traced back to the period of persecution, when the bones of the martyrs were collected and worshipped, and ultimately buried in Christian *martyria*. With the growing importance and interest in the possession of relics throughout Europe in the early middle ages, the synthronon seating arrangement of clergy started to go out of favour. As Radford observed:

> "The small chest (at Gerasa), designed for representative relics, would cause no inconvenience to the functional use of the synthronon. But in parts of the West, particularly in Gaul, it became usual to place in this position the sarcophagus with the body of the martyr or founder and to adorn this shrine with more and more elaborate ornament. As early as 574 the shrine of St Denis, in the abbey church outside Paris, stood near the altar and was built up like a tower (*turritum erat tumulum*). In the middle of the 7th century St Fursey's shrine at Peronne is explicitly described as a little house on the east side of the altar (*constructa ad orientalem partem altaris domuncula*). In Carolingian churches the practice went even further and a separate altar or shrine was being sometimes provided by the interposition of an extra bay between the transept and the apse. This is the type of plan adopted in the abbey church of Centula (St Riquier) begun about 790. The original draft shown in the parchment plan of St Gallen, dating from about 820, indicates a church following the same model. The internal arrangement of these two churches is either known or can be reasonably inferred. The two Carolingian plans recovered under the Cathedral of Cologne show a similar type of arrangement. These and similar Carolingian models lie behind the Saxon cathedral at Canterbury and doubtless influenced other pre-Conquest churches in England".[76]

With the Norman invasion, apse-ambulatories were introduced in the newly-built greater churches in England, as at Bishop Losinga's Norwich Cathedral and Gloucester Abbey, where relics could be accommodated behind the high altar. The east end of Bishop Walkelin's New Minster at Winchester was ready for use by the monks in 1093, where, on the feast of his translation (15 July), the

Fig. 1.24 St Peter's Rome. Chair of St Peter. Drawing after de Fleury (1883–89), II, pl. 144. Society of Antiquaries of London.

feretrum of St Swithin was deposited near, or on, the high altar.[77] The church possessed an apse-ambulatory plan with a square return, but followed the Conqueror's tradition at Caen in having few other relics.[78] Although Archbishop Lanfranc's rebuilt cathedral and monastery at Christ Church, Canterbury, completed in 1077, was conservative in plan with its Continental apse-echelon design, it perpetuated Canterbury's Anglo-Saxon and Early-Christian tradition of placing the choir at the west end of the presbytery, in the manner of a *schola cantorum*.[79] The earlier cathedral, categorised by Kevin Blockley *et al.,* as Period 4A, and its later extended version, Period 4C, were variously dated from the early-8th to the late-9th century.[80] At that time the archbishop was accommodated on a raised seat in a galleried chapel at the *west* end, with an altar to allow him to officiate at services in the nave.[81] This arrangement is similar to that at the Old Minster, Winchester, dedicated in 980, with its raised seat for King Aethelred at the west end.[82]

The isolation of the episcopal throne at the east end, in conventionally arranged churches, was exacerbated by the tendency to place reliquary chests upon the shrine, or shrines,

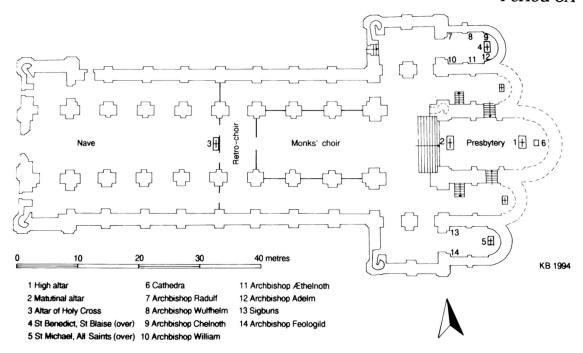

1 High altar   6 Cathedra   11 Archbishop Æthelnoth
2 Matutinal altar   7 Archbishop Radulf   12 Archbishop Adelm
3 Altar of Holy Cross   8 Archbishop Wulfhelm   13 Sigburis
4 St Benedict, St Blaise (over)   9 Archbishop Chelnoth   14 Archbishop Feologild
5 St Michael, All Saints (over)   10 Archbishop William

Fig. 1.25 Christ Church, Canterbury. Plan of Archbishop Lanfranc's post-Conquest cathedral. After Blockley et al. 1997, Period 5A. By permission of the Canterbury Archaeological Trust.

east of the high altar. This blocked the view of the synthronon, making it inconvenient to use. The tendency was to abandon the traditional arrangement, the bishop or celebrant positioning himself in *front* of the altar for the celebration of the eucharist, with seating being provided for the other officiants on the south side. This separation is typified in Prior Conrad's early-12th-century high altar screen at Christ Church, Canterbury. It was described in some detail by the monk Gervase, who recorded a great beam, resting on the capitals of two pillars, which stretched across the width of the sanctuary. This carried seven reliquary chests containing the bones of Canterbury saints.[83] Doors were placed on either side, so that the relics could be processed around, as exemplified in the early-15th-century drawing of the arrangement at St Augustine's Abbey, Canterbury (see Fig. 4.34).[84] Ultimately, the throne was moved to a privileged position at the east end of the choir-stalls, from which the bishop would be conveniently close to both his choir and clergy. Canon Phillips stressed that, at Christ Church, Canterbury, by at least the late-13th-century this wooden seat was known as the *sedes lignea*, to distinguish it from the ancient surviving marble throne, the *sedes marmorea*.[85]

Although there was a *cathedra* in the eastern apse of Lanfranc's cathedral (Period 5A), it must have been largely symbolic (Fig. 1.25). The clergy-stalls were in timber, and so, presumably, en-suite with an oak throne for the bishop.[86] Norwich Cathedral, with its late-11th-century apse-ambulatory, has retained the mid-12th-century siting of the bishop's seat. The medieval throne, of unknown date and origin, was raised up behind the high altar.[87] As at Canterbury, this location would have been distant from the monks' choir, under the crossing (Fig. 1.26). The extant throne itself is essentially inauthentic, the only hard fact being that the ancient stone on the north side resembles a chair side.[88] John Crook's forensic archaeological contextual study of the former furnishing scheme confirms that the throne is still in its mid-12th-century position.[89] The stone-lined vertical shaft in the west wall of the probably shelved reliquary cupboard in the centre of the east side of the ambulatory arcade (Fig. 1.27), would have linked directly with the throne above.

This reliquary cupboard is of interest on account of its setting and position at the crown of the apse. The large niche-like recess is provided with a moulded arch and elaborate capitals to emphasise its sanctified status within the thickness of the wall. On the basis of its intimate relationship with the throne directly above, the imperial throne at Aachen, which was provided with accommodation for relics behind it, was the prestigious *comparandum* instanced by Eric Fernie (Fig. 1.28).[90] The latter is traditionally held to have been built of marble fragments from the church of the Resurrection in Jerusalem. With regard to Norwich, Fernie stated that:

> "In these circumstances it becomes possible to argue that the throne itself was a relic, and such a status would only have been likely if the object was already old when the cathedral was begun. Indeed the very position of the throne at the head of the apse supports this contention. … The throne at Norwich could (therefore) have been placed in this position to stress the connection with the arrangement at North Elmham before the transfer of the see in 1071 or 1072".[91]

In his telling comparison with the arrangements at Winchester Cathedral, Crook adduces the parallels with that cathedral's "Holy Hole", through which a pilgrim could crawl to achieve closer contact with St Swithun's relics above.[92] At Norwich, however, the significance of the connection provided would have been, not solely on the link with the throne immediately above, but to the inferred display of relics within the sanctuary, any visual contact with the latter being unavailable to visitors. On archaeological evidence it has been shown that at Norwich, on both sides of the throne and at two different levels, relics were most probably displayed. Thus, Crook argues, that the benefits of the emanations via the niche shaft from both the venerable throne and the relics would have had a powerful attraction for the devout pilgrim.

English episcopal thrones *c.* 1100–1300

There is an historical tradition that the oak turned chair at Hereford Cathedral, with its bobbin-baluster decoration and round headed arches, was the chair of King Stephen (1135–1154) (Fig. 1.29).[93] Unfortunately, it is difficult to be positive of such an early provenance, as it was only first recorded in 1827, as having come from the bishop's palace. However, the evidence of its substantial size, and its formerly possessing a footboard, indicates that it was a chair of estate.[94] It is recorded in the 19th century as having displayed some vermilion and gold paint "in several of the narrow bands".[95] Penelope Eames mentioned

Fig. 1.26 Norwich Cathedral. View of bishop's throne from choir. J. Crook.

Fig. 1.27 Norwich Cathedral. Relic cubiculum behind bishop's throne. J. Crook.

a French 12th-century carved and polychromed figure of the Virgin seated in a similar chair, in the Statens Historisks Museet, Stockholm. A chair in this style, of *c.* 1100, can be seen in the church at Husaby, Sweden.[96] The Hereford chair is heavily bobbined throughout, and displays a similar Romanesque-style arcaded lower front rail. A well respected authority on

Fig. 1.28 Aachen imperial chapel. The imperial throne at first-floor level. Wikimedia Commons. Holger Weinandt.

Fig. 1.29 Hereford Cathedral. King Stephen's chair. S. Mather.

early English furniture, Eames suggested that the Hereford chair:

> "is one of the most important pieces of medieval furniture in Britain, representing a group which was once common, as is established by written records as well as by pictorial evidence, for instance, the round chair *with columns* provided by Stephen 'le Joignur' for Edward I (1272–1307)".[97]

The early-13th-century archbishop's stone throne at Christ Church, Canterbury is a precursor to the flowering of Gothic episcopal thrones in England (Fig. 1.30).[98] The occasion for its construction was the resolution of the dispute (in 1201) between convent and archbishop in the former's favour, following the prelate's intention to set up an alternative diocesan administrative centre elsewhere, which would have robbed the monastery, as the monks saw it, of its historic authority.[99] The chair is well documented, and it is very probable that its deeply panelled back and sides, were constructed in wood before their approval by the chapter.[100] Each panel is provided with fictive frames and mouldings, that seem to foreshadow a much later wooden joinery technique. In sum the monument's interest is more as an historical relic than a work of art.

The commissioning of a new chapter house at Christ Church, Canterbury by Prior Henry Eastry was part of his lavish early-14th-century refurbishment scheme, mainly concentrated in the cathedral choir, where he commissioned a set of seventy new choir-stalls, three new choir doors, a stone pulpitum and the elaborate stone parclose.[101] His throne in the chapter house is a fine tripartite canopied stone structure, with a central seat and places on each side for chaplains (Fig. 1.31). The painted and gabled canopies, which are inset with cusped oculi and spandrel tracery, were originally richly decorated with painted foliage, inset gilded fleurons and enamelled glass.[102] The delicate early-Decorated carved foliage crockets, finials and canopy bosses surmount plain seat backs.[103] The throne's formal design is somewhat analogous to the late-13th-century stone Gothic papal throne at S. Francesco, at Assisi (Fig. 1.22, above).

It will soon become evident that, by the 14th century, the placement and form of most medieval British episcopal thrones was quite unrelated to the conditions of the Early-Christian church. As at Norwich and pre-Conquest Canterbury, the throne would have fulfilled a function as much ceremonial and symbolic, as liturgical. In five of the six cathedrals whose thrones will be the subject of close analysis in the following pages, we find an imposing free-standing monument, set within a spacious Gothic architectural setting most often in the choir, long-since by then the object's usual location. From his vantage point, at the choir's south-east end, the bishop could continue to keep watch over his religious community, thus strengthening his immemorial function of the shepherd guarding his flock.

Notes

1   The term *cathedra,* as the term for the bishop's seat within his cathedral, was probably not adopted in the Roman church before the 13th century.

2   Examples can be seen in the underground basilica of the Ostrianum cemetery, on the Via Nomentane, the cemetery of S. Agnese fuori le Mura, and that of S. Hermes. As John Crook has pointed out, under Roman law cemeteries were prohibited from being located within the confines of the city of Rome, see Crook 2011, 4–5, who also cites J. M. C. Toynbee, *Death and Burial in the Roman World* (London 1971), 51. A basic source for a record of these and other catacomb cemeteries is Marchi 1844, but see also Cabrol and Leclercq 1913, *Chaire épiscopale,* cols 23–5.

3   Matthew 16:18. Christ named the apostle *Cephas*, meaning "rock" in Hebrew, and *petra* means rock in Latin.

4   Cabrol and Leclerq 1913, *Chaire épiscopale*, Col. 21.

5   After the Peace of the Church in 313 AD, synthronons were used by bishops to conduct the ecclesiastical courts.

6   The Edict of Milan was promulgated by the western Roman Emperor Constantine the first, and his eastern colleague Licinius. It was an edict of toleration by which the Christians were allowed complete liberty to practise their religion without molestation.

7   Radford 1959, 121 and Mango 1986, 25.

8   This translation is by D. J. Chitty, published in 1938 and cited in Crowfoot 1938, 184.

9   Gibson 1903, *Didascalia* cap. xii. This passage is based on the useful discussion of the origins of the synthronon, in Radford 1959, 121–9, pls viii–xiv.

10   Also see Radford 1959, fig. 1, for a ground plan of the early-6th-century cathedral of St Procopius, at Gerasa, with its synthronon indicated.

11   Crowfoot 1938,184.

Fig. 1.30 (left) Christ Church, Canterbury. Presbytery. Archbishop's throne. Early 14th century. With kind permission the Dean and Chapter, Canterbury. C. Tracy.

Fig. 1.31 (above) Christ Church, Canterbury. Chapter house. View of prior's throne from north-east. C. Tracy.

12 Radford 1959, 126. In the western Church, Synaxis normally refers to the liturgy of the Word, or the routine non-Eucharistic service. It is equivalent to the Anglican Mattins. See Cross 1958, 1314, and below for more on the Synaxis liturgy.

13 This practice was a hangover from Apostolic times. Note that the term "cathedral", to describe the principal church of a diocese, was not employed until the 16th century. However, from the 13th century, it was used adjectivally, as in "cathedral church". The concept of a bishop's *familia* was based on the early, quasi-legal, status of a bishop as a type of *pater familias*, where the faithful were his family.

14 Dix 1945, 38–41.

15 *Ibid.*, 28.

16 *Ibid.*, 37.

17 *Ibid.*, 40.

18 *Ibid.*

19 *Ibid.*, 41.

20 McNeill 2011, 4–8, fig. 1. The northern basilica at Concordia also had a double row of synthronon benching.

21 The basilica at Poreč was almost certainly the prototype for that at S.Vitale, Ravenna. See Deichmann 1969–76, II. 2, 235.

22 Terry 1984, 233–39.

23 *Ibid.*, 22, 36–7, 38–44, 50.

24 The main altar betrays a strong resemblance to one in the south apse at S. Maria Assunta, Torcello. Terry 1988, 43.

25 *Ibid.*, 52–3.

26 Grabar 1954b.

27 *Ibid.*, 358.

28 See Gaborit-Chopin, in Alcouffe 1984, 98–105.

29 Hüller 2009.

30 *Ibid.*, 168.

31 Agnellus 2004, 184–97.

32 See, in particular, Corrigan 1988, 6 and Simson 1948, 63–4.

33 Pers. comm. J. McNeill.

34 For discussion of Solomon's throne see Chapter 3, 95–7.

35 Schapiro 1980, 35.

36 The style of the ivories is considered to be most closely related to the ivory diptych of Christ and the Theotokos now in the Staatliche Museen zu Berlin, inv. 564, 565.

37 Schapiro 1980, 37.

38 Simson 1948, 64. For other sources for Maximian's throne, see Lowden 1997, 116–18; Morath 1940; Loerke 1984, 42. ff.

39 Simson 1948, 68.

40 Surprisingly, perhaps, there is evidence from the presence of housings in the catacombs, that some portable furniture was used there.

Cabrol and Leclercq 1913, *Chaire épiscopale*, cols 23–4.

41 A superb typological comparison with the throne of Dagobert is the 9th- or 10th-century version of the classical folding portable stool, the *sella plicatilis*, in the Musei Civici, Padua. See Stiegemann and Wemhoff 1999, vol. 1, 53–4. Pers. comm. J. NcNeill.

42 Nees 1993, 64, and n. 27, where the relevant passage from Suger's *De Rebus Administratione* is provided.

43 For the catalogue entry, see Lanc 2002, 1, 377–8.

44 For this reference and the images, I am indebted to Christian Opitz, who discusses them briefly in a blog < http://historienerrant. wordpress.com/2013/07/20/a>.

45 The latter was worn by Constantine's soldiers at the Battle of the Milvian Bridge in 312 AD.

46 Nees 1999, 778. For ancient *cathedrae* in England, there are the stone seats at Beverley and Hexham, the latter quite possibly the throne of St Wilfrid, d. 709. For Beverley, see Clapham 1950, pl. 30, and Monkwearmouth, Clapham 1950, 1–6, pl. 1. For important early thrones on the continent of Europe, in Germany, there is St Emmeram, Regensburg (late-10th century), Augsburg (12th century) and, in Spain, Girona (12th century). Walcott 1868 lists a number of other former or existing thrones, in France, at Vienne, Autun, Metz, Arras and Rheims, and in Italy, at Milan and the legatine thrones at Palermo and Monreale.

47 For the S. Maria-in-Cosmedin throne, see Gandolfo 1974–75, 201–18.

48 The symbolism of the juxtaposition of lions on episcopal thrones is the subject of more detailed discussion in Chapter 3, 96–8. See Radford 1959, 124 and fig. 1 for a reference to the porphyry slab.

49 For her commentary on this throne, see Stoll 1991, 11–15.

50 Stoll also stressed that the presence of lions on papal thrones underscored the pope's secular authority.

51 *Ibid.*, and Gandolfo 1974–75, 211–16, figs 4–6.

52 The same could be said for the Italian white marble throne of the Holy Roman Emperor at Aachen (Fig. 1.28). For the throne of Solomon, see Chapter 3, 95–7.

53 Nees 1999, 777; Guidobaldi and Lawlor 1990.

54 Gandolfo 1984, 5–29; Guidobaldi and Lawlor 1990.

55 Nees 1999, 777.

56 Grabar 1954a, 7.

57 Bertaux 1903, 448; Nees 1999, 773–6.

58 Grabar 1954a, 10.

59 Nees 1999, 774.

60 Belli d'Elia 1974.

61 Bonsanti 2002, *Schedi*, 575–6; Smirke 1836, 472, with drawing.

62 Giotto's *Ognissanti Madonna* is now in the Uffizzi Gallery, Florence.

63 The stalls are dated 1491 by contract. Pers. comm. Joanne Allen.

64 The imposing example at Naples Cathedral is thought to have been erected between 1371 and 1435.

65 *Catholic Encyclopedia, Chair of St Peter*. This is the most up to date theological source for the Roman chairs and feasts of St Peter. See also, Cabrol and Leclercq 1913, *Chaire épiscopale*, col. 87, which is still worth consulting.

66 Cabrol and Leclercq 1913.

67 The fruits of the rigorous historical and scientific research programme, undertaken in 1969, and sponsored by the Vatican, was published by a team of distinguished academics. See Maccarone 1971, pt ii, appendix 4, M. Alessio *et al.*, "Datazione con il metodo del Carbonio-14 di alcune strutture della cattedra lignea in S. Pietro", in which the timbers, mostly of chestnut, but with pine standards, were dated by radiocarbon to the second half of the 9th century, 173–83; and pt iii, appendix 2, K. Weitzmann, "The Reverse of the Plaque with 'Heracles's Lion Fight'", 247–51.

68 Weitzmann in Maccarone 1971.

69 *Ibid.*

70 The re-attribution of the *cathedra Petri* has spawned a considerable bibliography. The most important scholarly contributions are referenced in Nees 1991; 1993; 1999.

71 The chair's eventual fall from grace in the 17th century is described in Nees 1993, 64–8.

72 Farmer is sceptical of the traditional linkage, in the *Acts of the Apostles*, of Prisca and Aquila. According to him, the dedicatee is more likely to have been a Roman lady who lived on the Aventine Hill in the 4th century. Farmer 1997, 418.

73 See "Calendars" in Wormald 1934; 1939/1946.

74 For a discussion of the feasts of St Peter's Chair, see Klauser 1969, 88.

75 *Ibid.*

76 Radford 1959, 129. For the most recent study of the early development of saints' cults, reliquaries, contact relics, graves, shrines and crypts on the Continent, see Crook 2011, 1–40.

77 The ritual choir at Walkelin's cathedral was beneath the lantern tower. In the 1150s Bishop Henry of Blois moved the bones of the Anglo-Saxon kings and queens into the new cathedral, and relic chests were placed on the outer line of the apse-ambulatory, where the inscriptions, in part, survive. See Crook 1993, 57–60, figs 6.2, 6.3.

78 Crook 2011, 124.

79 For the reconstructed ground plans of Christ Church, Canterbury's pre- and post-Conquest cathedrals, see Blockley *et al.* 1997, 102, 105. The *schola cantorum* was the body of trained singers, who occupied the middle of a church. This practice was probably first introduced by Pope Gregory the Great in the 7th century. Hitherto, the singing was performed by the clergy from the synthronon. It was probably St Augustine who introduced this custom at Canterbury. See also the conjectural plan of the pre-conquest cathedral, which assumed there to have been a clergy synthronon in the eastern apse, flanking an altar. Brooks 1984, fig. 2, 38.

80 Blockley *et al.* 1997, 103.

81 The liturgical arrangements at Canterbury's sequence of cathedrals are drawn and discussed in Blockley *et al.* 1997, 103–6. For the west galleried chapel at 4A, the authors adduce German *comparanda*, such as the later St Cyriakus, Gernrode, St Peter, Soest, *c.* 800, and the former abbey church of St Alban, Mainz *c.* 805.

82 Kjølbye-Biddle 1993, 16, figs 2.4a, 2.4b.

83 Stubbs 1879–80, 13. For a tentative reconstruction of the Christ Church, Canterbury high altar reredos, see Tracy and Woodfield 2003, 52–3.

84 Trinity Hall, Cambridge, MS 1, fol. 77r.

85 Phillips 1949, 29. He stated that the *sedes lignea* was certainly in place before the enthronement of Archbishop Winchelsey in 1295. *Ibid.* 27.

86 The text of "The Instruction to Novices", in Archbishop Lanfranc's *Monastic Constitutions* is conclusive evidence of the clergy choir ordering, stating that during all psalmody "both choirs shall stand facing each other". Also, the *parva sedilia,* in "sitting and bowing *super parva sedilia*" can only be interpreted as the projecting ledge on the underside of the tip-up seat or misericord. However, it is not definitively stated that there was a chair for the bishop. Knowles and Brooke 2002, 205.

87 The neo-Classical stepped platorm leading up to it was inserted in 1959.

88 In discussing the Anglo-Saxon stone fragments on either side of the throne, Radford claimed that the piece on the north side is a former throne arm, and its companion, possibly, a component of a synthronon. He ascribed the abraded indications of decorative carving on both stones to the 8th century, i.e. from before the Danish conquest of East Anglia, and the possibility that they had come from the former cathedral at Thetford. Radford 1959, 113–18.

89   Crook forthcoming.

90   For the Aachen throne, see Geary 1978, 44; Mann 1995–97; and Airlie 2003, 132–6.

91   Fernie 1993, 66.

92   For the arrangements at Winchester, see Crook 1993, 61–3, figs 6.7, 6.8.

93   Havergal 1869a, 123–6; *RCHME, Hereford,* Vol. I, *South-West* (1931), 106 and Pl. 127, fig. facing page. Eames 1977, 210–11, pls 54–5; Chinnery 1979, 98–101.

94   The dimensions of the chair are 45 × 33 × 22 in (1143 × 838 × 559 mm).

95   Havergal 1869a, 123.

96   Appuhn 1978–79, fig. 12. There are several other chairs in the same style in Sweden. Eames mentioned the important group of stylistically similar furniture at Vallstena, Gotland, including an armed bench.

97   Eames 1977, 211; Brown *et al.* 1966, I, 224.

98   For a fuller discussion of medieval British episcopal stone thrones, see Chapter 4.

99   Reeve 2003. This article builds on Canon Phillips's ground-breaking text. See Phillips 1949.

100   Reeve 2003, figs 1–3.

101   Tracy 2006, 139–40.

102   The central gable is very similar to that on the slightly earlier St Edward's Chair or "Coronation Chair" in Westminster Abbey, which was also provided with similar glass covered decoration. This chair was not originally intended to play a role in the Coronation ceremony, but was probably a reliquary to display the Stone of Scone, a symbol of Edward I's victory over the Scots at Falkirk in 1298. It was, almost certainly, designed by the royal mason, Michael of Canterbury, and made sometime between the summer of 1297 and March 1300. Two 13th-century documents claim that it was located in St Edward's Chapel next to the altar and before the royal shrine. Rodwell was not happy with either of these positions, and, fortuitously, the forthcoming unpublished research by James Alexander Cameron supplies a fresh insight into the problem, by claiming that the term *cathedra* was routinely applied to clergy stalls in the medieval abbey records. In this case, the chair must have been intended not for an English monarch, but for the priest serving the royal shrine. Appropriately, on the *interior* seat-back is an image, most probably, of a sanctified English king, probably Edward the Confessor. See Percival-Prescott 1957, 5–10; Binski 1995, 136–7, figs 184, 186; 2003, 207–17 and *passim,* Rodwell 2013, 21, figs 91–8, and Cameron forthcoming.

103   A thorough restoration of the chapter house was undertaken by Sir Arthur Blomfield in 1896–97, including the painting and gilding of the stalls at the east end.

CHAPTER 2

THE TIMBER EPISCOPAL THRONES
OF MEDIEVAL BRITAIN

2

The timber episcopal thrones of medieval Britain

Of the 17 medieval cathedrals in England, four in Wales and 12 in Scotland, only one-fifth of their former episcopal thrones survive.[1] The main focus of this book is on the six extant high-medieval British thrones in stone and timber, all constructed in the 14th century. The two prominent pre-1300 British stone episcopal thrones at Benedictine Canterbury and Norwich have already been touched on. In Chapter 4 Andrew Budge will explore the mid- and late-14th-century freestone canopied *cathedrae* at Wells and Durham.

1. Exeter Cathedral

Description and physical analysis
In its Gothic positioning at the south-east end of the choir and its sheer monumentality, the Exeter bishop's throne represents an emphatic break from the traditions of the Early-Christian era (Fig. 2.1.1, Tip-ins 2.1.1, 2.1.2). Together with its, now lost, stone plinth, it would have risen more than 53 feet (16.15 m) into the choir vault. Not for nothing, it was described by Nikolaus Pevsner as "a monument of unprecedented grandeur … the most exquisite piece of woodwork of its date in England and perhaps Europe".[2] A trawl through a thin selection of coeval thrones in Europe confirms its uniqueness. Significantly, apart from the refashioned and repositioned choir-stalls, it was the first component of bishop Walter Stapeldon's superb suite of clergy-choir furnishings. It was planned and installed over

a 14-year period from approximately 1312 to 1325 (Fig. 2.1.2; Appendix I).[3]

It has been convincingly argued that the remodelling and rebuilding of the cathedral presbytery and choir, the second major phase of the institution's architectural rebirth between 1297 and 1342, was the achievement of Master Roger, in post from 1297 until his death in 1310.[4] From that date to 1342, the second major professional protagonist was Master Thomas of Witney. Christopher Paterson has reiterated that, throughout this momentous period, the role of the presiding bishops, Bitton (1292–1307) and Stapeldon (1308–1326), was no more, and no less, than as patrons and facilitators. Both men delegated the ultimate responsibility for the architectural design and project management to their master-masons and master-carpenters.[5]

The design of the throne's canopy consists of three tiers (the original *sedes episcopi*, or chair, has not survived). The base section is now in the form of a low rectangular arcaded screen, although, originally, the monument may simply have emerged from the four massive corner buttresses resting on a stone plinth.[6] Before it was dismantled in 1941,[7] it stood on a three-tier plinth in Ham Hill stone, a material that was only rarely used in the medieval cathedral.[8] Although it was only shown on a plain and shallow plinth in the Britton/Le Keux engraving (Fig. 2.1.3), prepared for John Britton's publication of 1826, a deeper plinth is indicated in John Carter's watercolour and

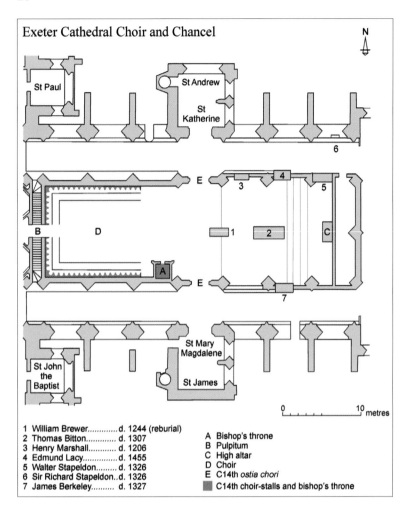

Exeter Cathedral Choir and Chancel

N

St Paul	St Andrew
	St Katherine
	6

E 3 4 5

B D 1 2 C

E 7

St Mary Magdalene

St John the Baptist St James

0 _____ 10 metres

1 William Brewer............d. 1244 (reburial)
2 Thomas Bitton............d. 1307
3 Henry Marshall............d. 1206
4 Edmund Lacy...............d. 1455
5 Walter Stapeldon.........d. 1326
6 Sir Richard Stapeldon..d. 1326
7 James Berkeley..........d. 1327

A Bishop's throne
B Pulpitum
C High altar
D Choir
E C14th *ostia chori*
■ C14th choir-stalls and bishop's throne

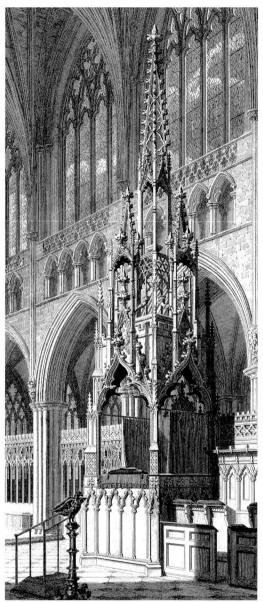

Fig. 2.1.2 (above) Exeter Cathedral. 14th-century choir ground plan. After Jones and Coffin, The Ichnography of the Cathedral Church of St Peter at Exeter (1757). Note that the entrance to the bishop's throne is shown as being on the north side. This is not definitive and, equally, it could have been on either of the two other sides. J. Read.

Fig. 2.1.3 (top right) Exeter Cathedral. Engraved view of bishop's throne by Shaw and Le Keux. After Britton 1826, pl. XI.

engraved elevations of 1797 (Fig. 2.1.4).[9] In that case, the prominent beaded moulding suggests that it could have been the original stone plinth. Carter's drawing, and that by the Devon architect Edward Ashworth, *c.* 1840, show the throne to be tucked into the east end of its arcade bay[10] (Figs 2.1.2, 2.1.4 and 2.1.5). The fact that some of the decorative carved elements on the eastern canopy niche, and a sliver from the arcade arch, had to be sacrificed, betrays an original intention to push the throne as far to the east as possible, presumably to allow maximum room for the choir-stalls. It was George Gilbert Scott who moved the throne into the centre of the bay, where it remains today.

Apart from the screen panelling on the south side, which is mostly authentic, there is no evidence for the existence of a former fence screen around the other three sides, possibly except for the drawing by John Carter, which shows a Gothic-decorated closure at

the front. Diane Walker, who has carried out extensive research on the post-Civil War history of the Exeter throne, has convincingly argued that Carter, followed by Britton and Le Keux a quarter of a century later, were using artistic licence in their drawings, in an attempt to show how the 14th-century Gothic fence might have looked.[11] As for the position of the original entrance, we have no evidence for this, although one would reasonably expect it to have been on the east side. On the other hand, one could argue that the pair of carved censing angels, positioned on the front canopy cusps, might present evidence that it was from the north side that the bishop was habitually censed, presumably unimpeded by any barrier.[12] Scott's replacement fence screens on the east and west sides are copies of the ancient tracery at the south side, but his enlarged nodding ogee-arched screen at the front is a felicitous flight of fancy in the spirit of medieval Hereford. In practice, these prominent mid-19th-century fixtures represent a conscious casting-off of the cathedral choir's previously accumulated Baroque ornamental components.[13]

Each of the pairs of corner buttresses of the throne support a tall gable, with a nodding ogee arch in front, behind which is the episcopal canopy of honour. From the haunches of the ogee arches, emerge three finialled and canopied tripods on the east, west and north sides (Fig. 2.1.6, Tip-in 2.1.1). Within is set an upper and lower tower stage. The latter is now closed-in with crenellated panelled sides, and above are four massive buttresses clasping the panels of the "fishscale" tracery of the lantern section (Fig. 2.1.17). From the level of the crown of the tripod vaults, smaller buttresses project up to form a large statue housing to accommodate a life-size sculpture, sheltered by a straight-sided gabled vault at the base of the canopy's final stage. This rises from the springing of these triangular gablets, and consists of a four-sided crocketted and finialled spire. This is secured by cusped and intersecting tracery. The south face of the throne does not project like the others, but carries a substantial flat gable decorated with high-relief foliage (Fig. 2.1.7, Tip-in 2.1.2).

Turning for a moment to the process of manufacture, by the summer of 1313, Galmeton and Membiri, evidently both West-Country craftsmen, must have already agreed a fixed fee of £4 for making the throne. This was at the point when the master-mason, Thomas of Witney, had been called from Winchester to oversee the choice of timber from the bishop's woods at Norton and Chudleigh.[14] Unfortunately, there then follows a crucial *lacuna* of 4 years. One must assume that, by the time that they reappear in 1316–17, all work on the throne was finished. There is no reference to it, apart from the statement that, at the end of the Midsummer Term, 1316–17, "Galmeton and his associate" were paid off *pro factura sedis episcopi ad tascam*. Inescapably, the choice, seasoning and preparation of the timber, the carving of the components, and the

final assembly and installation, were achieved within the space of just over 3 years.

It is probably worth trying to encapsulate the most salient activities in train from 1312–13 to 1323–24, the principal period of activity on the throne, as well as the development of the entire choir refurnishing project.[15] The throne is first mentioned in the cathedral fabric accounts at the start of the Midsummer Term, 1313 (25 June), where the item *Cost of timber for the bishop's throne* appears. There follows an intensive 3-month period of activity, starting with the master-mason's visit to the bishop's woods. Witney stayed for 3 weeks, after which he returned to Winchester. Doubtless, he oversaw the felling of the most important trees, and would have had an opportunity to make some initial design suggestions. Of the two master-carpenters, Galmeton, the project manager, was on site for 4 weeks out of the

Fig. 2.1.4 Exeter Cathedral bishop's throne. Drawing by J. Carter 1797. Society of Antiquaries of London.

Fig. 2.1.5 (above) Exeter Cathedral. Pencil and wash drawing of bishop's throne from east end by Edward Ashworth, c.1840. Note the 17th-century arcade fence screen front and side. Devon and Exeter Institution. G. Young.

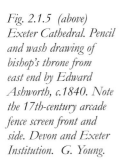

Fig. 2.1.6 (top right) Exeter Cathedral bishop's throne. North side mid-elevation. H. Harrison.

12, and his partner, Membiri for 5 weeks. Although the first tree trunks, and, probably, sawn planks, were submerged in the mill pond in Week 4, already by Week 7 they were hauling timber out of the water, and "carrying … (it) from Norton to Exeter". More activity followed, as, by Week 8, they started to saw "a certain great tree trunk", and one carpenter was sawing a further two tree trunks. At the same time labourers were paid "For carrying certain planks (*tabulis*) to the water 1d". Also two sawyers were paid for half a week, and during the final recorded 4 weeks of the accounts, two sawyers were paid just over £2.

The unfortunate 4-year break in the accounts lasted until Michaelmas Term, 1316–17, when we find Galmeton busy making centering, with the "other" carpenter for the high roof. That would have been for the eastern bay of the nave. There was no activity on the throne for the rest of the year,

although at the close of the Midsummer Term, the £4 contract fee agreed with Galmeton and Membiri for making the throne, is recorded. Over the next 9 years, all we have is a few embellishments listed. In 1317–18, there is an item for the cost of six images for the bishop's throne, and, 2 years later, in 1319–20, another for 2 lb (0.91 kg) of white lead, at 10d, for "the image of the bishop's throne", presumably, but not definitively, that of St Peter. This implies a 2-year campaign of carving and polychromy, planned to fit in with the carving and decorating of the nave roof bosses. In 1323–24, there are items "For writing 250 letters around the throne 5d" and "ironwork around the throne 3s 7d".

With regard to the commission, which included an unprecedented and highly ambitious canopy, Erskine was surprised that there was no mention anywhere of a stone chair (*cathedra episcopi*).[16] Although a small number of stone thrones retained their ancient position at the east end in a few cathedrals, such as Christ Church, Canterbury, and Norwich, timber episcopal chairs, placed at the east end of the suites of wooden choir furniture in the body of the church, were pioneered in the late-11th century at Christ Church, Canterbury by archbishop Lanfranc, and appeared in due course at Norwich, Rochester, Salisbury and Winchester.[17] Given Stapeldon's earlier commission of a new set of timber choir-stalls at Exeter, sourced from the oak woods on the episcopal estate, it would not be unreasonable to surmise that the new throne would also have been in the same material. Leofric's stone *cathedra*, if it still existed, would have been unsuited to this position. The lack of any detail about the making of a timber chair for the new canopy, for one must have been provided, is an unfortunate *lacuna* in the accounts. The phrase *Custus meremii ad sedem episcopi* leaves no doubt that we are dealing with a wooden chair. In this context it is understood to consist of a canopied chair of oak.[18] It is noteworthy that it is not referred to as a *cathedra*. This might suggest that Leofric's stone *cathedra* was still in existence.

The timber for the throne was obtained from the capitular woods at Norton (now Newton St Cyres) and the episcopal manor at Chudleigh. Both locations were traditional sources for the constructional timber supplied to the cathedral, and material from the bishop's estates was normally supplied free of charge. Although the accounts do not spell this out, it may be assumed that the timber from both locations was, for the most part, sawn into planks and carried to a storage depot adjacent to a mill pool at Norton.[19] During the months of June and July, when the trees were felled, the sap would have been rising, and it would have been the right time of year to season the wood by driving it out of the timber by submerging (*mergend*) the planks into the running water of a mill pool. The accounts relate that, after approximately 4 weeks, the boards were hauled out of the water and carted from Norton to Exeter. A coloured 1792 parish map of Newton St Cyres shows a "Pond Meadow" (letter "a"), which must be the site of the 14th-century mill pool (Fig. 2.1.8).[20] John Allan has provided a commentary on the logistics of taking timber from Chudleigh to Norton and back to Exeter at that period (Appendix V).

Although the master-carpenters were

Fig. 2.1.7 (left) Exeter Cathedral bishop's throne. South side elevation. Detail. G. Young.

working to task, the £4 fee had nothing to do with a modern-style fixed price contract, but, rather, it was a bonus for completion. The missing accounts would have detailed the payment of their daily wages when working on the project. The remuneration of the carvers, joiners and the other artisans, would also have recorded, not just their weekly wages, but the pattern of their activities, a few of which would have been specifically articulated. This lost information has robbed us of a definitive estimate of the cost of manufacturing the canopied episcopal chair. By contrast, such data can be elicited from the accounts of the other choir and presbytery furniture, particularly the high altar, reredos and sedilia, which were grouped together in the rolls as the "altar account". The latter has recently been estimated to have added up to between £750 and £800.[21] Despite the attentions of antiquarian and modern scholars up to now, no serious attempt has been made to estimate a true cost for the throne project. Even in a relatively recent study, John of Banbury's charge for constructing the three-vault tabernacle in the centre of the high altar reredos, of £5, was compared to the received cost of the bishop's throne of £4, with the conclusion that the stone structure must have

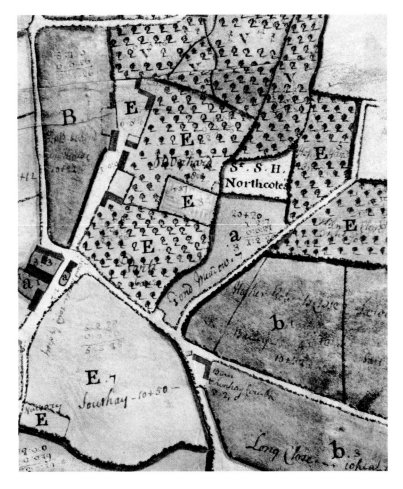

Fig. 2.1.8 Newton St Cyres parish map, 1792. Letter "a" shows position of "Pond Meadow", site of the medieval mill pool. Devon County Council.

than £6, the additional items of statuary and polychrome, and an estimate for the true cost of the materials (mostly supplied free of charge), a fair comparison with the cost of the reredos and sedilia would be in excess of £200, or more than a quarter of the cost of the total "altar account".

Returning to the description of the throne, on the east, north and west sides, the positions for three of the six sculptured images were provided on the massive finials at the top of the straight gables. These figures would have appeared to be standing beneath the miniature vaults of the open tripod canopies, although they stand a short way forward of them. It is suggested they were facing diagonally across the choir (Figs 2.1.6 and 2.1.9; Tip-in 2.1.1). Two slightly smaller figures were probably placed on the pair of candelabra branches emerging from the north straight gable, although the plinth on the east side now lacks a mortise. The shallow panelled tabernacle on the south side of the throne must have contained a painted image. Although we have no information about the systemic polychroming process, the fabric rolls indicate that six "images for the bishop's throne" would have been put in place before *c.* 1320. The statue in the top niche on the north side may have been of St Peter, an apt choice in the circumstances, and gold, silver and various colours for painting his image are mentioned in the fabric accounts for 1341–42.[24] If the upper tabernacle of the throne was occupied by then, which is highly likely, this figure must have been needed elsewhere in the cathedral, and the lofty northern image may not have been of St Peter.

On the lower part of the back buttresses are scored lines, presumably intended to provide a key for an applied gesso ground, which, along with the entire throne canopy was originally painted. Scott recorded that: "The whole of the old work was cleansed of its paint and varnish, but where it had been decorated in colour (*sic.* the bishops on the base of the front buttresses), this was preserved and restored".[25] The deposits that Scott refers to could be consistent with the application of black and/or brown paint at some time, as well as the repeated application of graining. A few unattributed late-19th-century sources claimed that beneath them were concealed traces of white and gold, and "profuse" medieval colouring.[26]

As for the carved decorative ornament, the "dogs" heads, which, on the choir-stalls

been pretty considerable.[22] An attempt is made here to remedy the situation, by estimating the work-force required to manufacture and install the throne within a period of a maximum of 4 years, broadly based on up to 1 year for felling, seasoning and preparing the timber, and 3 years for manufacture.[23] The study has concentrated, principally, on the amount of skilled carving which would have been involved, as this is likely to have been the most expensive element. The total came to 27¼ years' work for one man. Assuming Galmeton and Membiri worked full time for 3 years, they would have required seven other carvers to support them. If they received 2s 6d a week for 50 weeks a year, and the seven other carvers were paid 2s a week, their wages would have totalled £142 10s, excluding the joinery. The latter would have added, perhaps, a quarter to the carving costs (£35 10s) making a grand total of £178. If we add in the cost of cutting, seasoning and sawing the timber recorded in the accounts for the Midsummer Term, 1312–13, of more

at Winchester Cathedral appear only on the "Witneyesque" secondary buttresses, are here applied ubiquitously.[27] In the latter case, there is a greater variety of types, but we can still recognise the bat-shaped ears and quiffs of hair on top of the heads, which are even reminiscent of those on the gables of the arcades in the crypt of St Stephen's Chapel, Westminster, refounded by Edward I in 1292.[28] The foliage carving on the throne is thoroughly conventionalised, although the use of the trailing stalks strikes a realistic note. There is a tendency to bring this high-relief carving forward so that it all lies on the front plane. Foliage sprays tend to be squared off. The leaf forms can be categorised into various botanical types – oak, water-lily (for diapering), vine, long tresses of common hawthorn (within the gable on the south side), sycamore, maple and "marguerite".[29] The popular Decorated-type voluted trefoil leaf also features prominently. Ball-flower occurs but rarely, for instance, on the cusp pendants of the tripod arches. There is also some very unusual cusping, or denticulation high up in the tracery of the tripod arches, presumably, placed there to promote visual articulation.

Pevsner pointed out that the cusped nodding ogee arches on the throne canopy are amongst the earliest in the country.[30] Earlier architectural examples on a comparable scale do not exist, and the form in which the ogee arch is presented is the original conception of a master-carpenter. The exploitation of the motif here is audacious and, unquestionably on this occasion, the executant has outflanked the mason. Structurally, the Percy tomb at Beverley Minster, completed in 1340, is no match for the Exeter throne.[31] The nodding ogee canopies over the niches on the porch of Bishop Salmon's hall at Norwich must be later than 1318, when a license to crenellate was received.[32] The nodding ogee arches in the clearstorey of the choir at Selby Abbey, *c.* 1315–1335, are also, almost certainly, too late.[33] There are nodding canopies in the window jambs at St Alban's Cathedral Lady Chapel, of 1302–1308, and the exterior tabernacles at Newark Church, of 1312, but neither are large enough in scale to compare with Exeter.[34] Here large-scale nodding ogee trefoil arches sweep forward, sufficiently far to allow the massive diagonally-set supports of the tripods above to intervene between them and the straight gable

behind. The forward projection of the front gable contrasts with the perpendicularity of the subsidiary gable. By contrast, on the Percy tomb at Beverley, the leading edge of the rear gable sweeps forward to shelter the nodding ogee canopy.

The designer of the Exeter throne has invented a structure that capitalises on the essential characteristics of wood – lightness and tensile strength. Even though, as Hugh Harrison points out, on the lower half the continued use of the masonry-dependent additive techniques still rules, the tower section introduces the novelty of frame construction, which was to revolutionise joinery and constructional timberwork from then on. Another novelty is the device of hanging the main vault from the base of the tower section, which can be closely paralleled with the structural carpentry of the wooden vaults in the cathedral transept towers.[35] Like the Eleanor crosses, this baldacchino-like structure is free-standing, but the lower and middle stages are skeletal, giving the impression that the main structure is floating in space. The crenellated panelling, which wraps around the lower part, behind the massive straight gables, hides the top of the vault and the massive supports of the great tower, whose tapering profile accelerates upwards. Thanks to the 25 ft (7.62 m) crowning filigree spire, the entire structure is then visibly accelerated heavenward.

That the design of the throne was substantially modified has been recognised for some time. A radical alteration occurred during the construction phase, whilst still allowing for the completion within a demanding schedule of 4 years. Before discussing the most important changes to the original design, it would be profitable to examine the reconstruction drawing of the first project adduced by Hugh Harrison and Peter Ferguson (Figs 2.1.9 and 2.1.10; Appendix III). In comparison with the proportions of the extant monument, it will be readily seen that the main vault was originally lower, and that above it rose a harmonious three-part elevation of no great height. One can understand this comparatively modest design not fully satisfying a patron already well on course to complete the construction of an architecturally distinguished cathedral. It is also probable that he regretted the modest pretensions of his earlier choir-stalls, although he could hardly now reinvent them. When it

Fig. 2.1.9 Exeter Cathedral bishop's throne. North elevation showing the three tripod towers with figures conjecturally restored. Commissioned by Hugh Harrison. P. Ferguson.

planned height by approaching a third. In it the later tower section shoots up behind the finials of the original superstructure, carrying a substantial crowning vaulted image tabernacle for the large figure, with a spire above. The insertion of the new tower is graphically illustrated in a sectional elevation, where the massive tapered cross beams can be seen to be tenoned into the four corner posts, and, in turn, the posts of the new tower tenoned into them (Fig. 2.1.11). Unsatisfactorily, the highest image tabernacle is effectively obscured from view from below, behind the spire of the northern tripod, this perhaps being a small price to pay for such a radical change of plan (Tip-in 2.1.1). Appendix III dilates instructively on the throne's construction, and is supported by a raft of useful annotated drawings.

This co-terminal imposition of an over-weening taller central tower can be seen to have negated the original design, which featured, as its visual climax, the high level image gallery. It is most probable that this constituent, which also features on the sedilia (Fig. 2.1.12), and, most probably, the reredos, was, most likely, the defining architectural characteristic of Stapeldon's interior furnishing scheme.

In a recent article, Christopher Wilson has suggested that Exeter's nodding ogee arch appears to have been an adaptation of the trilobed arches on the wall arcade of the main upper chapel at St Stephen's, Westminster, created "by combining the ogee form of their central sections with the angling of their side sections"[36] (Fig. 2.1.13). He also cites the small nodding ogee arch over the image niche above the west door of the Berkeley Chapel at St Augustine's, Bristol, suggesting that it may very well be the first *exemplum* of the form, and, could have been an "internal adaptation" of Michael of Canterbury's wall arcading at St Stephen's.[37] Unlike the miniature arch in the jamb of the tomb of Thomas II Lord Berkeley and Joan Ferrers at the east end of the south choir aisle at Bristol, the Berkeley Chapel arch is no longer in two segments with the upper one projecting forward, as at St Stephens's, but has a smooth ogee forward trajectory.[38] By this and other means, Wilson sets out to demonstrate the extent to which, by *c.* 1300, Michael of Canterbury had influenced the Bristol Master. It is noticeable that, in outline, the nodding ogee arches in the lower stage of the Exeter throne canopy follow closely Michael of Canterbury's

came to the throne, however, Stapeldon may have felt it was not too late to literally raise his sights in regards to the all important throne. He was, after all, a prelate with plenty of personal and professional ambition.

The recent structural analyses by Hugh Harrison (Appendix III), and John Allan in the 1980s, have attempted to explain the evident equivocation at the base of the tower, where, for instance, the decorative carving on the interior faces of the tripod legs is hidden by the apparently secondary crenellated panelling. Their posited change of plan involved a secondary raising of the main vault, and the imposition of a tall skeletal tower and spire above. It was intended to raise the throne's

St Stephen's wall arcading. Thomas of Witney, when he was working there, would have had access to Master Michael's architectural models, even when the construction of the upper chapel had not yet begun. Although Wilson has demonstrated the Bristol master's familiarity with various aspects of the Exeter master's designs, and that he must have visited the cathedral, there seems to have been no dialogue between them over the Exeter throne, with Thomas sticking to his comfort zones at Westminster and Winchester.

By comparison, the sophisticated design of the Exeter sedilia is orthodox, yet it was probably manufactured within 5 years of the completion of the throne.[39] The seat canopies retain the hexagonal plan used for nearly all the later 13th-century French image housings, and the junctions of their gablets are adorned with small forward-facing beasts of a kind used on the south transept facade at Notre-Dame, Paris, and frequently thereafter. It has been pointed out that such beasts are extremely rare in early 14th-century England, and that their use is usually indicative of direct French *Rayonnant* influence.[40] Moreover, the style of the foliage carving on the sedilia is quite distinct from that on the throne canopy. Because it is on such a large scale, and the colour of the stripped oak timber is so dark, the throne appears unnecessarily heavy in comparison with the stone sedilia (the original colouring and gilding would have lightened its appearance considerably). The theme of the uprights intersecting the line of a gable on the throne is repeated in miniature on the tabernacle frame on the south side. Although managed differently, the same motif is found on the early 14th-century Easter Sepulchre at Hawton, Nottinghamshire.[41]

The Decorated sculpture of north-east England, and the contents of the chapter house at Ely, are too late in date to allow any meaningful stylistic comparisons. The place to be seriously considered is Winchester Cathedral, from where Thomas of Witney was called to Exeter in the summer of 1313. At that time, under Thomas's supervision, the consolidation of Winchester's troubled choir-stalls was still in progress. One of the most striking features on the Exeter throne canopy is the use of buttresses similar to those at Winchester with plain set-offs, inset panels and crocketted gablets with dogs' head terminals

Sketch showing Conjectural Reconstruction of Throne as Originally Planned.

EXETER CATHEDRAL, DEVON, BISHOP'S THRONE

surveyed, measured and drawn by PETER FERGUSON Dip.Arch(UCL), RIBA., 2012 – 2013.

(Fig. 2.1.14). The buttresses at Winchester were being employed as consolidants to prevent the stalls from collapsing, and were butted-up against the inner component of the original quatrefoiled supports of the major divisions of the earlier stalls (Fig. 2.1.15). It is noticeable that, at Exeter, the frequent jointing of buttress to buttress, and buttress to column, has become an integral part of the architectural syntax.

On the whole, the carving style at Exeter is more conventionally decorated than that at Winchester, less naturalistic and more broadly conceived. Yet the hawthorn foliage in the spandrel of the south gable, and on the crockets of the straight pediments, is quite close to that on the Winchester choir-stalls.

Fig. 2.1.10 Exeter Cathedral bishop's throne. Sketch showing conjectural reconstruction of throne as originally planned. Notice that the choir-stalls are copied from 19th-century photographs of those commissioned by Bishop Stapeldon in 1308, then at St Lawrence's Church. Commissioned by Hugh Harrison. P. Ferguson.

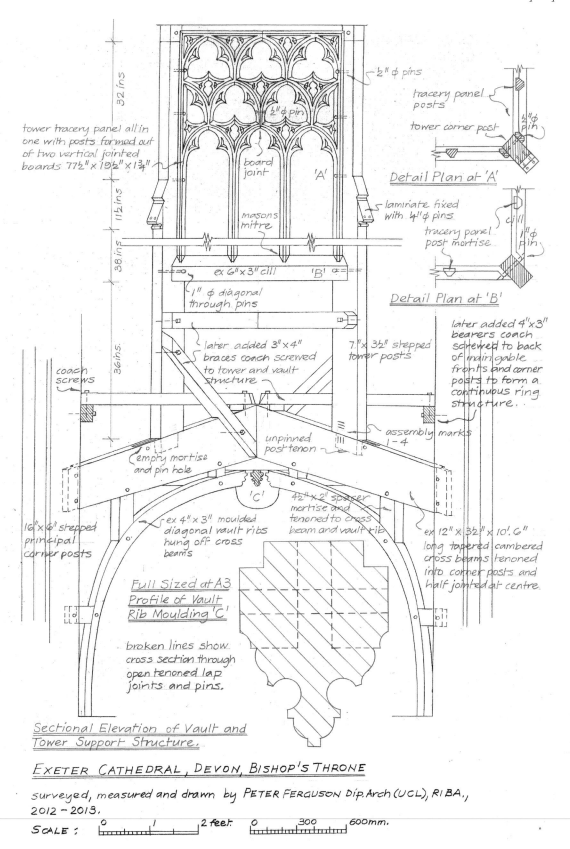

tower tracery panel all in one with posts formed out of two vertical jointed boards 77½" x 19½" x 1¾"

½" φ pins

tracery panel posts

tower corner post

½" φ pin

Detail Plan at 'A'

board joint

'A'

32 ins

masons mitre

11½ ins

laminate fixed with ¼" φ pins

tracery panel post mortise

cill

1" φ pin

Detail Plan at 'B'

38 ins

ex 6" x 3" cill   'B'

1" φ diagonal through pins

later added 4"x3" bearers coach screwed to back of main gable fronts and corner posts to form a continuous ring structure.

36 ins

later added 3" x 4" braces coach screwed to tower and vault structure

7" x 3½" stepped tower posts

coach screws

assembly marks 1-4

empty mortise and pin hole

unpinned post tenon

'C'

4½" x 2" spacer mortise and tenoned to cross beam and vault rib

ex 12" x 3½" x 10'.6" long tapered cambered cross beams tenoned into corner posts and half jointed at centre.

10"x 6" stepped principal corner posts

ex 4" x 3" moulded diagonal vault ribs hung off cross beams

Full Sized at A3
Profile of Vault
Rib Moulding 'C'

broken lines show cross section through open tenoned lap joints and pins.

Sectional Elevation of Vault and
Tower Support Structure.

EXETER CATHEDRAL, DEVON, BISHOP'S THRONE

surveyed, measured and drawn by PETER FERGUSON Dip.Arch (UCL), RIBA.,
2012 - 2013.

SCALE :   0   1   2 feet.   0   300   600mm.

Fig. 2.1.11 Exeter Cathedral bishop's throne. Sectional elevation of main vault, and tower support structure. Commissioned by Hugh Harrison. P. Ferguson.

The heads on the cusps of the arch within the south gable could well be a direct quotation from Winchester, where human-headed cusp terminations are ubiquitous.[42] However, Exeter does not share William Lyngwode's specialist interest in figure sculpture.

The foliage at Exeter shows no obvious links with that found on the shrine at St Alban's, of before 1308, although the crockets there do have spines curling up into pronounced volutes, as they do on the ribbed hawthorn at the base of the Exeter throne. As to any influence from the West-Midlands, the use of ball-flower is limited to the cusps on the tripods. The heads of the angels, holding the instruments of the papal Mass have the same hair-style, smooth faces and straight aquiline noses, as those on the cusps of Sir Richard de Stapeldon's tomb in the Exeter presbytery, of *c.* 1320, and other Devonshire sculptural examples, particularly the monuments at Haccombe and Modbury.

Whereas the throne was the first major piece of free-standing furniture to be set up in the new choir, a fresh set of choir-stalls, equipped with Bishop Brewer's 13th-century misericords, had already been ordered by the newly appointed bishop, Walter Stapeldon, most likely, in his first year of office. The Fabric Rolls record that, during the Christmas term 1309–10, a Master John of Glaston was paid to "remove the stalls".[43] In practice, the new stalls were set up in the recently completed Gothic choir, further east than they had hitherto been located at the east end of the nave and under the transept in the Norman church. There is now only one small stall component extant, the furniture having been replaced in the 18th century. However, Bishop Brewer's set of mid-

Fig. 2.1.12 Exeter Cathedral. Sedilia from south. H. Harrison.

Fig. 2.1.13 St Stephen's Chapel, Westminster. Detail of wall arcading. From Topham 1805, pl. xv. Society of Antiquaries of London.

Fig. 2.1.14 Exeter Cathedral bishop's throne. Butted decorated stanchions on east face of the northwest buttress of the lower zone. G. Young.

Fig. 2.1.15 Winchester Cathedral. Choir-stalls, north-west side. Detail of a secondary decorated buttress replacing the inner component of an original quatrefoiled column. C. Tracy.

the new stall design, with its modest echelon of gablets fixed to the back of the seat capping rail, suggests that the speed of this reordering was of the essence.[44] Glaston must have been an experienced joiner if, as seems probable, he had been involved in the provision of new choir-stalls at Glastonbury Abbey between 1291 and 1303.[45] His wage, of 3s 9d a week, was exceptionally high.

The Fabric Rolls for the year 1312–13 give a list of the men specially employed on the bishop's throne.[46] Besides Thomas of Witney, the cathedral's master-mason, who received 33s 4d a quarter and the use of a house in the close, for the first few weeks, there were the two head craftsmen, William Membiri and Robert Galmeton, whose weekly wages were 2s 3d and 2s 2d, respectively. Galmeton is later referred to as *custos carpentarie,* and he continued to be head-carpenter on the cathedral building staff after his special work on the throne was finished. After being paid off for his work on the throne in 1316–17, William de Membiri does not appear again in the accounts. Galmeton evidently supervised the provision of woodwork of all kinds needed for building operations. He is frequently referred to as making centering – *cinternas,* for which he received direct payment. The additional penny a week that was paid to Membiri may have been in recognition of his extraordinary skills as a wood-carver.[47] It will be recalled that no less than eight carvers would have been required to complete the job within 3 years. We have no record of their activity because of the lacuna in the records. In the summer of 1313, the carpenters referred to as receiving 2s a week (Robert Grosp and John Lock), and 1s 9d a week (Richard de Briggis, or Brugges, Walter Umfrey and Alexander de Holecomb) must have been competent craftsmen. At the same time, five carpenters, paid between 1s 9d and 1s 6d a week, are mentioned by name. A large number of sawyers, paid from 1s 1d to 1s 3d a week, were required to prepare the felled timber for seasoning.[48]

As already mentioned, John Harvey argued that the Thomas de Winton recorded in the Exeter Fabric Rolls was one and the same as the Thomas de Witteneye (Witney), who worked as an apprentice mason at St Stephen's Chapel, Westminster, in 1292–4,[49] and about a decade later at Winchester Cathedral.[50] There used to be an indenture at Winchester, which gave an

13th-century misericords, which Stapeldon salvaged, are still in residence in their fourth set of choir-stalls. The relative simplicity of

account of proposals for the rebuilding of the presbytery.[51] It was an agreement between Prior Richard (1309–1327) and the convent, and "Master T. of W. mason" – *cementarius* –, for the repair – *refeccione* – of the presbytery. On or before 1311, a Thomas de Wyteneye, mason, and his wife Margery were selling a tenement and garden in Calpe (St Thomas) Street, Winchester.[52] In November 1313, St Swithun's Priory, Winchester, obtained a licence to hold in mortmain 6 acres (*c.* 2.4 ha) of meadow in Michelmersh, granted to the priory by Thomas de Wytteneye.[53]

Of interest is to what extent, the design of the Winchester choir-stalls and the Exeter bishop's throne was the work of the same master. The Winchester choir-stalls betray a strong East Anglian flavour, having been designed by a Norfolk master-carpenter and carver.[54] However, after the departure of Lyngwode, an urgent consolidation of the structure had to be undertaken by the cathedral's new master-mason, Thomas of Witney. The manner and decoration of the remedial work betrays an assimilation of the earlier metropolitan-style architecture and stone furnishings in the crypt at St Stephen's Chapel, Westminster, and the funerary furniture at Westminster Abbey. Harvey argued that, when Master Thomas was summoned to Exeter, to advise on the sourcing of timber for the new episcopal throne, he was also required to supply suggestions for the monument's design. The resulting throne is redolent of the expertise of which Witney had already gained experience. The novel semi-structural ogee arches and the intersecting tracery of the spire, for instance, strongly suggest an intimate collaboration with a specialist joiner. We have no evidence that either Galmeton or Membiri were themselves considered seriously as architects or designers, as most master-carpenters would have been. On the other hand, their knowledge of the propensities of the material would have been invaluable. In the early part of Witney's professional career, his work tended to centre around the production of high-class, mainly stone furniture, for which he had developed a peculiar talent. Although he appears to have had little experience in designing timber furniture before Exeter, it is probable that his limited intervention on the Winchester choir-stalls had given him the confidence to attempt the commission. He would have become

used to collaborating with joiners, listening to their advice and incorporating some of their technical as well as stylistic ideas.

Master Thomas's salary at Exeter of approximately 2s 9d a week, may seem modest in comparison to the weekly wages of the two master-carpenters, but for site work, he was paid an attendance allowance of 3s a week. At this time, he seems to have been receiving a similar stipend from the Winchester chapter. Also in both cities as well as receiving the usual perquisites of office during residence, not to mention the profits from the supply of any building materials, his total emoluments would have left his master-carpenters at Exeter a long way behind.

Whilst it has already been possible to make certain stylistic comparisons between the Exeter throne canopy and the Winchester Cathedral furniture, the architectural similarities between the two timber monuments are even more convincing. Richard Morris went so far as to suggest that the two skilled masons, whom Witney introduced to Exeter, may already have been working with him on the feretory screen and in the presbytery at Winchester.[55] This argument depends upon the date of the feretory screen, however, about which there are currently two schools of thought, supporting either *c.* 1310 or *c.* 1320.[56] On the furnishings in wood and stone in both buildings, Morris pointed out a number of common elements in the architectural mouldings. For instance, at Exeter Witney seems to have introduced the Winchester-type undulating moulding profiles.[57] He gave special emphasis to the introduction of the additional bead mouldings on the necking of most of the capitals on the Exeter throne canopy, a trait that is significant for the attribution to Witney, and which was probably encountered for the first time in England in the undercroft of St Stephen's Chapel, Westminster, where the apprentice architect was employed in the 1290s.[58] This, probably, French *Rayonnant* characteristic seems to have been "popular with craftsmen like Witney who worked in wood: the easier carving quality of wood encouraging extra embellishment".[59] Witney probably worked alongside William Lyngwode, who used the same device at Winchester shortly before 1310. Morris pointed out that "its other main distribution was in East Anglia", which was the latter's native soil.[60] He also discusses:

Fig. 2.1.16 Exeter Cathedral. South-west nave clearstorey, second window. Detail of fishscale tracery. G. Young.

"a memorable feature of the pulpitum (being) the exquisitely carved foliage in its cusped and sub-cusped spandrels;[61] and exactly the same idea appear(ing) in the throne, in the tympana of the gables of the main canopy, rather hidden by the ogee arches in front of them.[62] The usage in a gable suggests a link in design, if not in execution, with the excessive foliage in its cusped and sub-cusped tympana of the north aisle tomb recesses in St Thomas's church, Winchelsea (1312 sqq.), virtually contemporary with the Exeter throne. And the ultimate source may well be the foliate spandrels of Lyngwode's choir-stalls at Winchester, a year or two earlier".[63]

It is clear that it is not possible to divorce the foliate style of the bishop's throne from its mouldings, and that any apparent waywardness at Exeter can be explained in terms of Witney's characteristic "robust" mouldings and the differences in local workmanship. The evidence in both locations discloses an ultimate dependence on the metropolitan *rayonnant* characteristics of the Court works, and subsequently, the tombs at Winchelsea and choir-stalls at Chichester Cathedral.[64]

Other examples of this expatriate style, consistently in Beer stone, can be found in both Devon and Cornwall.[65] In the latter, at the destroyed Glasney College, founded by Bishop Bronscombe, and with later bishops of Exeter as benefactors, has turned up many important archaeological fragments in the style. The heavily-rebuilt St Michael, Penkevil, offers more Beer stone work in the expatriate style.[66]

Winchester's influence on Master Roger's rebuilding of the presbytery and choir at Exeter, especially the latter, can be recognised from the mouldings of the presbytery north-east arcade, the gallery balustrades, the feretory screen, and the east arcade of the wall above it in the former.[67] The architectural dynamics between the two buildings are necessarily imprecise, due to the paucity of dating evidence at Winchester. However, the east side of the feretory screen, with its haunched and trefoiled gables, is comparable to the design of the lower level on the bishop's throne. Moreover, the possibility that the refugee arcading in St Andrew's Chapel, Exeter, which also has Winchester overtones, could have been a component of the Exeter high-altar reredos, has again been raised.[68] One final clue to Witney's fingerprints at Exeter cannot go unmentioned. Harvey focussed on the most characteristic of Master Thomas's window tracery patterns, a series of cusped trefoils set in curved triangles (Figs 2.1.16, 2.1.17).[69]

One side of each triangle is omitted, to create what we shall call a "fishscale" pattern, seen in its simplest form in the aisle windows of bays 2 and 4 of the Exeter nave, and in the bishop's throne. A characteristic detail is that the trefoil is kept intact within the fishscale frame, supported on a small "eye" or dagger.[70] The precursors of the fishscale pattern are likely to be the impaled trefoils and delicate curved triangles which appeared in the 1270s and 1280s in the east arm of St Paul's Cathedral, London, the greatest building of its generation and on which numerous masons from the home counties and beyond would have worked. Subsequently, a more ornamental version of the curved triangle with split-cusping appeared in the south-east, as in the diaperwork of sections of Prior Eastry's choir screen at Canterbury Cathedral (1304 sqq), and the aisle windows of St Thomas's, Winchelsea (before 1312). Without doubt, Witney was familiar with these examples, but it was not until his work at Exeter that the fishscale pattern developed from them.

Fig. 2.1.17 Exeter Cathedral bishop's throne. Fishscale tracery detail on tower lantern section. H. Harrison.

The case for personal attribution to him rests particularly on the evidence of the bishop's throne, where the motif appears seemingly for the first time, in the openwork tracery of the superstructure.[71]

As already stated, the entire throne is always referred to in the Fabric Rolls as the "*sedes episcopi*". During the Christmas term 1328–29, there are references to the provision of a *cathedra domini episcopi*, almost certainly a new chair for the bishop whilst officiating at the high altar.[72] The first item is noted in the Christmas Term, 1328–29, "For the part of the lord bishop's chair which is put out to task 12s 1d", and another "2 great (gross) and 20 small nails bought for the lord bishop's chair".[73] Then, in the following Midsummer Term, was an item "for making 2 bars, 4 'clomp', 4 staples and 4 hinges".[74] In the Michaelmas Term, 1329–30, a ring was bought for the chair,[75] and during the Easter, "One ox-hide (was) bought for the lord bishop's chair", a "cloth (*panno*)" and 2s was spent "For fretting (*frettenda*) (diapering/ornamenting/embroidery) the bishop's chair".[76] In the Michaelmas Term 1330–31, another metal fitting was purchased for the "lord bishop's chair".[77]

Erskine referred to this item as a "stone chair", although it is, surely, more likely that this "*cathedra*" was made of timber. Freeman had followed John Britton, who also claimed that it must have been made of stone, but his interpretation of "*frettenda* the bishop's throne" as "for scraping" is suspect. Erskine translated this word as "to decorate with fretted carving etc., which could apply to either medium".[78] The evidence is not clear-cut, but for what purpose would you need a gross of nails at the outset of commissioning a stone chair? Then there is the raft of iron fittings, and finally, the leather, which could have been used for serving as a seat, or covering a cushion? The use of the term *frettenda* is, admittedly, ambivalent, but if it relates to decorative carving, and the throne was made of stone, the carving would have been carried out during the manufacturing process, rather than a year later. By contrast, some low relief wood carving could easily have conveniently been undertaken on the wooden chair later *in situ*. The carved depictions of a throne in the mantel jamb of the stone fireplace of Bishop Vesey's time (1519–1551), now in the Deanery, has traditionally been thought to depict Bishop Leofric's *cathedra*.[79] We shall

never know whether the distinction being made during Grandisson's time, between *sedem* for his predecessor's massive choir throne and *cathedra* for a new bishop's chair, implies that Leofric's venerable stone chair was to be finally dislocated under the new regime. With the completion of the straight-ended Gothic presbytery with its tall reredos, one could speculate that his predecessor's ancient *cathedra,* might have been set up by Bishop Stapeldon on the north side of the altar. Chairs during the middle ages were important mediators of hierarchy, and given this particular one's ancient physical and spiritual provenance, it would, surely, have earned a place somewhere at the east end of the later building, representing a reassuring retrospective bridge to the institution's foundation.[80]

For whatever reason, John Grandisson, who was nominated bishop in 1327, commissioned this wooden *cathedra episcopi*. Its original placement is inferred from the list of expenses for 1346–47 (Easter Term), including an item for wages paid "for cleaning the reredos of the high altar, and the bishop's *cathedra (mundant' retrodors' maior' altar' cathedr' episcopi passionar')*".[81] Erskine noted that the almost illegible reading *passionar'* "may perhaps refer to a sculptured panel representing the Passion on or near the high altar". Given the entries relating to metal fittings, whilst Grandisson's *cathedra* cannot have been structurally canopied, it was fitted up to support a less formal "cloth of estate".[82] As a portable throne, it would have been more impressive, if less practical, than a traditional faldstool. If for whatever reason, it was subsequently considered to be no longer "fit for purpose" and removed from the sanctuary, it would, most probably, have enjoyed a long afterlife. Although in 1759 it was affirmed, by Andrew Brice, that there stood a bishop's chair on the north side of the high altar, there is no evidence to confirm that this was Grandisson's wooden *cathedra domini episcopi*.[83]

Before exploring some of the circumstances surrounding the commissioning of the throne, we need to gather up as much information as remains about the monument's later history. The 17th century was a dangerous time at Exeter for choir furnishings. Disastrously, in early 1638, with Charles I still on the throne, Witney's reredos was replaced by a substitute, inscribed with the name of the donor, Helyer, Archdeacon of Barnstable.[84] Presumably emanating from the turbulent 1640s, there is a tradition that the throne was deconstructed and buried for safety by one of the sons of Bishop Hall (bp 1627–1641).[85] At this time, random attacks were carried out by the soldiery occupying the Royalist city. Extant evidence of it can still be recognised, particularly in the damage done to the bishops' tombs.[86] On 16 January, 1658, during the Protectorate and the bishopric of Ralph Brownrigg, an order in the cathedral chapter states: "The late Bishop's seat and side walls in the inner choir of St Peter's Church each to be removed for better carrying on and perfecting that work".[87] At the same time, a petition was addressed to the House of Lords, which speaks of "an excellent Episcopal seat, not the like as is supposed in England, and seats for the Dean and Canons and a communion table railed in such curious work as cost near £100, 'were taken away etc'".[88] We cannot know what really happened, but surmise that Stapeldon's throne raised the ire of the Presbyterians, who were occupying the choir.[89] One could speculate whether Stapeldon's choir-stalls were then mutilated, or even destroyed, and, perhaps the throne canopy hidden away somewhere. More likely, it was left in position and camouflaged in some way. A considerable disincentive to its removal would have been the fact that the canopy weighs in excess of 10 tons.[90] Any further speculation on this point is obviated by a letter, dated 31 January, 1944, in the cathedral archives from Herbert Read, the respected timberwork conservator. In it he states that "… we found the original oak pins *still in place*".[91]

After the Restoration of the monarchy, of considerable interest is the visit of Cosimo III de Medici, Duke of Tuscany, to the cathedral in 1669, which was recorded by Count Magalotti, his secretary and friend. The party visited the cathedral at the hour of prayer, and the account continues:

> "On the Gospel side stands the ancient seat of the Bishop, but the present one is in a large marble tabernacle surmounted by a very high lantern; the ornaments of which, being taken from the Passion of Christ our Lord, show it to have been formerly (as was the custom in ancient times) the Pix of the most Holy sacrament. Now the seat of the bishop is there, in which he assists at the service, and curtains of taffeta are stretched from pillar to pillar; this throne is placed on the Epistle-side, at the head of the choir, which is in the body of the church, in the middle aisle".[92]

This passage has led to some confusion, and Edward Freeman was of the opinion that the "marble tabernacle", on the south side, referred to the sedilia.[93] This seemed to Vyvyan Hope to be most unlikely, particularly since Worth, referring to the restoration of the throne, had stated that "upon removing the brown paint with which it was coated, traces of white and gold colour were discovered".[94] Whereas "a large marble tabernacle surmounted by a very high lantern" hardly describes the tripartite sedilia, it could fit a monument that we know from the paint analysis contained a great deal of lead white. One could, surely, understand how a 17th-century visitor from Italy might have assumed that the polychromed white and gold throne was made of marble. Sinclair's polychromy analysis evidenced the widespread use of lead white on the monument in both the medieval and post-medieval periods. In any case, we know that a decade earlier, in the winter months of 1660–61, the throne was painted to resemble marble, which explains the continuing widespread appearance of lead white on the monument to this day (see Fig. App. 4.1).[95] The impact that it had on the Duke's secretary, of a gilded and painted marble monument, is not as unlikely as one might imagine. Given the parsimonious combination of white and gold in much of the medieval scheme, one could be tempted to suggest that Stapeldon was intending to embody an overt reference to King Solomon's ivory throne.

The first phrase of Count Magalotti's description contains a useful piece of information referring to the "ancient seat" standing on the Gospel (north) side. One would expect this to have been a wooden chair placed adjacent to the high altar for the convenience of the bishop. As it is described as "ancient", it could have been the "*cathedra*" commissioned by Bishop Grandisson in 1328.

Canon Freeman's obsession with the sedilia led him to claim that the item in the rolls for the Christmas Term 1317–18, relating to the carving of six images *pro sede episcopi*, referred to the sedilia, rather than to the canopy of the bishop's throne.[96] He claimed that there were only five sculpture platforms on the throne, but a total of six on the sedilia. We found on the recent inspection that it is not possible to be certain exactly how many there originally were, since some are modern replacements and lack fixing mortises. Freeman maintained that the sedilia must have been used by the bishop

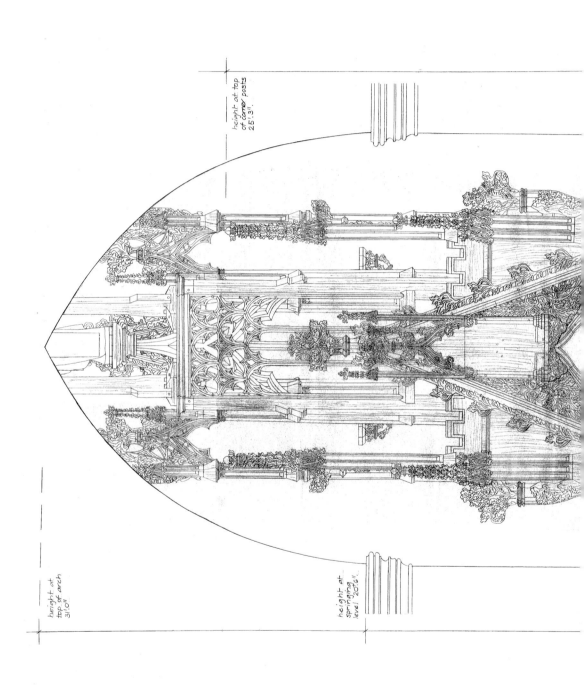

height at top
of corner posts
25'.3"

height at
top of arch
31'.0"

height at
springing
level 20'.6"

height at
springing at
vault 10' 6"

datum at
finished floor level

vault

fence

datum at
finished floor level

SOUTH ELEVATION

EXETER CATHEDRAL, DEVON, BISHOP'S THRONE

surveyed, measured and drawn by PETER FERGUSON Dip.Arch.(UCL), RIBA.,
2012 - 2013.

SCALE :   0   1   2   3 feet.   0   500   1000 mm.

Tip-in 2.1.2 Exeter Cathedral bishop's throne. South elevation. P. Ferguson.

when officiating at the high altar, and recounts the tradition that, at Leofric's consecration, the bishop was led by each arm by Edward the Confessor and Queen Eadgytha to the sedilia. Unfortunately for the historian, the sedilia is not separately referenced in the Fabric Rolls, but, rather, subsumed within the Altar Account. But there seems to be no evidence that it was ever referred to as the *cathedra*.

Sir George Gilbert Scott (1811–1878), whose involvement at Exeter covered the period 1870–1877, stated that:

> "The lower part (of the throne) was nearly all modern, and much of it was in plaster: indeed some of the parts of the old work (on the corner buttresses) remained, and those indications have been precisely followed, excepting that I yielded to pressure in making the front open".[97]

This statement is confusing, because the present arcaded front, usually considered to have been designed by Scott, is closed. However, there are two early photographs showing it backed by a draught-excluding cloth.[98] Thus, it seems that, quite soon after Scott's departure, the bishop had had second thoughts about the prescribed arrangement, and ordered the apertures to be filled in. Discussing the privileged treatment of the fence front in *Professional Recollections,* Scott continued:

> "This front is magnificently carried out, in exact imitation of the old work at its angles, which still existed; the sides and back are simpler, and follow evidences attached to the several angle buttresses". [99]

Although we cannot now know the sequence of events, we may assume that, with the exception of the south side, which appears to have been left untouched, the rest of the enclosure is now to Scott's design.[100]

Scott added that on the throne enclosure "The whole of the old work was cleansed of its paint and varnish, but where it had been decorated in colour this was preserved and restored".[101] This does not necessarily refer to medieval polychromy, although the portraits of four robed bishops, which were revealed, and, unfortunately, overpainted, would have been. It has been suggested that the figures may represent a quartet of famous Exeter bishops, selected from a choice of Warelwast, d. 1137, nephew of William the Conqueror; Quinil, d. 1291; Bitton, d. 1307; Stapeldon, d. 1326; and Grandisson, d. 1369.[102] However, if the paintings are coeval with the erection of the throne, it would have been too early

to include Grandisson. Is it not more likely that the second bishop would have been Bronscombe, d. *c.* 1280, who laid out the plan for the momentous eastern extension of the cathedral? The modern over-painting precludes the possibility of reaching any definitive conclusion.

The loss of the original bishop's chair is regrettable, and the extent to which the incumbent was originally raised up, and how the chaplains were originally accommodated must remain an open question. In the mid-18th century, Brice claimed that the "Seat" was erected on a "Supereminence, the Ascent to which is by 6 steps and its Area squares several Foot, in which the Episcopal Chair itself is placed, the same being cover'd with Crimson Velvet".[103]

The profile of the baldacchino-inspired canopy holds itself within the confines of its footprint, in the same way that the canopied figures in the east window, stay within their more fanciful architectural receptacles and the rigid margins of the glazing frames (Fig. 2.1.18).[104] Both compositions are tall and narrow, but the throne canopy has particular architectural and stylistic pretensions, such as the novel tracery, the layering of an ogee arch in front of a straight gable, the latter to become a commonplace of the mature Decorated style in church furniture, e.g. the choir-stalls at Gloucester and Lincoln, and finally the openwork spire with intersecting tracery, also seen on a smaller scale at Gloucester (Fig. 2.1.19).[105]

Given that, apart from the 19th-century documented evidence that the repainted images of bishops on the throne buttresses are copies of degraded medieval originals, there is today little indication that the monument was ever polychromed. Eddie Sinclair's report on the original painted decoration is welcome. Her painstaking analysis has revealed that the structure was, originally, "aglow" with colour (Fig. 2.1.20).[106] There is also the probability that "… large sweeps of mouldings, are likely to have been decorated with devices such as sheets of tin-relief imitating beaten metal or textiles", and marbling, thus resembling a more luxurious medium than timber. Although no medium analysis was carried out, it is probable that it is oil based. The lead white oil paint seen on the cathedral's timber vaults in the transepts, although dating

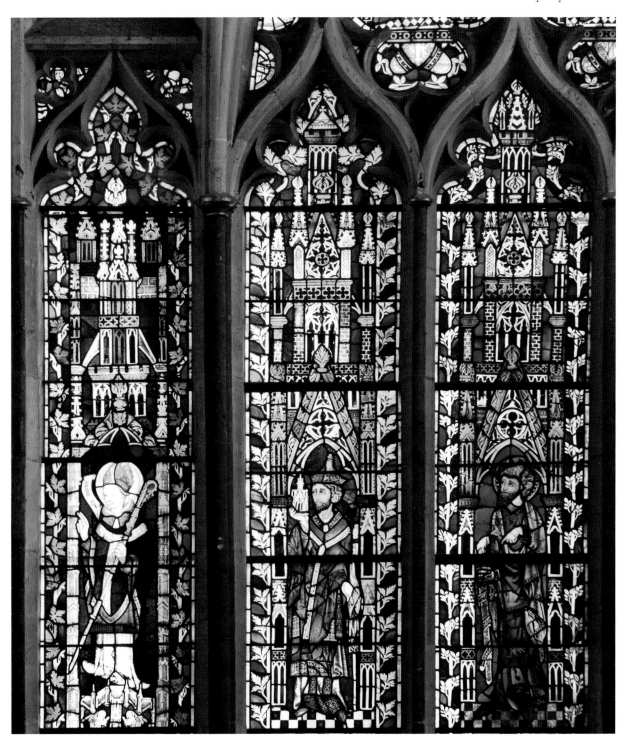

Fig. 2.1.18 Exeter Cathedral. Presbytery east window. Glazed triplet on south side with canopied images of St Peter, Matthew and Andrew. G. Young.

from Scott's restoration, echoes the original preparatory layers of all decorated elements of the medieval scheme.[107] On the throne it is likely that the same range of pigments was used as featured elsewhere in this important location, and a palette dominated by red, green and white, with some gold or yellow, and black, survives. Whilst the costly blues, azurite and indigo, were only found at ground level, it is likely that they were used elsewhere, given that the presbytery bosses and corbels were predominantly gold and azurite.[108]

The decorative sculpture is rich in its variety of human, animal and vegetal motifs. The

portrait-style male and female human heads on the south gable, popularly thought to represent Master Galmeton and his wife, are well known, but the images of a king and a bishop, presumably Edward II and Bishop Stapeldon, as well as the face of a woodling (with eyes closed) in the canopy vault, are harder to spot but uncommonly good. These heads must have been taken from the life, the bust of the king having more than a little in common with that of the albeit sharpened visage of the crowned monarch on the sedilia. The heads of king and bishop on the south side of the throne demonstrate psychological insight, predicating the work of a specialist metropolitan sculptor (Figs 2.1.21, a–c). The angels presenting the instruments of the papal mass, are both competent and sculpturally ambitious. They were the work of a different hand. The loss of up to five large free-standing figural sculptures, particularly that at the top, is regrettable, given the quality of some of the above.

Sinclair has observed that:

"From the west end of the cathedral, visitors would glimpse in the distance, beyond the lavish stone pulpitum, a pinnacle of green, red and white soaring to the vault, enclosing, a life-size figure, possibly of

St Peter. The patron saint in this position would… be appearing at the same height as the carved rood group above the pulpitum. Such effects were not accidental, but indicate that, although each individual sculptural element had its own liturgical function, the individual components worked together to create a theatrical liturgical ensemble".[109]

Discussion

Walter Stapeldon, for whom the canopied episcopal throne was created, was probably the eldest of seven children born to William and Mabil Stapeldon, whose ancestral land holdings lay in the parish of Cookbury, some forty miles north-west of Exeter. As farmers, the family cannot have been rich, as the inferior agricultural soil is only any good for cattle grazing.[110] Walter was probably born in about 1260, and was referred to as *magister* in a legal record of 1286. As John Maddicott has suggested, he must have displayed academic potential early, with his father managing to send him to a grammar school, most probably in Exeter.[111] We have no inkling of the patronage that Walter, and his brother Robert, managed to obtain to get themselves into Oxford. In Walter's case, that it was a West-Country contact is indicated on the basis that, by 1293, he was ordained and provided with a country living in South Devon. He quickly built up his

Fig. 2.1.21 Exeter Cathedral. Bishop's throne decorative sculpture: a. Sleeping "woodling" canopy vault boss; b. face of a bishop; c. head of a king; b. and c. are both head stops from south gable. H. Harrison.

connections with the cathedral at Exeter, was made a canon, and by 1305 precentor, and, soon after, Bishop Thomas Bitton's deputy.

Stapeldon's career has been well-documented, and we can build up a picture of a clever, hard-working self-starter, who through loyalty to his city, cathedral, and king, coupled with his innate administrative and diplomatic skills, carved himself out a successful career as an effective prelate, public servant and cathedral builder. The keys to this achievement were his knack of self-enrichment, if sometimes by dubious means, to facilitate his apparent generosity, and the ability to siphon-off the resources of his diocese to support his ambitious building programme. Paterson has also pointed out that:

> "Exeter was fortunate in the timing of its building. A stable chapter provided regular funding during the growing prosperity of Edward I's reign, and bishop Stapeldon was in a unique position to garner resources during the turbulent times of Edward II. The building had progressed sufficiently by the lean times of the thirteen thirties to make it possible for it to be completed before the Black Death. The short period of its construction allowed Exeter a unity of design which is unusual in English cathedrals".[112]

From the time of his appointment as precentor, Walter Stapeldon (bp 1307–1326) would have been greatly encouraged by the generosity of the endowment in the will of Bishop Peter Quinil (1280–1291), which had provided the cathedral with a reliable income.[113] Nonetheless, he was aware that the progress of building had so far been slow, notwithstanding the probable, mostly unrecorded, generosity

of Bishop Bitton (1291–1307).[114] He found himself in a position to give his time to prosecuting a scheme for raising money for the project from the diocesan sources. For example, from 1303–4, he is recorded as paying in to the building fund the not inconsiderable sum of £124 18s 8d, and, from then on, this became the regular episcopal contribution.[115] The annual subventions of the dean and chapter added up to £62 9s 4d, this sum representing exactly half the bishop's contribution, with the result that "a building programme could be planned with a staple sum of £187 18s guaranteed for it".[116] After 1325 the bishop's regular payment ceased, and he presented the fund with 1000 marks. At the same time, the chapter's contributions continued. The latter had the benign effect of preventing the collapse of the building programme after Stapeldon's unexpected demise. The dean and chapter regularly contributed small amounts of money, collected in various ways, and, finally, there were the generally small testamentary bequests from the diocesan clergy and laity.[117]

Veronica Sekules's analysis of the liturgical significance of Stapeldon's unique high-medieval suite of cathedral furnishings, is based on the individual contributions of the various components.[118] Apart from claiming that the reredos may well have been the first of its kind in England, she argued that the fragment of stone arcading in St Andrew's chapel is a refugee element from it.[119] Percy Morris maintained that this hypothesis was impossible, because it shows every sign of having been fitted flush to a wall. However it is now known that there was a wall behind the reredos, and that only the highest parts of the tracery would have risen above it.

Although the form of the reredos may have been inspired by the low-walled structures established by the 13th century, with saints' shrines placed above them (Fig. 4.34), Exeter Cathedral possessed no major relics, and was not a significant pilgrimage site. Although the reredos was provided with doors at each end, on the model of cathedrals like Winchester, there was no room, or need, for a feretory behind. The reredos itself housed a forty-five-strong sculptured hierarchy, headed by the Virgin, St Peter and St Paul, to whom the altar was dedicated. One wonders if the refugee relief figures, now on the south side of the entrance to the south choir aisle, could have come from the reredos, and whether the lost smaller sculptures on the bishop's throne canopy also adopted this somewhat classicizing style (Fig. 2.1.22). This seems doubtful, given that the six "images for the bishop's throne", were supplied as early as 1317–8, and would, more likely, have followed the refined and innovatory carving style of Galmeton's remaining workshop.[120] It is also possible to speculate that the 'putative' great figure of St Peter on the throne canopy was stylistically cognate with the decade-earlier, and restored, image of the saint in the presbytery east window. On the contrary, however, the style of the relief carvings seems closer to the glass painting than to anything else.

Sekules's thesis was that:

> "Walter Stapeldon was determined to overcome whatever perceived deficit the cathedral exhibited, by means of the Gothic classicism of its internal architecture and fittings, the complexity of its liturgy and sophistication of its music".[121]

Fig. 2.1.22 Exeter Cathedral. Displaced fragmentary early-14th-century relief carving of an apostle or prophet holding a book. G. Young.

She goes so far as to suggest that:

> "… the formidable group of holy images at the high altar rising from the floor to the stained-glass window above, was intended to simulate the effect of a vast reliquary. All this suggests a possibility that the Exeter liturgy was elaborated to the extent of being an attraction in its own right, equivalent to that of a cult".[122]

As far as the throne is concerned, it is important

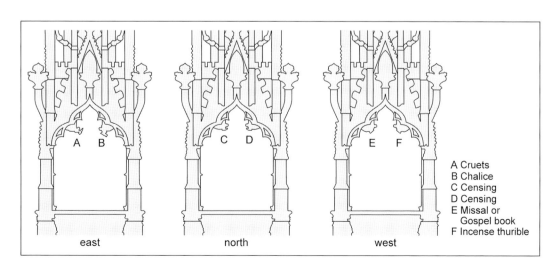

east   north   west

A Cruets
B Chalice
C Censing
D Censing
E Missal or
   Gospel book
F Incense thurible

Fig. 2.1.23 Exeter Cathedral. Vaulted throne enclosure. Diagram of throne canopy at ground level. Six carved cusp figures of angels on east, north and west aspects, presenting the instruments of the papal mass. G. Young.

*Fig. 2.1.24 Exeter
Cathedral. Bishop's
throne. Instruments of
the papal mass series of
angelic cusp sculptures
on the vaulted throne
enclosure: a. West face
north side. Angel holding
a Gospel book or Missal;
b. West face south side.
Angel with towel on wrist
holding a water jar or
thurible; c. North face.
One of the pair of angels
swinging censers; d. East
face south side. Angel
holding water and wine
cruets; e. East face north
side. Angel holding the
chalice. G. Young.*

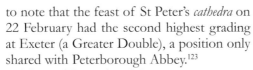

to note that the feast of St Peter's *cathedra* on 22 February had the second highest grading at Exeter (a Greater Double), a position only shared with Peterborough Abbey.[123]

The sedilia and pulpitum are two more liturgical fittings in the cathedral of crucial importance, but we need to focus on the issues emanating from the current research on the throne, that can amplify or finesse the findings of this most recent dissertation. To begin

with, it is profitable to assess the symbolism of the six surviving angels on the cusps of the ogee gables of the canopied enclosure on the west, north and east sides of the throne (Fig. 2.1.23). On the north side of the west face (E on diagram), an angel holds the Gospel Book or a Missal (Fig. 2.1.24a). Its counterpart is an angel (F), over whose wrist a large towel is draped, holding a cylindrical container (Fig. 2.1.24b). As Vyvyan Hope remarked, the presence of the towel or napkin on the angel's wrist, suggests the use of water for the bishop's hands following censing.[124] It has also been suggested that this was an unguent jar, although it is probably too large for that. A third suggestion, that Hope preferred, was that it was a container for incense. He quoted from Bishop Grandisson's Ordinal of 1337, which would support this:

> "*The Bishop then ascends to the altar steps, kisses the altar in the middle and the missal., and then puts incense into the golden thurible*".

He concluded:

> "Is it just coincidence that both in the Ordinale and on the throne itself the missal and the vessel in question are so closely connected?"[125]

On the north face (C, D) both angels swing censers, which are very damaged (Fig. 2.1.24c):

> "In each case the hand nearest to a spectator standing in the Quire holds a circular stop, which prevents the chain from slipping through his hand when the censer is swung. In between the hands, which are close to one another, the chains hang down in loops. But as the links cannot be carved in wood in three dimensions, these loops look like cords, or even strips of cloth. In each case the censer must have protruded from the further hand, but has been broken off".[126]

These censing angels are appropriately located on the side of the throne, from which incense would have been broadcast. As Sekules noted: "Much was made of the censing of bishops during Mass, whether they were officiating or not, and this was done immediately after the censing of the high altar".[127] Under Bishop Grandisson, the censing of bishop's tombs, unless the bishop was canonised, was prohibited. Under Stapeldon, it is clear that this practice had previously been permitted.[128]

As one would expect, on the east face of the throne we encounter Passion symbolism. There is an angel holding the wine and water cruets on the south side (A), and another with the chalice on the north side (B) (Figs

Fig. 2.1.25 Bishop Quinil's capitular seal. Exeter Cathedral Library. G. Young.

Fig. 2.1.26 Bishop Quinil's episcopal seal. Detail showing his mitred head under a canopy. Exeter Cathedral Library. G. Young.

2.1.24d,e). The theme is underlined by the application of copious carved vine foliage. The latter only occurs here, whereas the north and west sides display their own individually distinctive decorative foliage types.

Bishop Quinil (bp 1280–1291) was the third Exonian in succession to become bishop of Exeter, and as Sekules has demonstrated, he was ambitious and pretentious. His seal resembled that of the cathedral chapter, which shows St Peter under a canopy (Figs 2.1.25 and 2.1.26).[129] This was almost unique for the period, and it was argued that he may have been preparing to promote a cult of bishops at Exeter.[130] He exhibited a strong independence of spirit, consonant with the decision to deny

the communion cup to the laity, which had been ordained by the English Church in the provincial Synod of 1281. "You may depose me as a schismatic, you may burn me as a heretic, but, Bishop while I am, I will never deprive my flock committed to my charge of that which Our Lord died on Calvary to give them".[131] About this incident, the cathedral's Canon Collier remarked: "From hence it appears that the laity received the Communion in both kinds in the Diocese of Exeter, notwithstanding the late provincial constitutions of Lambeth to the contrary etc.".[132] The interesting question is whether this institutional defiance outlived Bishop Quinil, and influenced, in any way, the supercharged liturgical practices during Walter Stapeldon's tenure of office. The extraordinary scale of the chalice on Stapeldon throne canopy, seems to suggest that, in this regard, little had changed since Quinil's day.

Stapeldon's project was carefully thought out. As someone who was to become an Oxford Professor of Law, Vatican office-holder, diplomat, and civil servant with the ear of the king, he seems to have had an early premonition that he would spend most of his professional life in the limelight. His magnificent cathedral project must also have been intended to promote the institution's reputational profile. By the same token, he would have had every reason to bask in its glory himself, and quite possibly, have been infected somewhat with pretensions of grandeur.[133]

On entry to the cathedral, the imprint of Stapeldon's wealth and artistic ambition would have been signalled to visitors by the unprecedentedly tall canopy of the throne, rearing up behind the pulpitum. The design of his seal is also a measure of his self-confidence, featuring a canopy of honour, almost identical to that of his predecessor but one, Bishop Quinil (Fig. 2.1.27). By contrast, Thomas Bitton, his immediate predecessor, seems to have eschewed the use of a canopied episcopal seal.

Following his sudden and untimely death, the cathedral chapter was anxious to accord Stapeldon the most prestigious location for his burial, adjacent to both the temporary Easter Sepulchre (the tomb of Christ), when it was set up each year in Holy Week, and the high altar.[134] Sekules suggested that this was probably part of a long-term strategy to have Stapeldon canonised, which, in the event, was prevented by the bishop's unexpected end.[135] This was consistent with the long-established interest in a cult of bishops at Exeter, starting with Bronscombe's plan to move his predecessors tombs into the Lady Chapel.

Stapeldon was a model of a relatively new breed of civil-servant bishops, whose number in England rose to a high point of 12 in 1325.[136] Throughout their episcopacies, these men were required to undertake a range of additional duties over and above their administrative and pastoral diocesan responsibilties. Thus Stapeldon was a man of his time. However, over and above his meticulous attention to the needs of his ministry, including the routine conduct of confirmations, ordinations, and an impressive record of visitations, he applied himself with considerable energy to raising funds in the diocese for the great building project, as well as founding grammar schools, as well as Hart's Hall and Stapeldon's Inn, at Oxford (now Exeter College), endowing several hundred bursaries to these institutions for poor scholars.

Longer and longer absences from the diocese became a fact of life, the bishop only spending six Easters in Exeter during the 18 years of his episcopacy.

Were the surviving larger and more impressive British high-medieval episcopal thrones, at Exeter, St Davids, Hereford, Wells and Durham, supposed to stand as a continual reminder of the authority of the office, whether or not it was occupied or vacant at any one point in time? This raises the question of whether the blank spaces on throne backs were used to display the patron's image, or that of a venerable forebear. In a secular royal context, on the St Edward Chair at Westminster Abbey, it has been suggested that the attested painted seated figure in this position was probably St Edward the Confessor.[137] Unfortunately, no trace of any painted imagery on episcopal thrones survives in Britain or elsewhere.

Whether we can detect a whiff of hubris emanating from the unashamed architectural ambition of some of Britain's episcopal thrones is a question we shall be perennially considering. In Stapeldon's case, however, his institutional preoccupations were uppermost, to bolster the prestige of his cathedral and diocese and boost the cathedral's reputation and honour, not to mention its income. Or was this a patron who also hoped to bequeath a memorial to himself, even a monument perhaps worthy to become the relic of a sanctified prelate? Up to this point, episcopal thrones had changed little over time. In Britain the monumentality of the Exeter throne, and doubtless a good number of its successors, represented a new departure, which in European terms had seldom been attempted before. Moreover, at Exeter the project was ambitiously tied into a wider musical, liturgical, political and institutional strategy.

Notes

1   An early 16th-century copy of the Worcester *Chronologia aedificorum* (WCL MS A XII) records the building of the episcopal throne at Worcester Cathedral, probably *en suite* with the new choir-stalls, in 1380. Luxford 2005, 102.

2   Pevsner and Cherry 1989, 377.

3   Exeter's unique set of Fabric Accounts record 25 of the first 50 years of the 14th century. They were translated and edited by Audrey M. Erskine in two volumes, Erskine 1981 and 1983. John of Glaston's new stalls were placed in the new choir during the Christmas term 1309–10, see Tracy 1986.

4   Paterson 2009 unpublished, 10. For other recent discussions of the rebuilding of the east end at Exeter, see Jansen 1991, 35–56 and N. Coldstream, in Swanton 1991, 47–60. For the main sources on the medieval rebuilding and refurnishing of the cathedral, see, in particular, Ashworth 1853, Freeman 1873, 9–62, Oliver 1861, 175–80, and Glasscoe and Swanton 1978, 4–8.

5   Paterson's recent analysis and interpretation of the Exeter fabric rolls provides invaluable insights into the great rebuilding project at Exeter. For an accessible summary of his research, see Paterson 2011.

6   The question of whether the lower section was ever provided with screen work, except at the back, will be discussed below.

7   The decision to dismantle the throne and remove it to a place of safety, was taken in May 1941, probably in reaction to the bombing of Plymouth in March and April of that year. *Exeter D & C*, 17 May 1941.

8   This was probably Scott's plinth, the details of which can be recognised in a photograph in the Exeter Cathedral Library and Archives (ED 120/3/19). Its mouldings seem to conform well with Scott's fence screen above. Today the throne stands on a relatively shallow wooden plinth.

9   See Britton 1826, pl. xi; Carter 1797, pl.x and *Society of Antiquaries of London* 1792–96 unpublished, 1, 4.

10 The Ashworth drawing is in the collection of the Exeter Institution. It also provides a good view of the 18th-century choir-stalls. They were made by the joiner, John Gale, who was paid, following the repaving of the choir under Dean Milles (1762–1784). The asymmetrical positioning of the throne within its bay, is well illustrated in both Carter 1797, and Jones and Coffin, *The Ichnography of the Cathedral Church of St Peter at Exeter* (1757). A careful inspection of the drawing reveals that the front of the throne enclosure seems to have been embellished with carved figures and swags at each end. An early stereoview by G. W. Wilson, provides a more nuanced impression of its treatment at the time of Scott's intervention. Some of the additional carving, of unknown date, seems to have been in plaster. Scott 1879, 347.

11 Pers. comm. D. Walker.

12 A third alternative for the position of the original entrance was adduced by Hewett, who claimed that "There can be little doubt that it was originally open on the sides towards the choir, its platform being level with the adjacent stalls". At that time he would have been referring to the 18th-century stalls. See J. W. Hewett, *History and Description of Exeter Cathedral*, 1848.

13 An early photograph shows the fence panels on the exterior of the east side to be decorated with Baroque cartouches, probably dating from *c.*1660, when we know that a joiner was called in to remove the old choir-stalls, and to erect new ones. Their Baroque-style treatment is visible in the Ashworth drawing, on both the east and the north aspects, and

in the early photograph cited above, see University of Aberdeen, George Washington Wilson Special Collection, negative F0743X, available online at http://www.abdn.ac.uk/ historic/gww/index.htm. The photographic image shows that the entrance, at that time, was on the east side where it is today, although the throne was surrounded on three sides by choir-stalls and pews, those at the front for the use of the bishop's family.

14 Chudleigh, which is some 8 miles (*c.* 13 km) from Exeter, would have been well known to Stapeldon, as it was the location of his episcopal manor.

15 Appendices I and II.

16 Erskine 1983, xxxi.

17 For a pioneering account of the development the bishop's throne at Christ Church, Canterbury, see Phillips 1949. In monastic cathedrals the bishop was provided with another throne at the south-west stall entry, with the prior seated opposite him on the north side.

18 *Custus meremii ad sedem episcopi* is the heading of the bishop's throne project in the Fabric Rolls for Midsummer Term, 1312–13. Erskine 1981, 71 and Appendix I.

19 Appendix I, 1312–13, Midsummer Term, weeks 4, 7.

20 See Church Commissioners 98/8788, parish map for Newton St Cyres. The 1889 Ordnance Survey map seems to indicate a body of water adjoining the road. In September 2011, an inspection of the location was made, and the site of the former mill pool, now devoid of water, confirmed.

21 Pers. comm. C. Paterson.

22 Sekules 1991a, 172.

23 My grateful thanks to Cameron Stewart, the professional woodcarver, and Hugh Harrison for this estimate.

24 Erskine 1983, 269, Week 12, Christmas term, 1341–2.

25 Scott 1879, 348.

26 Cited in Worth 1878, 26; *Western Times*, 5 May, 1873.

27 At Winchester Cathedral, it must have been Thomas of Witney who was required, in *c.*1312, to shore-up the Norfolk master-carpenter/sculptor, William Lyngwode's, recently erected choir-stalls.

28 Witney almost certainly embarked on his career as a master craftsman in the early 1290s in the crypt of St Stephen's Chapel, Westminster. See Harvey 1984, 339.

29 The trailing common hawthorn-leaf tresses at Exeter on the south gable of the throne canopy, are developed out of similar ornament at Winchester and elsewhere. The three front gables are thematically differentiated, the east side featuring exclusively vine, the north voluted trefoil, and the west sycamore maple. I continue to deprecate the use of "seaweed" in discussions of Decorated foliate ornament.

30 Pevsner and Cherry 1989, 377.

31 For Beverley, see Pevsner and Neave 1995, 290–1. The monument has been associated with Lady Eleanor Percy, d. 1328, see Coldstream 1994, 150 and frontispiece.

32 For Bishop Salmon's hall, Pevsner 1962, 229, 230, and Pevsner and Wilson 1997, 219–20.

33 Hutchinson 1948, 14, 15.

34 For Sekules's discussion of the Decorated style in the East Midlands, see Sekules 1986.

35 Allan and Jupp 1981, figs 1–9.

36 Wilson 2011, 101–2.

37 *Ibid.*

38 For the Berkeley Chapel nodding arch see *ibid.*, fig. 4.28.

39 The sedilia is never mentioned, as such, in the Fabric Rolls. It was subsumed within the High Altar accounts. Mackenzie Walcott's dating of *c.* 1320, for the completion of the sedilia, has not been challenged by later historians.

40 The canopy above the image of the Virgin in the north nave aisle at York Minster is instanced, and the tomb chest of the de Valance monument at Westminster Abbey, in Wilson, 1979 unpublished, chapter 4, n. 94.

41 For the Hawton Easter Sepulchre, see Sekules 1986, fig. xxvia.

42 Tracy 1987, pl. 60.

43 Tracy 1986, 99–103, figs 21–3. For the relevant entry in the Fabric Accounts, see Erskine 1981, 49.

44 Tracy 1986, figs 21–3.

45 Harvey 1984, 118.

46 See Appendix I.

47 Pers. comm. Hugh Harrison.

48 The individuals involved in the supervision, felling, processing, sawing and labouring, with their weekly rates of pay, during the Midsummer Term, 1312–13 were as follows:

Master Thomas of Witney	3s
William Membiri	2s 3d ? Master-carver.
Robert Galmeton	2s 2d Master-carpenter.
John Loch	2s/1s 10d
Robert Grosp	2s
Richard Briggis	1s 9d
Walter Unfrey	1s 9d
Alexander de Holecomb	1s 9d
2 sawyers	1s 8d
Thomas Atta Wichie	1s 7d
J. Prodomme	1s 6d
J. Schere	1s 6d
3 sawyers	1s 3d/1s 1.5d

Benedict Scrogeyn   1s
Robert Crop   11d.

49 Harvey 1994, 338–41, for his putative account of Witney's career.

50 "Winton" identifies Witney's current abode in Winchester (archaically Wintonceastre).

51 *Ibid.*, 339.

52 *Ibid.*

53 *Ibid.*

54 For a comprehensive discussion of the Winchester Cathedral choir-stalls, see Tracy 1986, 16–24.

55 R. K. Morris 1991, 57–62.

56 *Ibid.*, 69.

57 *Ibid.*, 58.

58 *Ibid.*, 58–60, and R. K. Morris 1979, fig. 16r.

59 *Ibid.*, 60.

60 *Ibid.*, n. 19. The other moulding devices employed by Witney at Exeter are the elaborate bases on the throne, pulpitum and sedilia, symmetry, hollows and prominent fillets, the omission of scroll and keel mouldings, and foliage spandrels. *Ibid.*, 58–61.

61 *Ibid.*, pl. xia, i.e. the hawthorn-type foliage on the west side of the pulpitum.

62 *Ibid.*, pl. xiib. This foliage is most visible on the rear gable of the canopy.

63 R. K. Morris 1991, 61. See Tracy 1987, pls 64, 67.

64 For the architecture and ornament on the Chichester Cathedral choir-stalls, see Tracy 1987, figs 29, 38, 46, 50, 51.

65 In Devon, their work is also found at Bere Ferrers, Haccombe, Littlehempston, Landkey, Kingskerswell and Broadclyst. Pers. comm. John Allan, who points out that the fabric rolls tell us that the masons working at the cathedral, prior to *c.* 1300, were from outside the county, especially from Somerset and Dorset, whereas, by the early 14th century, they were Devonians.

66 For Glasney, see Allan and Blaylock's "The Architectural Fragments", in Cole 2005. The principal general reference to Cornish churches is now Orme 2010.

67 R. K. Morris 1991, 66.

68 *Ibid.*, n. 59. That the St Andrew's fragment was part of Witney's reredos was first suggested by Scott, and later by Bishop and Prideaux 1922, 57, 112. Most recently, the suggestion was revived in Sekules 1991, 174.

69 Harvey 1984, 340.

70 R. K. Morris 1991, n. 70.

71 *Ibid.*, 72–3.

72 1328–29, Christmas Term, Week 13. Erskine 1983, 218.

73 1328–29, Christmas Term, Weeks 13, 14. Erskine 1983, 218.

74 1328–29, Midsummer Term, Week 3. Erskine 1983, 221.

75 1329–30, Michaelmas Term, Week 12. Erskine 1983, 226.

76 1329–30, Easter Term, Weeks, 2, 3, 10. Erskine 1983, 229–30.

77 1330–31, Michaelmas Term, Week 12. "One bar (*barra*) for the lord bishop's chair 6d". Erskine 1983, 236.

78 1329–30, Easter Term, Week 10. Erskine 1983, 230, 233, n. 7.

79 Leofric was bishop of Exeter from 1050–1072.

80 For a discussion of the hierarchical distinction between an earlier and a later archbishop's throne at Christ Church, Canterbury, see Phillips 1949, 30–6.

81 See 1347–48, Easter Term, Week 1. Erskine 1983, 276 and 278, n. 3.

82 *Ibid.*

83 Brice 1759, where the author states, in parenthesis to his description of the bishop's *sedes*, "Another the like hath Station at the Right Side of the Altar", 542–3.

84 Huxley Thompson 1933, 42.

85 Exeter was a centre of loyal Royalist support. In 1645 the episcopacy was abolished in England in the Long Parliament.

86 Lehmberg 1996, 29, 33, 40.

87 Morris 1940 unpublished.

88 *Ibid.*

89 Lehmberg 1996, 49, and n. 78.

90 Pers. comm. H. Harrison.

91 In the letter Read states that: "It is true that the Throne had undergone considerable repairs on more than one occasion – for I saw much evidence of this & it is also quite within the bounds of possibility that the whole thing in its entirety might have been moved slightly – indeed I think it had been lifted bodily – but I am sure it had never before been taken to pieces – which of course would have been necessary if it had been removed from the Cathedral. There is no doubt about this". *Exeter D & C.*

92 Chope 1918, 108–9.

93 Freeman 1873, 38. For his full account of the sedilia, 37–42.

94 Worth 1878, 26.

95 C. Brooks, "The building since the Reformation", in Swanton 1991, 220.

96 1317–18, Christmas Term, Week 9. Erskine 1981, 94.

97 Scott 1879, 347.

98 There are two photographs showing Scott's final open front fence arcade, with the later cloth backing, available from "Images Online", in the Devon Heritage Centre, <http://

99   Scott 1879, 348.

www.devon.gov.uk/localstudies/151428/6. html&s=2TVUBS494vP>. <http://www. devon.gov.uk/localstudies/151494/34. html&s=lvC0kJ1b1qz>.

99   Scott 1879, 348.

100 Scott's presentation of the front of the fence screen at Exeter is reminiscent of the authentic example at Hereford Cathedral, where he had supervised the root and branch re-ordering of the choir furniture some 15 years earlier. See Chapter 2.3, figs 2.3.1, 2.3.3, 2.3.6b, 2.3.11.

101 Scott 1879, 348.

102 Addleshaw 1898, 82.

103 Brice 1759, 542.

104 For a discussion of the comparable stained glass windows at Hereford Cathedral, see Chapter 2.3, 81 and fig. 2.3.16.

105 Tracy 1986, pls 164a, b.

106 See also Appendix IV, Fig. App. 4.1.

107 Scott's further colouration is misleading. Conservation work carried out on the choir and presbytery vaults indicated that the 19th-century painting is a poor representation of the original decoration beneath.

108 The fabric accounts of Midsummer 1301–2 record the purchase of "gold, silver, azure and other colours", which Anna Hulbert identified as being intended for this group of carvings. This was subsequently confirmed through visual and microscopic analysis. Erskine 1981, 24; Hulbert 1991, 189.

109 Sinclair 2012 unpublished.

110 The principal sources for Stapeldon's life are Oliver 1861, 54–70; Buck 1983; 2012 and Maddicott 2009 unpublished.

111 Whilst his worldly brother, Sir Richard, inherited the manor, Walter's brother, Robert, was also educated at Oxford, and ended up as doctor of civil law. He was later principal of Checker Hall. Maddicott 2009 unpublished, 2, Buck 1983, 27.

112 Paterson 2011.

113 *Ibid.*, 9.

114 Erskine 1983, ix.

115 *Ibid.*, 10.

116 *Ibid.*

117 Such as, excerpted from the annual account of "John de Schyreforde Chaplain Warden of the Work of the Church of the Blessed Peter of Exeter etc.; ... After the feast of St Michael 1323. ... And of 20s from the testament of dom. John de Cnowille in part payment of 40s on the feast of the said John for the Work of the Blessed Peter of Exeter aforesaid. And of 6d from the testament of William Attehope of the parish of Clyst Hydon. And of 20s from the testament of

dom William de Traci rector of the church of Morthoe". Erskine 1981, 146.

118 Sekules 1991a and 1991b. The Saxon minster was dedicated to the Virgin and St Peter.

119 Sekules 1991a, 174; 1991b, 114.

120 In any case, the most active period for the stone carving of the images for the reredos was in the period 1320–1325.

121 The argumentation for a highly sophisticated liturgy begins with Bishop Bronscombe's statute of 1275, "that no vicar or other inferior minister or clergyman was allowed to officiate in choir, whatever his learning or emolument, unless he could play a musical instrument or had knowledge of singing" (Sekules 1991a, n. 60); "… the extensive directions for singing in polyphony, which are evident in Grandisson's books, would seem not to have been entirely his initiative" (n. 61); it is pointed out that Bronscombe instituted the feast of St Gabriel in 1278 as a feast of major grading (ns 61, 62); "Exeter had more double feasts than any other English church – 65 as opposed to the 50 according to Sarum – and one extra grade of double feast" (n. 62); Sekules also mentioned, amongst others, "genuflection to the altar at the *Incarnatus* in the Creed rather than inclination as practised elsewhere, and a distinctive sequence of colours" (n. 63).

122 *Ibid.*, 178.

123 *Ibid.*, 175. In the 11th century the feast had only a minor grading. See "Calendars" in Wormald 1934.

124 Hope *c.* 1940 unpublished, 4.

125 *Ibid.*

126 *Ibid.*

127 Sekules 1991a, 176, n. 47.

128 *Ibid.*, 176. n. 49.

129 This fragmentary wax impression of the top of the seal in the Exeter Cathedral library shows another, if somewhat perfunctory, architectural canopy, which is missing on the Society of Antiquaries impression. For the latter, see *ibid.* fig. xxvid.

130 *Ibid.*, 175.

131 Quoted from a lecture by J. M. Neale, and excerpted in Hope c. 1940 unpublished, 5. Quinil's Synodal Statutes for the diocese of Exeter 16 April 1287, and the *Summula*, are transcribed in Powicke and Cheney, 1964, 982–1077.

132 Allegedly the words of Canon Collier of Exeter. Quoted in *ibid.*, 5–6.

133 Oliver 1861, 54–66.

134 Thomas Bitton, had been buried on the lowest step of the high altar.

135 Stapeldon was beheaded on 15 October 1326 by the London mob, which supported

Mortimer and Queen Isabella's landing on the coast of Suffolk, to depose Edward II.

136 Pantin 1955, 9, 12.
137 See Rodwell 1982, 32, figs 91, 97.

2. St Davids Cathedral

Description and physical analysis

The episcopal throne at St Davids Cathedral, an ancient college of secular canons, is one of only three medieval timber examples of monumental proportion in Britain (Fig. 2.2.1, Tip-ins 2.2.1, 2.2.2). It is surprising, given its precocious architectural design and stylistic ambition, that it is so little known and regarded.[1] An attempt here will be made to place it in a stylistic context, in order to suggest a credible date for its manufacture and a motivation for its installation in the cathedral at that time.

The liturgical choir at St Davids remains under the crossing tower, where it has been since the late-12th century.[2] Curiously, it shares with Hereford Cathedral this confinement of the clergy stalls, it being usual in the High Middle Ages for the latter to occupy the east end of the nave as well as the crossing.[3] The extant late-15th-century furniture consists of 28 back-stalls, including the six returned seats at the west end. This is a comparatively small number, but it fits comfortably within the confines of the crossing tower. By comparison with the larger 14th-century English back-stall sets (Winchester Cathedral, 66, Wells Cathedral, 55, and Chichester Cathedral, 48), the Pembrokeshire furniture is modest in scale.[4] In the 14th century, at St Davids the seating capacity was even smaller than it is today. Browne Willis lists only 24 members of the medieval cathedral, who were accommodated in nine lateral back-stalls on each side, and the existing number of returned seats at the west end, and a matching quota of sub-stalls (Fig. 2.2.2).[5] The present total of 28 stalls contains four unallocated seats, which would not have been required in the 14th century.

It has been suggested that the present stalls were set in train as early as the 1470s under Bishop Tully (Fig. 2.2.3).[6] However, if the latter did initiate the project, the process would have dragged on over three episcopates. In practice, it seems that the furniture was paid for by the bishop and a prebendary, and that the carved Tully arms are retrospective.[7] It seems more likely that the construction phase was contained within reasonable bounds, completion being before 1501, the date of the marriage of Prince Arthur and Katherine of Aragon. The carved stall-ends with the Prince of Wales's feathers, pomegranates and the heraldic Tudor rose clearly celebrate this occasion. The painted coat of arms of Bishop Vaughan (bp 1509–1523), formerly on the back of the episcopal stall, must be retrospective.[8] The construction of a new set of choir-stalls must, at least, have been partly necessitated by the need to increase the clergy accommodation. It will be argued that the throne is a component of Bishop Gower's 14th-century choir furniture.

The bishop's throne partially blocks the south *ostium chorum* in the open fourth bay west of the high altar. These arcade openings at the east end of a presbytery were routinely used in greater churches by both choir and clergy for rapid ingress and egress to and from the choir. However, in this case the throne could have been set back into the bay opening, but would have isolated the bishop somewhat from his choir. Its present eccentric position was clearly a compromise, intended, whilst leaving the arcade open, to ensure that he was as near as possible to his clergy and choir. The attempt to fence off the resulting ensemble

Fig. 2.2.1 (far left) St Davids Cathedral bishop's throne. H. Harrison.

Fig. 2.2.2 (below) St Davids Cathedral. Choir ground plan. J. Read.

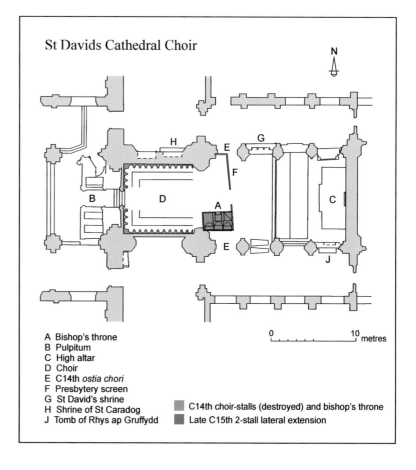

St Davids Cathedral Choir

N

A Bishop's throne
B Pulpitum
C High altar
D Choir
E C14th *ostia chori*
F Presbytery screen
G St David's shrine
H Shrine of St Caradog
J Tomb of Rhys ap Gruffydd

0   10 metres

  C14th choir-stalls (destroyed) and bishop's throne
  Late C15th 2-stall lateral extension

of choir furniture with a screen, only serves to emphasise a somewhat untidy appearance (Fig. 2.2.4). Where the presbytery screen runs up to the south-east corner of the throne, it will be noted that the end double-panel dado section has been truncated to make room for a secondary entrance to the throne (Fig. 2.2.5). It is most likely that, in the first place, the entrance was from the choir side.

The similarity of the chancel screen's dado panels to the throne's fence screens, and the mid-14th-century appearance of its superstructure tracery, indicates that, in one form or another, they played a part in Bishop Gower's mid-14th-century choir furnishings. Although of similar date, the present screen is probably fulfilling a function secondary to the construction of the throne to fence off the *cathedra* from the choir. Notwithstanding its somewhat inept reconstruction after the consolidation of the tower under George Gilbert Scott in the mid-1870s, it has a liberally decorated dado containing figure paintings on both sides, probably of saints and prophets, and must formerly have enjoyed a prominent position. An identical dado screen is also employed to fence off the south side of the bishop's throne, and there is no reason to question whether or not this application was coeval.

On the presbytery screen's eastern architrave, the evidence of a, presumably, 15th-century polychromed enrichment with painted vine-scroll frieze can still be made out (Fig. 2.2.6). Jones and Freeman, and others, have pointed out that the long cornice exactly fits the space between the north and south tower arches.[9] Various opinions have been aired over the years about the screen's original function. The evidence of the painted vine-scroll decoration on the east face suggests that it was recycled from a late-15th-century re-assemblage, presumably associated with the reordering of the choir-stalls in the late 15th-century.[10] The hypothesis that the superstructure of the presbytery screen may have functioned as a parclose behind Gower's stalls was rejected by Crossley and Ridgway, on the basis that it is neither panelled nor canopied, and that the distance between the uprights suggests that it would not have worked effectively behind the normal spacing of choir-stalls. Significantly, in the 19th century, part of a finialled ogee canopy was discovered behind the choir-stalls. This suggested to Jones and Freeman that Gower's stalls had been canopied. Although this is likely, such treatment may have only been applied to the dignitaries' returned stalls at the west end.

The editor of the 18th-century edition of the *Menevia Sacra* commented that "This throne

Fig. 2.2.4 St Davids Cathedral. South-east end of presbytery screen. H. Harrison.

Fig. 2.2.5 St Davids Cathedral. Detail of 14th-century-type foliate dado-panel carving on the south-east side of the presbytery screen, hard up against the throne. Note the botched 19th-century reconstruction of the original double panel, to make way for a new ceremonial entrance, and the mismatch between the upper and lower dado levels; also the ephemeral outline of a haloed human head on the panel. H. Harrison.

Fig. 2.2.6 St Davids Cathedral. Presbytery screen. Detail of vine-scroll painting at south end of architrave. H. Harrison.

was much larger and fuller of work than at present; but as some of it decayed, other parts were taken away to preserve it uniform etc." By the mid-19th century, the received view was that the monument, in its surviving form, was little more than a 15th-century carcase, adorned with discarded fragments from Bishop Gower's choir-stalls. The recent careful archaeological examination of the throne, by Hugh Harrison and Peter Ferguson, suggests that all of the losses referred to were made

good by George Gilbert Scott in 1869, and that the architecture of the superstructure is unaltered.[11] Scott's careful restorations amount to about 40% of the coeval fabric. Crossley and Ridgway had complained that the throne does not match the watercolour drawing by the Rev. John Parker, which they illustrated.[12] Their main concern seems to have been that, in the drawing, the top lantern appears to have been shown as open, "but now it is boarded up". Our research has confirmed that the superstructure has always been fitted on three sides with painted panels, most of which still display medieval polychromy. In any case the panel boarding is clearly indicated on the drawing by John Chesil Buckler, inscribed 1815, which, in all respects, has been shown to be an accurate representation of the unrestored throne.[13] It is probable that Parker did not visit the cathedral until 1836.[14]

The monument consists of three stages.[15] At the base, are the seats, for the bishop at a higher level, and his chaplains on either side. Above, is the pierced and buttressed skeletal semi-hexagonal central canopy, from which rises a two-tier rectangular blind lantern tower, the panels in total containing the images of six saints. The structure is topped by a crocketted and finialled spire, the centre part rising to a height of about 29 ft (8.8 m).[16] From a joinery perspective, the techniques employed are transitional, on the one hand, employing a monumental structural frame, whilst at the same time, harking back to the solid constructive techniques found at Exeter (Appendix III).

From the ubiquity of the traces of gesso ground and original polychromy on most of the woodwork, but particularly on the superstructure, one can state with confidence that the throne was decorated all over in the traditional medieval colour scheme of red, green and blue.[17] It is regrettable that it probably survives only because of the difficulty of removing it, a job that was, however, methodically undertaken at ground level. Even there, where the original surface is pretty much lost, the faintest vestiges of formerly painted haloed profiles are discernible on some of the dado panels of the throne fence screen on the north side, and particularly on the south-east side adjacent to the modern throne entrance (Fig. 2.2.5). What are certainly the earliest surviving sketch drawings of the throne, from the library of Browne Willis, are signed by a certain E. Pigott and dated 1729 (Fig. 2.2.7).[18] The image of the north elevation faintly outlines three, apparently, Baroque-style painted empty fictive recesses "in black leading paint", that were, presumably, visible at this time. The companion ground plan of the front part of the seating area, including the entrance and fence-screen, is only diagrammatic, but at least it shows the position of the, now lost, lectern "standing and turning on a pillar

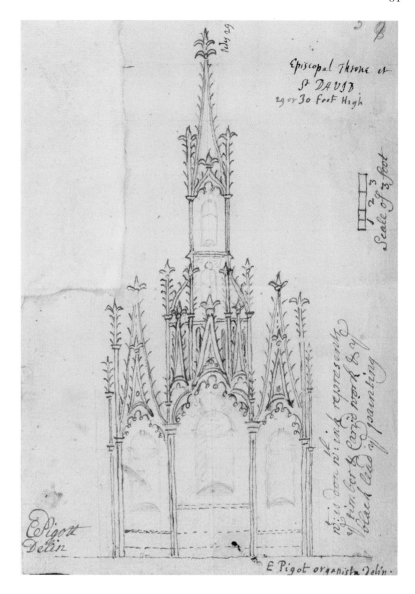

of timber for my Lord's book". Of the five surviving early structural British thrones in stone or timber, those at Hereford, Wells and Durham can definitely be said to have used an integral book-rest, in the place of a lectern.

The outline of the pencilling on the panel above suggests that, at that level, the image was medieval and probably still recognisable. The panel at the second level, however, seems to be another of the overpainted empty classical tabernacles. Behind the seats at ground level, and in spite of, or perhaps because of the evident Baroque overpainting indicated in the ink drawing, it is no surprise that the faintest traces of medieval figurative painting are still visible.[19] On the back of the bishop's seat, there are the faintest traces of a single central figure.

Fig. 2.2.7 Ink drawing of the St Davids Cathedral bishop's throne, with the remains of painted panels outlined in pencil. Dated 1729, by E. Pigott. Oxford, Radcliffe Library, Ms Willis 37, fol. 5r. Oxford, The Bodleian Libraries, The University of Oxford.

Fig. 2.2.8 St Davids Cathedral bishop's throne. Image of St Andrew on the lower half of the bishop's throne's lantern tower. East side. H. Harrison.

Fig. 2.2.9 St Davids Cathedral bishop's throne. Image of the reverse. H. Harrison.

The outline of what may very well have been a throne side can be detected on the right. Was this possibly an image of the enthroned Christ? There were two figures on each of the flanking panels. Were these angels? From Eddie Sinclair's fastidious gleanings at Exeter,[20] the abundance of polychromy on the superstructure of the St Davids throne would not have been out of the ordinary.[21] Other than Sinclair's ground-breaking research at Exeter, very little, if any, formal analysis has ever been undertaken on the existence of polychromy on English choir furniture, yet one would expect that evidence of the phenomenon would be freely elicited.[22] With the exception of the ground level, the St Davids throne is lucky to have escaped any repainting or scraping in 600 years. For this is reason alone, its historical significance as an ecclesiastical monument is secure.[23]

From the scaffolding, as well as ground level, the remaining fugitive images of five of the originally six painted saints can be observed. Although the female figure on the north-facing upper niche is unidentifiable, by tradition, it represents the Virgin Mary. The east-facing male saint at this level is still identifiable as St Andrew, the cathedral's joint dedicatee since the 12th century (Fig. 2.2.8). It is possible to make out the form of his cloak to the right and the saltire cross at his feet. The other readable images are standing figures in profile, as one might find them on the dado of a 15th-century chancel-screen. It is clear that these images, and probably the even more fugitive ones behind the three stalls at ground level and on the front of the fence screen, are part of a secondary late-15th-century programme. This would probably have been evidenced by richly decorated and prominent haloes like that still recognisable on the figure of St Andrew, and reminiscent of those on late-15th-century East Anglian chancel screens.[24] An interesting feature of the image's strikingly graphical character is the use of black hatched shading lines, which also appear in a slightly different form on the figure of the same saint at Marker's Cottage, Killerton, Devon. The dating of that screen, from a rare secular setting, cannot be earlier than the mid-1520s, given that it also contains Renaissance candelabra decoration. The St Davids image is linear in character, and experiments with perspective. It was most likely a copy of a late-15th-century German or Flemish woodcut.

The throne appears to have been intended

to be read through 360°, there being less, but enough, evidence to confirm the former use of polychromy on the back of the lantern tower (Fig. 2.2.9). The panelled reverse evidences the plentiful use of red oxide pigment on the stacked lanterns and two side gables. There is also an area of recent panelling close to ground level, which, if removed, might reveal more original paintwork. Be that as it may, at the lower level above the modern panelling there remains the fugitive suggestion of human shoulders in frontal profile, figured in red ochre. This is almost certainly 14th century in origin. The outline is admittedly faint, particularly on the left side, although it is traceable for some depth (Figs 2.2.10, 2.2.9). The most diagnostic feature is what appears to be a splayed tassel or fringe at the surviving extremity on the figure's left side. Was this the bishop's maniple, either suspended from the crozier or held in the left hand, and was the image originally the figure of a vested bishop or archbishop? As a saint, David would have been vested as an archbishop. Bishop Gower's seal shows the maniple very well (Fig. 2.2.11).[25] The throne's free-standing position in an open arcade would have exposed the reverse of the tower to full view from the south aisle, and provided an opportunity to promote the image of St David to passing pilgrims. At the same time, from the partially open bay of the south *ostium chorum,* pilgrims would have enjoyed an unobstructed, if distant, view of the south side of the shrine (Fig. 2.2.12).

Given the paucity of surviving episcopal records at St Davids, the dating of the bishop's throne has always been contentious. Antiquarian sources suggested the episcopate of Bishop Morgan (1496–1504), which would make it coeval with the early-Tudor choir-stalls.[26] However, modern writers have adduced a variety of dates from the 1340s (Lovegrove), the episcopacy of Adam de Houghton, 1361–1389 (Crossley), and the late-14th century/early-15th century (Scott). Whilst acknowledging the mid-14th-century style of both the presbytery screen and the throne, Crossley remarked that one would expect such provincial monuments as St Davids to be *retardataire*. However, there are cogent reasons for incorporating the throne within Bishop Henry de Gower's refurbishment of the choir, commissioned in 1342.[27] Surely for him, the completion of the

Fig. 2.2.10 St Davids Cathedral bishop's throne. Lower part of main panel on reverse of lantern tower. Detail of fugitive figure. H. Harrison.

Fig. 2.2.11 Seal of Bishop Gower (bp 1328–1347). Society of Antiquities of London.

episcopal throne would have had almost as high a priority as that of his tomb in the pulpitum? If his death, followed soon after by the onset of the plague, had delayed the completion of the project by a year or two, it is unlikely that it would have been abandoned during the two short-lived episcopacies of his successors, John Thoresby (1347–49) and Reginald Brian (1350–52), who would not have stood in the way of a project that was almost certainly pre-funded. Unfortunately, we know little of their successor, Thomas Falstoff (1352–1361), who was described by Jones and Freeman as "in no way distinguished".

In view of the lack of documented evidence of Gower's agency in respect of the throne,

Fig. 2.2.12 St Davids Cathedral. Shrine of St David from south, as refashioned. J. Tate.

his colleague and later successor, Bishop Adam Houghton should be taken seriously as a possible candidate for its patronage, albeit that the monument's mid-14th-century style mitigates against Gower's protégé's involvement. Although Houghton was consecrated bishop nearly 15 years after Gower's death in 1347, he was born in the locality,[28] and had already been admitted precentor in 1339.[29] Thus he would have been acquainted with the bishop's plans for the renovation of the cathedral. Should the throne not have been completed before Houghton's sponsor's demise, surely Houghton would have had the influence to push it through well before his own consecration in 1361.[30] Admittedly, during that period he was busy making a career as a royal clerk and civil lawyer, and was ultimately to reach the pinnacle of a legal career as Chancellor of England. Once consecrated, the focus of his patronage at the cathedral, apart from founding a choir-school, and a college for a master and seven priests, was to make a decisive architectural statement through the erection of the ambitious collegiate chapel on the north side of the cathedral with a set of cloisters that linked it to the church.[31] In any case, one cannot but help feel that, had Houghton designed a new throne, it would have looked very different to the one we see today.

The architecture of the throne is innovative for its time, and betrays distinct Perpendicular tendencies. Nonetheless, if the evidently mid-14th-century panels in the throne fence-

screen are genuine components of it, a proposition that our research supports, this represents strong circumstantial evidence that the monument is coeval with Gower's stalls. Also, as already touched on, the discovery of a fragment of a finialled ogee canopy by Jones and Freeman in the upper part of the existing stalls "agreeing nearly in character and detail with the Decorated work in the throne",[32] strongly suggests that both stalls and throne were designed *en suite*.

This unique British *cathedra* seems to have been the final flourish of a bishop's 19-year love affair with ecclesiastical architecture, which included the reconstruction of his palaces, at St Davids, Lamphey and Swansea, and, probably, that at Llandewi in Gower.[33] The substantial improvements and embellishments to his own cathedral are well-attested, and include various additions to the Lady Chapel, and the installation there of a chantry for his predecessor.[34] Bishop Gower, often described as the "Welsh Wykeham" was at the forefront of 14th-century British ecclesiastical patronage. His reconstruction of the St Davids palace has been described as "the most complete and probably the most remarkable surviving secular building of the second quarter of the fourteenth-century".[35]

Bishop de Gower (1277/8–1347) was of aristocratic descent, of a family with its roots and considerable landholdings in the Gower penisula.[36] He studied at Merton College, Oxford, became a doctor of civil and canon law, a fellow, *c.* 1307, and was elected chancellor of the university in 1322. He became bishop of St Davids in 1328 at the age of 50. He played only a minor part in politics, but was active diplomatically on behalf of Edward III. As Glanmor Williams has stated: His "fame rests chiefly on his munificent benefactions and his distinction as an architect".

At the cathedral, his impressive pulpitum has recently attracted attention in connection with the archaeological reconstruction of the former pulpitum at Tintern Abbey.[37] Gower's interest in contemporary architecture, coupled with his professional connections, meant that he was familiar with the most innovative commissions being undertaken in the Bristol area. He was also a friend of Abbot Knowle at St Augustine's Abbey. The "Berkeley arch" in the inner courtyard at Berkeley Castle is essentially an half octagon. The motif also appears on the

Berkeley tombs at St Augustine's, and can be recognised at St Davids on the palace hall porch, in the cathedral on a tomb recess at the east end of the south nave aisle, as well as on a small doorway in the pulpitum screen. The latter's entranceway has flying ribs like those in the anteroom of the Berkeley chapel.[38] Turner *et al.* stressed that a team of masons, distinct from those working on the palace, could have been active in the cathedral.[39] Williams argued that the St Davids pulpitum screen must have been finished by 1342, at which point the bishop ordered the canons' stalls to be reconstructed.[40] Finally, it was suggested that one of the three master masons working at Bristol – Nicholas de Derneford, Thomas of Witney or William Joy may be linked to work at either the St Davids palace or the cathedral.[41] It is likely that Bishop Gower would have known all three men, and was familiar with the pulpitums at both Exeter Cathedral and Tintern.

If we compare the style of the St Davids bishop's throne with the earlier superstructure of the Edward II tomb, *c.* 1335 at Gloucester (Fig. 2.3.13)[42], the timber choir-stalls, *c.* 1350 in that cathedral (Fig. 2.2.13),[43] the stone bishop's throne at Wells, *c.* 1340 (Fig. 4.3), and the canopy of the timber bishop's throne at Hereford, *c.* 1344–1360 (Fig. 2.3.3), it is striking to confront the virtual abandonment in Pembrokeshire of the Early Decorated

encrusted embellishment so familiar from the Exeter throne. In return for this loss in ornamental richness at St Davids, there is a greater interest in the massing of coherent sculptural forms, typified in the tripartite arrangement of the seating. But this refined aesthetic is combined with a marked restraint, and betrays an interest in the Perpendicular style. Inevitably, this is not the Perpendicular of the inscribed fenestration and cage-like interiors of the choir and transepts at Gloucester Cathedral. Timberwork exploits the verticality of its host tree, but cannot compete with masonry window tracery, although the designer of the throne at Hereford makes a creditable attempt to do so.

By the middle of the 19th century the superstructure of the St Davids throne was in a lamentable state, but in an attempt to describe it, the normally reliable Jones and Freeman tended to sell it short:

> "Decorated canopies are flanked by Perpendicular pinnacles and propped by shafts in the worst style of the last century … the general effect is that of a framework of late Perpendicular date, with fragments of Decorated work affixed to it. In three or four places the finials of Decorated canopies are stuck on the top of Perpendicular pinnacles and produce a most gross effect".

Even allowing for the commendable rejection of the unacceptable methods of the pre-modern restorations, it remains evident that,

in it own way, "the design is quite consistent with the mid-fourteenth-century woodwork at Hereford and Gloucester".[44]

At St Davids, the decorative foliage is limited to the voluted "trefoil" leaf (Fig. 2.2.5), found also at Exeter, Wells, Hereford, Gloucester and Tewkesbury, and is used here on the cusping of the arches and the crockets of the gables and finials. The only other decoration is a simple rosette placed in the centre of the gables. For the rest, the ornament repertory is confined to blind lights and simple string-course mouldings on the buttresses, battlementing on the corner posts of the octagon, and egg and dart necking underneath the finials. This is a meagre ration of embellishment, but such is the architectural inventiveness of the monument, that we do not miss it. The diminution of the ascending stages is nicely judged by the sequence of solid and pierced forms. The lower stages of the superstructure are a thicket of gables, buttresses and pinnacles, the upper portion throwing up flying buttresses towards the next stage. This effect is reminiscent of the lower two stages of the Exeter throne, which metamorphose into a third stage. At St Davids the painted blind "lights" on the two-stage piled-up lanterns of the middle section, originally displayed the images of six saints. The lower lantern barely emerges from behind the clinging finials and buttresses, the upper offering a satisfying break in the monument's upward thrust. The somewhat modest openwork spire reinvigorates the spirit of the Decorated style, looking back to the Exeter throne, but springing from a closed, instead of open image housing.

Discussion

The tripartite architectural form of the St Davids throne is a significant variation from the more conventional discrete formulas at Exeter and Wells. It is reminiscent of Michael of Canterbury's late-13th-century tomb of Edmund Crouchback, Earl of Lancaster, at Westminster Abbey, which was neatly intruded between two piers at the north-east end of the sanctuary, and became a model for the early-14th-century English "ciborium" tomb (Fig. 2.2.14).[45] This, ultimately French *Rayonnant* motif is typified by the design of the south portal façade at Nôtre-Dame, Paris. Nearer to home is the tripartite portal to the anteroom of the Berkeley Chapel at St Augustine's Abbey, Bristol (Fig. 2.2.15), which, in turn, is in many ways closely modelled on Master Michael's tomb at Westminster.[46] This design formula is successfully developed at St Davids with the side canopies emphasising their lower status as discrete stalls. They provide the accommodation for the bishop's two chaplains.

It is true that the architecture of the St Davids throne lacks the unifying verticality of the approximately coeval Hereford throne, and Archbishop Stratford's tomb at Canterbury Cathedral (Fig. 2.2.16).[47] The Hereford and Canterbury monuments both excel in aesthetic richness and the exploitation of the effects of light and shade, but they are the products of a more sophisticated cultural context. The semi-hexagonal canopies on the Gloucester choir-stalls (Fig. 2.2.13) and the central tabernacle on the Hereford (Fig. 2.3.6c) and St Davids bishop's thrones, are sprung from uprights at the rear. The tabernacle above Michael of Canterbury's prior's throne in the chapter house at Canterbury (Fig. 1.31), 1304–1320, with the lower subsidiary stalls, is canted back on either side, and can be seen as an ancestor of the hierarchical architectural composition at St Davids.[48] Because of its wider central door opening, the entrance to the anteroom of the Berkeley Chapel at Bristol produces the same centralising emphasis.

It can be seen that at St Davids the architectural style is noticeably pulling away from Exeter. In stylistic terms, apart from the tripled elevation with its clear distinction of the status of its three users, there is the virtual absence of the ogee arch, and also the introduction of semi-circular and segmental arch-heads. A curiosity is the tall solid three-dimensional gables at the back of the side stalls, which in profile contribute a powerful impression of depth. Although this monument is evidently unaware of the work of William Ramsey III at St Stephen's Chapel in the 1320s, it is still influenced, if unconsciously, by the Perpendicular style, its open construction giving a free rein to an exhibition of verticality. This is in sharp contrast to the Exeter throne, whose most striking feature is its cage-like constriction and great height. The scarcity of architectural decorative ornament at St Davids, emphasises the designer's priorities. Here is someone consciously sloughing off the overburden of the early-Decorated style. Whereas St Augustine's Abbey, Bristol is the most likely source for the tripartite elevation of

the seating, there is surprisingly little evidence of influence from the concurrent furniture projects at Gloucester or Hereford. The earlier Edward II tomb at Gloucester (*c.* 1335) is perhaps another matter, its verticality and decorative reticence being to some extent shared at St Davids. At the same time, the tomb's sophistication and stylistic nuances are metaphorically miles apart.

The renewed programme of building activity at St Davids during the 1330s and '40s was not merely the product of a new bishop's architectural enthusiasms, but seems to have been an instrument of his determination

Fig. 2.2.16 Christchurch Cathedral, Canterbury. Archbishop Stratford tomb, c. 1348. A. Budge.

to breathe life into the liturgy, as well as the status and finances of the cathedral.[49] His determination to greatly increase the accommodation for high-status visitors at the palace was intended to publicise and promote an interest in the recently rediscovered bodily relics of St David. Gower was a capable financial administrator, and his astute housekeeping quickly produced a substantial increase in the institution's cash flow, particularly from the offerings of a growing body of pilgrims at the shrine of the patron saint. The bishop's register does not survive, but the Statute Book records the obtaining of licences to alienate property for the financial benefit of the cathedral, such as the manor of Saint Dogwel's, for which a royal licence was received in December 1329,[50] the church of Llanddewi,[51] and in 1334, the benefice of Manorowen, near Fishguard, was appropriated to maintain the subchanter and the vicars choral at St Davids.[52]

The High-Medieval cult of St David owes it origins to the Norman, Bishop Bernard (bp 1115–1148), who gained the support of Pope Callixtus II, who ruled that two pilgrimages to St Davids should be worth one to Rome. Also it is recorded that, in 1131, some relics were translated into Bishop Bernard's cathedral, and, presumably, a new shrine.[53] The rebuilding of the cathedral in the last two decades of the 12th century under Bishop Peter de Leia (1176–1198), and in particular the expansion of the east end, must have promoted further interest. However, it was the discovery of the whole body in the 1260s or '70s, that seems to have initiated a third round of cathedral building in the early-14th century, under Gower, that is pertinent in the present context.

A vision received by a certain John de Gamages, prior of Ewenny, Glamorgan, a dependency of Gloucester Abbey, led to the *inventio* of the intact corpse, and its translation to the south side of the cathedral.[54] Such clairvoyance could have been inspired by the writing of a new life of the saint by Gerald of Wales in the late-12th century. In any case, it was not until 1275 that an entry in the *Annales Cambriae* relates that "work was begun on the shrine of St David in the church of Menevia".[55] Bishop de Leia's choir aisles permitted inspection of the double-sided shrine by visiting pilgrims from both presbytery aisles. Presumably, only privileged

pilgrims were granted intimate access to the south side (Fig. 2.2.12). It is generally agreed that the original shrine base, albeit now in three pieces, is still *in situ* on the north side of the first bay of the presbytery. The shrine was provided with a wooden *feretrum* for processional purposes:[56]

> "The relics of St. David and St. Stinan (the former's confessor), were kept in a portable shrine or feretory, which may have rested on the stone table. Above this was a painted timber coving which survived the slighting of the shrine in 1538, as did the mural paintings of St David, St Patrick and St Stinan in the niches. Below the stone table there were stone receptacles for the alms of pilgrims kneeling before the shrine, offerings reflected in the fine quality of the medieval furnishings and fittings".[57]

The traditional identification of the painted head-bearing Stinan with the Northern-French St Denis, who suffered the same martyrdom, is no longer considered viable.[58] The latter had no known historical connection with the Welsh diocese.

Following the conquest of Wales in 1284, Edward I visited the shrine on 26 November. He was a keen relic hunter, and came away with an arm of the saint.[59] In addition, several of the body parts were distributed to key locations in England, such as Salisbury Cathedral and Reading Abbey.[60] Unfortunately, the recorded receipts at the cathedral shrine during the 14th century are too sporadic to provide a reliable record of either their amount or distribution. However, given the high number of Edwardian coins found within the curtilage of the cathedral, it appears that most of the financial superfluity stemming from this *renaissance* for the cult, accrued to Gower's episcopate. There is also evidence in the *Black Book of St David's* that, under their duty of service, the bishop's villeins were bound "to follow the relics of the Blessed David" on their occasional day-long parochial progresses, as well as during the longer events through the bishopric in times of war. At Maboris, tenants were expected to join the procession, and to pay a fine of 7s each.[61] This must have been the standard practice, and would have brought in a substantial sum of money.

The feast of St David (1 March), who died in 601 or 589, had been commemorated locally, probably since the 7th century.[62] It was celebrated as one of the highest grade in the diocesan churches dedicated to the saint. At St Davids, it was also:

"one of the eight occasions classed as Principal Double Feasts: Christmas, Epiphany, Easter, Ascension Day, Whitsunday, the Assumption of the Blessed Virgin Mary, the feast of the patron saint, and the feast commemorating the dedication of the church".[63]

It has been posited that

"… it is possible that St David's Day was also celebrated as a *Festum duplex principale* in churches dedicated to St David in the other Welsh dioceses, as well as in the nearby dioceses of Hereford and Exeter, from which early evidence exists of a devotion to the saint".[64]

At St Davids Cathedral, the bishop would have had an unencumbered view of the lavishly decorated shrine from his *cathedra* opposite, which would have increased his opportunities for personal devotion. As already noted, the throne itself was liberally decorated with the usual medieval palette of polychromy – red, green, blue and gilding. A more methodical study of this, than it has been possible to undertake so far, would elucidate the logic of the clearly hierarchical application of different colours, to maximise their combined symbolic and aesthetic impact.[65]

As already noted, the six stacked-lantern panels facing east, west and north, were filled with the painted images of saints. Tradition has it that the Virgin was placed at the lower level on the panel facing north, although only the ghost of a female figure is now evident. Regrettably, only one of the panel paintings, that of St Andrew, facing east at the upper level, is definitively recognisable from its saltire cross (Fig. 2.2.8). St Andrew became the dedicatee of the cathedral in the High Middle Ages, and a large chapel was erected in his honour on the north side of the choir in the late-12th century. In view of the comparatively recent failure, at that time, of the diocese to remain independent of Canterbury,[66] it would not be surprising if, as well as the putative image of David on the back of the throne, and perhaps another image higher up, the ensemble of painted images on the front would have included one or two of the remaining available honoured Menevian saints, such as Patrick, Non (St David's mother), Stinan, and even Caradoc.[67] Doubtless, the imposing size of the throne, and its ostentatious apparel would have amounted to an affirmation of the Welsh diocese's self-belief.

Apart from at Llandaff (see Chapter 3), we do not know whether the display of images of saints and former bishops as here and at Exeter, was a commonplace on medieval British episcopal thrones. As we have already seen, in one way or another, this practice can be associated with Early-Christian and Byzantine traditions. In the former it extends to the routine display of standing apostles, and the figure of Christ, on the mosaic and painted semi-domes of the eastern apse. Very occasionally, proprietorial inscriptions are also to be found on the chair itself. On the Ravenna throne the images are an integral part of the *cathedra* (Fig. 1.1). They include the Evangelists, St John the Baptist, the apostles, and even the Old Testament figure of Jacob.

Given that Gower's choir-stalls were liberally painted, the impact of the entire suite of furniture in the choir and presbytery would have been striking. Additionally, there is the possible archaeological evidence for a large-scale human figure painted on the back of the lantern tower. The identity of an upper one will never be solved, the lower ecclesiastic is more open to interpretation. The most likely suggestion is David, the patron saint, vested as an archbishop, which his status would have demanded. The effect of this unexpected confrontation on the pilgrims, who would otherwise be gazing in devotion across the presbytery towards the shrine, would have been overwhelming. With the possible exception of Exeter Cathedral, there is otherwise no precedent in Britain, or elsewhere, for a life-size sculpted or painted image of a patron saint on a medieval episcopal throne. The possible evidence presented here is, therefore, both unexpected and valuable.

Notes

1 The most recent studies of this episcopal throne have been, Tracy 1988 and Budge 2011 unpublished.
2 For a recent discussion of the architecture and fittings at St Davids Cathedral, see Lloyd 2004, 386–413.
3 In the case of Hereford, an abbreviated number of stalls were moved out of the tower space into the historic presbytery in the late 19th century.
4 All of these medieval choirs, including St Davids, would have had sub-stalls.
5 Willis lists the members of the cathedral in the back stalls, as the bishop, who was *quasi decanum,* and seated at the north end of the south returned stalls, the precentor adjacent to him, at the south end of the north returned

stalls, the chancellor and treasurer opposite each other in the east terminal stalls, and in addition four archdeacons, eight prebendaries, and six canons cursal (total 22). In the sub-stalls sat the remainder, e.g. the sub-chanter, four priest vicars, four lay vicars, the organist, four choristers, the master of the Grammar School, the verger, porter, sexton, and keeper of the church in prayer time (total 19). Willis 1727–30, 7, and Willis, *Parochiale Anglicanum*, 175.

6   Jones and Freeman, 1856, 86.

7   The date of the present choir-stalls is discussed in Evans 2007, 1.

8   Evans 2007, 1–11. The choir-stalls at St Mary's Priory, Abergavenny were also remodelled at that time. Tracy *et al.* 2002, 203–54.

9   Jones and Freeman, 91, and Lovegrove 1951. The footprint of the tower is a square.

10 Whereas, the presbytery screen appears, on the face if it, to be all of a piece, the dado is a patchwork of subtly varying styles of early-to-mid-14th-, and even late-13th-century date, which matches up somewhat haphazardly with the arcaded superstructure above. At the north end, it returns, unexpectedly, to the west, where a more stylistically primitive decorative form appears, both at dado and arcade levels. The dado turns into a plain trefoil shape, with no carved decoration in the spandrels and the tracery heads of the elevation become plain geometric trefoils. It seems that Crossley and Ridgway were not troubled by the disjunction between the upper and lower components of the screen. They were convinced of the structure's liturgical authenticity, and pointed to other recorded examples in Wales, at Brecon Cathedral and Ewenny Priory, and Dunster, in Somerset. They noted that the lower section of the screen is double-sided and could not have been part of Gower's choir-stalls. St John Hope thought that the screen may have once stood one bay to the west of the pulpitum, functioning as a fence (there are prominent empty sockets there on the piers in the first bay west of the pulpitum). At all events, since the last quarter of the 15th century, the screen has remained where it is today, even if it was temporarily disturbed in the 19th century. Its 19th-century rationalisation seems to have been to provide a liminal marker to the threshold of the presbytery. It is noticeable that the panelling of the throne fence is very similar to the presbytery screen dado. See Crossley and Ridgway 1957, 31; Vallance 1947, 64.

11 Yardley 1927, 20–1; Scott 1873, 25–7. When the throne was moved westwards in the late-15th century, as well as the provision of a new protective presbytery screen, it was given a new entrance from the east side. Both of these operations resulted in damage.

12 Crossley and Ridgway 1957, pl. iiia. The Parker drawing is not in the collection of this Victorian amateur architect and watercolourist's work at the National Library of Wales.

13 Buckler's drawings of the St Davids throne are in BL Ms Add. 36,397, fols 58, 62, 63, 68. This includes a detailed drawing from the east side.

14 His drawing of the nave taken from the west end, dated September 1836, is in the collection of the National Library of Wales, and was published in *Archaeologia Cambrensis* XCIV (1939), 95.

15 Edward Yardley described the throne as "erected … under a stately arch or pavilion of woodwork, rising with lofty Gothic pinnacles curiously carved, painted and gilt … It is 29 feet high, and may vie with most Episcopal thrones in the kingdom". Yardley 1927, 20. In 2011 a careful study of the joinery of the throne was undertaken by Hugh Harrison and the architectural draughtsman, Peter Ferguson.

16 For a full analysis of the construction of the St Davids's throne, see Appendix III.

17 The *Menevia Sacra* maintains that the woodwork was supposedly painted and gilt, see note 15.

18 The Bodleian Library, University of Oxford Ms. Willis 37, fol. 5r. (elevation). On folio 5v. there is a schematic plan.

19 There is substantial evidence of a former covering of a red base colour with green on top. These colours are particularly found on the architectural mouldings and decorative carvings. A scientific analysis would produce more information.

20 See Chapter 2.1, 43–5 and Appendix IV.

21 It is to be hoped that a full polychromy analysis will be carried out at St Davids before much more of the surviving paintwork falls off. Unfortunately, at the time when we were examining the throne's structure from a scaffold, the cathedral's limited funds could not stretch to undertake this potentially expensive procedure.

22 There are traces of gilding on the medieval abbey stalls at Gloucester. The former cathedral conservation officer has commented as follows: "When we catalogued the finials we scraped off the brown varnish from one and they were very respectably gilded. … These must be at least late medieval in order to be thrown out by Scott in 1868 (and to have several layers of varnish). …, it could be that only the finials were gilded? There are smaller gilded finials as well". Carolyn Heighway pers. comm.

23 As well as the polychromy's archaeological study and conservation, the monument's structural conservation is also a priority. Following the

initial careful inspection of the joinery in 2011, it is to be hoped that the cathedral will also be able to fund this work.

24 Mitchell 2000, figs 1–12.

25 Bishop Houghton's seal shows the maniple distinctly, but less clearly.

26 Yardley 1927, 20, 83.

27 BL Ms Harleian 6280, f. 13b. See Williams 1981, n. 45 and Jones and Freeman 1856, 91.

28 For a useful discussion of Houghton's patronage at St Davids, see Evans 2009, 177–9.

29 Houghton ceased to be precentor in 1352. It is even suggested that Houghton may have attended the cathedral school, and even have been a chorister. *Ibid.*, 177.

30 Houghton is described by Evans as possessing "initiative, drive, influence and ability". *Ibid.*, 176.

31 For Houghton, see Williams 2012a and Emden 1958.

32 Jones and Freeman 1856, 91.

33 Williams 2004a.

34 For Gower's architectural sources at the palace and cathedral at St Davids, see Turner *et al.* 2000, 160, 162, 167–8.

35 Turner *et al.* 2000, 87.

36 The following biographical synopsis is based on Gower's biography in Williams 2004a.

37 Harrison *et al.* 1998, 243–4.

38 For a suggested re-dating of the east end of St Augustine's, Bristol, see Wilson 2011.

39 In Harrison *et al.* 1998, 244, it is suggested that a separate "St David's master" from Bristol directed reconstruction work at the palace.

40 *Cal. Close Rolls*, 1330–3, 168 and Williams 1981, 9.

41 Turner *et al.*, 2000, 167.

42 Stone 1972, 160–4; Heighway and Bryant 2007, 1–2.

43 Tracy 1987, 44–8.

44 Tracy 1988, 115.

45 Lewes Gee 1979, 29–41.

46 For his comments on the Bristol master's handling of this frontispiece, see Wilson 2011, 107–8.

47 The Stratford tomb is usually dated to *c.* 1348. See also Chapter 2.3, 78–80.

48 For the Canterbury Prior's seat, see Chapter 1, 20.

49 Unfortunately, in spite of the commendable efforts of Owain Edwards, disappointingly little information seems to have survived with regard to the conduct of the liturgy at St Davids Cathedral.

50 Williams 1981, n. 36.

51 *Ibid.*, n. 37.

52 *Ibid.*, n. 40.

53 For the cult of St David, see James 1993, 110–12; Cowley 2007; Farmer 1997, 130–1.

54 Cowley 2007, 276–7. This section is based on this author's useful account.

55 *Ibid.*, 277.

56 *Ibid.*, n. 14. This has recently been reinstated with a conjectural feretory.

57 Evans 2001, 18.

58 Stinan and Justinian was closely associated with David. Farmer 1997, 282–3.

59 Edward also "acquired the head and other body parts of the skeleton of St David, and in the following year the Bury St Edmunds chronicler records that 'the King led a solemn procession from the tower of London to Westminster bearing the head of St David … which he had brought from Wales'". Cowley 2007, 278.

60 *Ibid.*, 278–9.

61 For the reference in the Black Book, see Williams 1981, n. 85.

62 Edwards 2007, 237.

63 *Ibid.*

64 *Ibid.*, n. 27.

65 See a similar demonstration of the hierarchy of palette on the Spring chantry mortuary chapel screen at Lavenham, Suffolk in Tracy and Harrison 2011, 253–4, fig. 26.

66 The Welsh dioceses initially lost their independent status in 1127. Jones and Freeman 1856, 27, 253.

67 The uncanonised Welsh saint, Caradoc, d. 1142, was buried at St Davids Cathedral, where exists the remains of his shrine. For St Caradoc, see Farmer 1997, 88.

3. Hereford Cathedral

Description and physical analysis

Although of exceptional intrinsic interest, the Hereford episcopal throne is today little regarded beyond the confines of a small circle of specialists (Fig. 2.3.1). This is largely a matter of presentation, as the monument was moved in the mid-19th century from its former position against a solid flat-faced pier at the south-west end of the presbytery, into the adjoining open arcade to the east within the confines of the sacristy (Figs 2.3.2–4, 2.3.10). In its present position, its intimate scale and delicate architectural superstructure are forced to compete with the powerful and unforgiving daylight emanating from the generous windows in the south choir aisle. On confronting the throne, the glare from behind it eats into the delicate traceried canopywork, so denying altogether any meaningful intelligibility and subtlety in the aesthetic experience.

The reason for the throne's removal is, indirectly, bound up with the parlous state of the cathedral's central tower by the mid-19th century, and the need to clear the transept in order to effect the necessary repairs. The 14th-century pulpitum on the west side had to be removed, along with the 48 clergy back-stalls, as shown by Willis, from their time-honoured positions.[1] On completion of the building work, there was a hiatus of some 15 years, before the decision to permanently exclude the choir-stalls from under the central tower. From the contents of his *Recollections*, it seems that George Gilbert Scott believed that, on his removing the pulpitum in 1840, Lewis Nockells Cottingham found no traces of ancient manufacture.[2] This may have been the impression the latter wanted to bequeath, since the pulpitum's final disposal appears to have been promptly arranged. In any case, according to Scott, Cottingham had "left no trace of it",[3] and the latter had decided to replace it with one of "Norman character".[4] By contrast, "The beautiful stall-work" had been "stowed away in the crypt, all in fragmentary pieces. It was part of my task to fit these together and rearrange them".[5] By the time of Scott's arrival it had been decided not to reinstate the formerly ten returned stalls in their original position, and that it was going to be necessary to reduce the number of lateral stalls from 40 to 31 (15 to the north and 16 to the south).[6] This drastic curtailment was necessitated by the decision to shoehorn a formerly substantial suite of choir furniture from under the crossing tower into the limited confines of a modestly proportioned presbytery.[7] In addition, the ten return stalls at the west end were either moved to the south side or otherwise disposed of, this amounting to a loss of 19 seats.[8] Scott's comments on what he had been asked to do with the furnishings are redolent of his disapproval of his client's priorities: "to make the eastern arm the choir, (and) giving up the transepts as well as the nave to the congregation. From an antiquarian point of view it was an error".[9] However, it is still possible to say that, in spite of this wanton loss and destruction, Hereford remains the only British cathedral to retain *en suite* most of its medieval choir-stalls and its bishop's throne.

Apart from the loss of so many choir-stalls, there was the contextual damage from the blocking of the *ostia chori* at the east end of the stalls and the bottling up of the choir and clergy at the south-east end of the presbytery. At this end it was critical, because the former breathing

Fig. 2.3.1 (far left) Hereford Cathedral. 19th-century arrangement of south side of choir, showing bishop's throne and junction with choir-stalls. To the right, note the pier against which the throne was originally placed. S. Mather.

Fig. 2.3.2 Hereford Cathedral. Choir and aisle ground plan. J. Read.

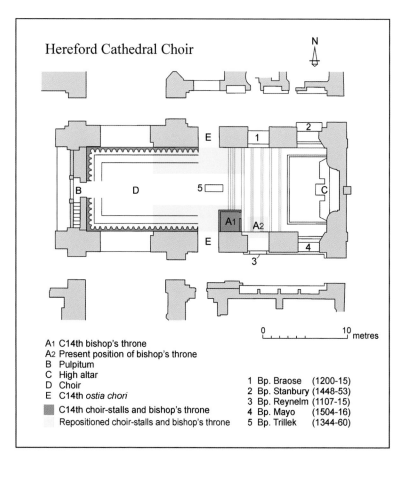

Hereford Cathedral Choir

N

A1 C14th bishop's throne
A2 Present position of bishop's throne
B Pulpitum
C High altar
D Choir
E C14th *ostia chori*
■ C14th choir-stalls and bishop's throne
□ Repositioned choir-stalls and bishop's throne

1 Bp. Braose (1200-15)
2 Bp. Stanbury (1448-53)
3 Bp. Reynelm (1107-15)
4 Bp. Mayo (1504-16)
5 Bp. Trillek (1344-60)

0   10 metres

Fig. 2.3.3 Hereford Cathedral. Front view of bishop's throne. H. Harrison.

of three wider return-stall seats at the west end of the south lateral stalls. This ill thought out arrangement has resulted in the south-lateral stalls and the throne confronting each other in the manner of a slow car crash (Figs 2.3.3, 2.3.4, 2.3.9) The insensitive removal of any meaningful physical break between the stalls and the throne, doubtless contributed to George Gilbert Scott's documented dissatisfaction with the whole process.

In this episcopal collegiate church, the occupation of the second arcade south-west of the high altar by the bishop's throne would have been considered unacceptable. Without the need to rehearse the arguments for identifying the burial on the south side of this bay as either one or other of the cathedral's "founders", Bishop Losinga or Reynhelm, suffice it to say that this grand and wholly reinvented canopied tomb occupies a key position at the head of the early 14th-century series of historicising episcopal effigies in the presbytery aisles.[10] It is placed within the main presbytery arcade, close to the high altar, because it would have represented an important presence to both users of the sacristy, as well as to the pilgrims in the choir aisle (Fig. 2.3.5). Today it is not immediately obvious that the tomb is double sided, with the ball-flower decoration and arch mouldings repeated on the north side.[11] It was naturally intended that the view of this monument from the sacristy should have been unobstructed.

In an attempt to outline the cathedral's 14th-century building history, it is a considerable drawback that there are no surviving fabric accounts, and precious little related documentation. Instead, one has to fall back on the more hazardous arts of stylistic analysis. The joinery and carving on both the throne and the choir-stalls appears to have been the product of two different workshops, and there are the unmistakable signs of a protracted manufacture.[12] The seat shapes and the carving style of the misericords characterise the product of an earlier patronage. The subsequent campaign accounted for the superstructure of both the stalls and bishop's throne. However, even on the stalls, there are differences in the details of workmanship and motifs between the north and south ranges, which led one commentator to suggest that the north side was constructed earlier than the south.[13] The pattern of repetition is certainly

space between the east end of the stalls and the bishop's *cathedra* was lost. These entrances into the choir stalls from the east end within the space of an arcade were a convenient facility for the clergy to effect an orderly and rapid arrival and evacuation into and out of their seats, for both practical and processional purposes. In the new arrangement, the present disparity in the number of stalls (15 on the south vs. 16 on the north) looks, on the face of it, to have been motivated by an attempt to prevent the complete merger of both stalls and throne on the south side. However, the reason for this discrepancy is the interposition

Fig. 2.3.4 (far left) Hereford Cathedral. Detail of junction of the throne and choir-stalls. Notice the remains of the original sacristy plinth, embedded beneath the east portion of the western arcade pier. H. Harrison.

Fig. 2.3.5 (left) Hereford Cathedral. View of the double-sided historicising tomb of Bishop Reynhelm from the second bay from east of the presbytery arcade. The back of the bishop's throne is just visible behind. H. Harrison.

haphazard, but it is very difficult to say which of the two sides is earlier, and, in any case, most of the work was the responsibility of the second workshop.[14] Whereas Bishop John Trillek (bp 1344–1360) seems to have been responsible for the more advanced style of the second phase, it is likely that the project was initiated under the previous Bishop Charlton (bp 1327–1344), using a team of craftsmen, quite probably from Wells (see below). It is not unreasonable to surmise, that, sometime after his consecration in 1344, Trillek decided to commission a new workshop from the West Midlands. As fate would have it, within a short time the rejuvenated project was overtaken by the arrival of the plague in 1348. This could have delayed its final completion until sometime before *c.* 1350. This hypothesis is speculative, but it is to be hoped that by the end of the debate that follows, an agreeable synthesis can be reached.[15]

On the bishop's throne, the miniature battlements on top of the buttresses, the buttress set-offs, the tall blind arches with gablets, the quatrefoil friezes, cusped nodding arches, rosettes and large free-standing finials, all go with the ornament on the adjacent screens, formerly on both sides of the choir entranceway, and also shielding the dean and precentor's stalls at the west end. The canopy

vaults over the seats of the bishop's throne are similar to the "improved" ceiling of the "dean's stall", which was moved by Scott to the west end of the south stalls.[16] Even the style of the seats in the throne are close to those in the choir-stalls (Figs 2.3.6a–c; 2.3.7; 2.3.8). This shows that the entire project was initiated at the same time.[17]

In considering the date of manufacture of the earliest work at Hereford in more detail, particularly the stall seating and some elements of the superstructure, as well as the seating of the bishop's throne, some assistance is provided by the close similarities in many cases on the choir-stalls at Wells Cathedral, of the iconographic motifs, the figure and animal carving and decorative ornament. This is particularly noticeable on the carved foliage, seat mouldings, and the style and subject matter of the misericords.[18] On the latter, the most striking iconographic *comparanda* are, probably, the left-handed dragon slayers, the bats and the quadruped-bodied masks. It is certain that one of the Hereford carvers was familiar with the earlier furniture at Wells. The latter can be safely ascribed to the years 1335–1340. The spandrel dragons in the surviving desk fronts at Wells, carved by the superlative executant, known as the "Master of the Alexander misericord" can be related to the style of the sculpture in the spandrels of the panelling on the lower part of

*Fig. 2.3.6 Hereford
Cathedral bishop's
throne. Decorative
detailing: a. bishop's
canopy; b. fence screen
west side; c. upper part of
throne from north-east;
d. bishop's canopy lierne
vault. H. Harrison.*

the former dignitaries entrance screens of the Hereford choir-stalls.[19]

Whilst stylistically retrospective in some ways, the total visual impact of the design of the Hereford furniture is startlingly innovative. For instance, on the stall canopy work, the three-dimensional treatment of the spandrels on the line of the sweeping full-ogee arcade arches, provides a visual diagonality, which breaks decisively away from the *rayonnant*

traditions of early-14th-century choir-stall design. To this is added the use of Perpendicular traceried grids, for instance, on the seat back of the "dean's stall", the outer panels of the dignitaries' stalls (now reused as the lateral stall terminations), and the inner panels of the bishop's throne (Figs 2.3.7; 2.3.9). This amounts to an experimental synthesis of styles, with generic up-to-date resonances from William Ramsey III's work at St Stephen's Chapel, as well as features of the Gloucester choir-stalls (Fig. 2.2.13), the latter an amalgam of "London" and Exonian formulae.[20]

The throne itself is of considerable distinction, and is a sophisticated exploitation, on a smaller scale, of the same tripartite architectural form that we have already seen employed at St Davids. It is 8 ft (2.4 m) broad, stands on a wooden plinth and was originally placed in front of a flat-faced pier of maximum width of 10 ft 9 in (3.28 m) (Fig. 2.3.10). It consists of a central panel, from which the spire and side canopies are hung, clasped at right-angles by a pair of side wings at each end, running north-south (Fig. 2.3.1).[21] The spire, which rises to a height of just under 22 ft (6.7 m), would have been well clear of the back wall, the whole structure jutting forward as shown on the Browne Willis plan, beyond the line of the lateral-stall desks.[22] It would not have overwhelmed the stalls, since the open arcade of the south *ostium chorum* would have intervened between them. The seating area of the throne, and both sides of the wings, are surrounded by tall crenellated panelling. At the front, is a low fence-screen, a feature which appears to have been a constant on all three of the surviving structural British timber thrones. At Hereford this feature is certainly authentic. The slender subsidiary arches of the elegant canopied frontal arcade display typical early-14th-century-type dog's head terminals, and each of the main arches shelters a pair of birds in the spandrels (Figs 2.3.3; 2.3.11). Given the confines of the space, it is most likely that a book-rest was attached to this screen, rather than the employment of a lectern. The bishop's stall is surmounted by a projecting semi-hexagonal canopy with a pair of miniature straight-sided forward-facing gablets at the springing of the front arch, in the spirit of William Ramsey III's architectural detailing at St Stephen's Chapel, Westminster. The chaplains' seats have bifurcated nodding ogee arches, with pairs of small flanking spires and a large spire at the back, very close to the Gloucester-type of nodding ogee arch, backed by a single spire. This formula appears to represent the West-Country's ardent embrace of the Decorated style, at first typified on the canopy of the Exeter bishop's throne, and later developed here and at Gloucester at about the same time.

The elegant diminishing central tower is an essay in micro-architecture, in five stages. Its projection begins with three ogee-cusped and crocketted arches of the throne canopy, but quickly metamorphoses into the lower semi-hexagonally-planned cage-like structure, fronted by three tall, empty, vaulted and

Fig. 2.3.7 (above) Hereford Cathedral. View of south side of choir-stalls. Notice the upright tracery grid on the back of the "dean's stall" (far right), and the "nodding" arcaded spandrels of the canopies. A similar grid is inset on the outer faces of the dignitaries' stall ends, now reused as lateral stall ends. S. Mather.

Fig. 2.3.8 (above left) Hereford Cathedral bishop's throne. Detail of seating. H. Harrison.

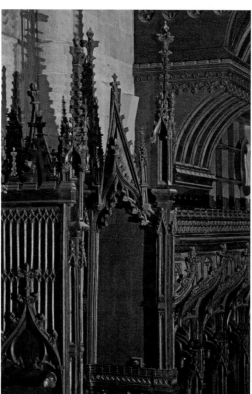

Fig. 2.3.9 (left) Hereford Cathedral bishop's throne. Junction of throne and stalls from east. Note the terminal lateral stall end on right, and the traceried grid on south-west face of throne's enclosing wing screen on left. H. Harrison.

Fig. 2.3.10 Hereford Cathedral. Flat-faced pier, on the north side of the presbytery, of the type in front of which the bishop's throne stood. C. Tracy.

prominently spired would-be sculpture enclosures (Fig. 2.3.6c). This stage is braced by three structurally improbable ogee-profiled flying buttresses, and appears to rise up by approximately 4 ft (1.2 m) above the top of the throne's winged panelling. It finishes with an echelon of deeply carved, pierced and foliated coronas. The next Perpendicular-style densely articulated traceried section, still hexagonal in plan and divided by a mid-height transom, is largely devoid of decorative features, and skeletal in appearance (Fig. 2.3.12). It is topped by three less detailed coronas. From ground level, this pair of stages thrusts upwards with its sheaf of crocket-free pared-back uprights, bound by the central transom, yet still accompanied by five semi-detached tall finials. One is conscious throughout of the deliberate shedding of ornament as the tower

ascends. This parsimony is deliberate, and more noticeable as the composition rises to its climax. Even at this level, the architectural ornament is not stinted, but its impact is intentionally restrained. The tower is screened at the back by what appears to be a vertical extension of the bishop's seat-back, breaking through the line of the crenellated cornice. This seems to support both the lower, as well as the higher tower stages. This bravura architectural performance is largely illusory, with the perspective effects of the half-scale elements exaggerating the impression of height. Catharsis is finally reached with the perfectly conventional crocketted and finialled spire thrusting its way to as yet unexplored heights.

The design of this impressive superstructure attempts to transform flat Perpendicular tracery into three-dimensions. For this purpose, the use of timber offers a head-start for a craftsman aiming at a filigree-like outcome. The light openwork hexagonal framework of the bishop's canopy extension could be built up to the height required using timber standards conveniently joined together by means of sprig nails and glue. Ultimately, the entire structure was supported on the side standards of the central throne, pinned to the cross member of the cornice and stiffened by the backboard, which, in turn, was nailed to the mullions of the ogee-shouldered frame. Visually, the finials and elegant flying buttresses appear to be securing the frame-like construction of the tower sections, both components of which are essentially hollow. Once these overt architectural gestures are abandoned, their semi-hexagonal cores dominate, being finally crowned by the *flèche*.

Hereford's canopied *cathedra* is worth studying in more detail. At ground level the crenellated parapet and the panels of blind stacked tracery lights flanking the throne recall William Ramsey III's wall decoration in the chapter house at St Stephen's Chapel, Westminster, probably of the early 1340s (Fig. 2.1.13).[23] The profusely decorated spandrels of the arch below the central throne canopy is reminiscent of the arch spandrels on the south elevation clearstorey windows at Westminster.[24] When it comes to the throne superstructure, the canopy work on Archbishop Stratford's stone tomb, *c.* 1348, in the south choir aisle at Canterbury Cathedral, is close to the mark, even though the two monuments are very differently

*Fig. 2.3.11 (far left)
Hereford Cathedral
bishop's throne. Fence
screen. Detail of archlet
composition with birds in
spandrels. H. Harrison.*

conceived (Fig. 2.2.16). Its superstructure is highly sophisticated, and was probably to the design of the architect, John Box, who was in the service of the prior of Canterbury Cathedral.[25] The scale of the decorative ornament on the Stratford monument is much more restrained than is the case on the Hereford throne. However, the paring down of the structural members is noticeable in both cases, resulting in a transparent skeletal appearance. Both monuments seek to explore new ways of projecting three-dimensionality into the emerging Perpendicular mode. At Hereford the designer exploits the relative lightness of his material, to create a structure on a scale and complexity of plan beyond the reach of stone.

An important stylistic analogy is provided by the tomb of Edward II at Gloucester Abbey, *c.* 1335 (Fig. 2.3.13). This was probably the work of a south-east-England mason, possibly Thomas of Canterbury, another pioneer of the Perpendicular style.[26] As such it is a monument whose artistic provenance was mainly metropolitan. The frontispiece of the Hereford throne, contains several quotations inspired by the Edward II tomb, even though few of them are used in exactly the same way. This suggests that the master-carpenter at Hereford had visited Gloucester, and it is possible that some of his craftsmen could have migrated between the two places, but in which order it is not possible to say.

A third significant English *comparandum* is the tomb of Hugh III Despenser, d. 1349, and Elizabeth Montacute, at Tewkesbury Abbey (Fig. 2.3.14).[27] This funerary monument is

*Fig. 2.3.12 Hereford
Cathedral bishop's
throne. Central tower.
Stage 2. H. Harrison.*

thought to have been erected before the death of Despenser's first wife in 1359, so the tomb could have been designed in the mid-1350s. It has been described as "one of the most ambitious and ostentatious of its period".[28] It is clearly influenced by the Edward II tomb, which is similarly tripartite and open, but lacks the latter's transom rail between the upper and lower arcade, and is stylistically related to the Archbishop Stratford tomb at Canterbury. But there are no fewer than four zones of open arches at Tewkesbury, which finally diminish upwards into a spire. In spite of being constructed in a different medium, the monument shares a number of characteristics in common with Hereford, although, perhaps suggesting that a superstructure of this apparent ambition might be achieved more satisfactorily in timber. The Hereford throne

Fig. 2.3.13 Gloucester Cathedral. North elevation of the tomb of King Edward II. A. Hornak.

Fig. 2.3.14 Tewkesbury Abbey. Tomb of Hugh III Despenser, and Elizabeth Montacute from south-west. Conway Library, The Courtauld Institute of Art, London.

was not intended to be free-standing, which the Tewkesbury monument seems, in the first instance, to have been, albeit to be viewed from one side only.[29] Its use of ornament is proportionate, rather than florid, although its architectural members are similarly pared down. Considering the weight of the material, this can have been no easy task. One wonders if the use of timber was ever considered, or whether it would have been ruled out as not a sufficiently prestigious material.

On the scale of the Hereford Cathedral throne's architectural importance, it is possible to point to a pertinent contemporary international *comparandum* at the former Cistercian monastery at Bad Doberan in Mecklenburg, Germany. There in the sanctuary, and throughout the church, is one of the most impressive ensembles of High-Medieval ecclesiastical wooden furnishings in Western Europe. In combination, the 38 ft (11.6 m) high, free-standing sacrament house on the north side of the high altar, the earliest in Germany, the gilded and painted altar itself, and its central three-stage spired ciborium-like tower, with a flanking lesser pair at each end, is nothing short of awe inspiring (Fig. 2.3.15).[30] The gabled reredos, has been dated to *c.* 1310, its superstructure to 1350–1360, and the sacrament house to 1360–1365. With tongue in cheek, it has been suggested that the tower canopy work had been the designer, Master Bertrams's, "journeyman's piece!"[31]

Whilst a direct comparison between Hereford's now monochrome semi-tower with Doberan's much taller polychromed free-standing monument is invidious, some remarks on the more detailed differences, and emphases, are in order. The Hereford structure rises almost imperceptibly from the crown of the vault of the episcopal canopy, whilst Doberan's plinth sits conspicuously on the roof of an earlier gabled reredos. Its first stage takes up the plinth's footprint, with its triangular concavities, but otherwise, the elevation is classically *rayonnant*. The open second stage is unconventional, contrasting an outer shell against an inner core, as on the lower phase at Hereford. The crown of Doberan's second phase is somewhat spoiled by the use of the curious "broken gable" motif, with still no sign of an ogee arch in evidence. The surrounding external standards rise up to announce the final half-scale component of the tower, which is untransomed, surprisingly delicate and elongated.

At Doberan the ciborium tower faces the east window, which, in this case, is not very large. The light from the rising sun would only have affected visibility for a couple of hours, at most, each day.[32] In this connection, it is interesting to note the almost exclusive use of gilding at Doberan, with colour employed only sparingly, mostly to highlight the architectural transitions and details on the figure sculpture.[33] As at Exeter and St Davids, at Hereford colour would have been used to emphasise the different architectural components of the structure. Against the backboard, a colour would have been chosen to provide as strong a contrast as possible to show-off the tower's design.[34] As on the Gloucester choir-stalls, gilding would have been sparingly applied to the finials and other decorative sculpture. It is to be hoped that a rigorous polychromy analysis will be undertaken on the Hereford throne in due course.

After an exhaustive discussion of the finer aesthetic attributes of the Hereford throne, and its stylistic context on a national and quasi-European stage, we need to briefly address its religious symbolism. At Hereford the fine early-14th-century, but restored, architectural stained-glass windows in the north-east transept resemble in their scale the ambitious monumental stone canopied tabernacles honouring and protecting the standing saints beneath them (Fig. 2.3.16).[35] By comparison with the superstructure of the bishop's throne, probably made some 30 years later, the architecture is cumbersome, with its thick uprights and schematic decorative carving. At the same time, the tiered elevation is nicely articulated with its jointed stone surfaces, quatrefoil friezes, a triplet of gabled windows and the solid flanking spires.[36] Their design is stylistically ambitious, and even resonates with aspects of the architecture at St Stephen's Chapel, Westminster. Its both architectural and symbolic resemblances to the three timber *cathedrae* at Exeter, St Davids and Hereford, and the stone *exemplum* at Wells, are undeniable. These windows, including those in the choir at Exeter (Fig. 2.1.17), and the three other West-Country thrones, betray a cousinage with the forms of the most religious objects of the Roman Church, such as the tabernacle, monstrance, ciborium, pix cover, sacrament house and reliquary. Their role is to display and protect either the sacred

Host or the relics of Christianity's historic witnesses. In the same way, the canopied *cathedra*, channelled the respect and devotion of the faithful to the office of the living representative of Christ in their midst.[37]

Discussion
This section contains a succinct consideration of the chequered cathedral building history at Hereford during the 14th century, as it impinged on the delayed installation of a set of choir furnishings. It also attempts to grapple with the challenge of reliably deducing the latter's patronage, a matter unsupported by any

Fig. 2.3.15 Bad Doberan, Mecklenburg, Germany. Cistercian abbey church. High altar with spired ciborium and sacrament house. M. Heider.

Fig. 2.3.16 Hereford Cathedral. North-east transept early-14th-century stained glass windows with figures of St Katherine and St Michael. H. Harrison.

Fig. 2.3.17 Hereford Cathedral. Memorial brass for Bishop Trillek, now on north-east side of presbytery. Detail. H. Harrison.

documentation, and which has been a bone of contention for a long time. It will be necessary to summarise the complicated architectural narrative in these respects in order to reach a robust conclusion.

It will be recalled that, at the opening of the 14th century, at St Davids Cathedral, apart from a few relics of a minor Celtic saint, there were the rediscovered bones of St David, a significant British saint. Although, by the end of the 13th century, Hereford had two patron saints – the 8th-century St Ethelbert and the Virgin Mary. The former's popular shrine left no traces, and there were no other relics of any importance in the cathedral.[38] It was a similar story at Exeter. Given the important financial benefits which could accrue to a religious house from hosting a flourishing pilgrimage cult, this placed both cathedrals at a relative disadvantage.

At Hereford, Bishop Thomas Cantilupe (bp

1275–1282) had been a distinguished scholar of canon law and theologian, who became chancellor of Oxford, Lord Chancellor of England and, later, a trusted advisor to Edward I. He was an exemplary pastor and a just administrator of his diocese. Under his successor, Richard Swinfield (bp 1283–1317), an altar tomb was prepared for him in the north transept, which was later converted into a shrine.[39] For about 20 years after the translation of his bones into the former tomb in 1287, there was a huge surge of interest in his miracle-working cult.[40] This eclipsed the status of St Ethelbert, although the Virgin Mary's was already secure, thanks to the magnificent Lady Chapel.[41] Cantilupe's cult helped to fund the rebuilding of a substantial part of the cathedral, and by the end of the 1320s, his fame easily outstripped that of St Wulstan at Worcester and St Swithun at Winchester.[42]

The later remodelling of the presbytery aisles was intended to provide convenient access to the Lady Chapel, in which it was ultimately planned to translate the saint's shrine. The ceremonial approaches from both sides of the presbytery aisles provided:

> "… an opportunity readily utilized for displaying the history and prestige of the cathedral. The choir aisles were lined with new recesses and effigies commemorating ten previous bishops, intended to form an impressive prologue to the reliquary: perhaps Swinfield had in mind the earlier series of posthumous tombs to Saxon bishops in the choir aisles at Wells Cathedral".[43]

There was also the rebuilding and consolidation of the new bell tower, which had, at least, partially collapsed and had to be rebuilt.[44] In 1319, in its appeal for financial assistance to Pope John XXII, the chapter claimed that they had already spent large sums of money on the superstructure, as well as on sumptuous workmanship, and that the tower threatened ruin.[45] In fact, Richard Morris believes that "the present tower is the one erected before 1319 and (is) not a rebuild after *c.* 1320 … The main reinforcement work … was directed at the arcades adjoining the north-west crossing pier, and did not extend to the tower itself".[46] It would have been underpinned, but the reinforcement of the arcades, was of equal importance. The ultimate completion date for this work is not recorded, but is likely to have been by the mid-1320s. It should have been followed by the construction of a stone

pulpitum, and the planning of a set of new choir furniture, although, as already proposed, it is inconceivable that any serious work, in the latter regard, could have been started until some 15 years later.

Morris observed that the successor 14th-century solid-screen pulpitum, although not conforming to the verandah type at Exeter (1317–1325), Tintern (*c.* 1330) and St Davids (*c.* 1340), is comparable to that at Wells (*c.* 1335).[47] These analogies should help to bring us a little closer to arriving at a date for the final consolidation of the Hereford central tower, and the possible onset of preparations for erecting a new set of choir furniture. If the adduced proposition that the choir fittings were commenced in the closing years of Charlton's bishopric, i.e. *c.* 1340, the pulpitum at Hereford could have been completed a few years after that at Wells. Given the almost constant building, and rebuilding, activities in train during the first two decades of the century at Hereford, this probable additional delay in the refurbishment of the choir invites the question as to what had been the arrangements for the conduct of the daily offices in the cathedral for possibly up to half of a century!

It has already been posited that the stalls and episcopal throne betray a protracted manufacture, looking back to both the Wells choir furniture, of the late 1330s, and, to St Stephen's Chapel, Westminster, where building and fitting-out works were still in train throughout the 1340s, and even to the choir-stalls at Gloucester Abbey, *c.* 1350. Irrespective of work on the choir at Hereford, unfortunately, any attempt to date the construction of the cathedral's new pulpitum, is problematic. During his episcopacy, Bishop Orleton (bp 1317–1327) seems to have been mostly occupied with public affairs, and may not have had the opportunity, nor the energy, to move things much further forward before his transfer to Worcester. For later historians, Bishop Charlton hardly seems to have put his head above the historical parapet, although the possibility that he initiated the fitting out of the Hereford choir is underscored by the marked difference in style of the early and later phases of the extant furniture. In trying to establish a reliable dating bracket in which to place the timber furnishings, including the bishop's throne, a cut-off point of 1360, when there was an even more severe plague epidemic than that of the Black Death, is inevitable. Following the demise of Bishop Trillek in the same year, the possibility that the furnishings were not complete by then surely stretches credulity.

For approximately 60 years, Cantilupe's tomb/shrine had stood where it does today in the north-west transept, and it was not until 1349, the year of the Black Death, that the relics were finally translated into the Lady Chapel in a previously constructed purpose-built shrine by Bishop John Trillek, D. D. (bp 1344–1360).[48] By then it was already 20 years since Cantilupe's canonisation by Pope John XXII in April 1320. The translation appears to have been a delayed response to the visitation of the Black Death, and possibly a memorial to those who had succumbed.

The proposition that Bishop Trillek must have been the patron of the choir furniture, even if not the initiator of it, may seem to be going against the grain of history, as he is not usually noted as a builder of the fabric.[49] Some years ago, it was suggested by this writer that the dating bracket for the woodwork was 1340–1355.[50] This is well within the period of Trillek's episcopate, although, when this claim was made, the latter's involvement had not been systematically investigated. Crucially, as has been pointed out by Morris, the bishop's choice of burial in the centre of the choir is *prima facie* evidence of his involvement in the refurbishment (Fig. 2.3.2). The burial position was verified in 1609 by Thomas Dingley, who noted "In the Quire near the high altar is seen the tombstone which I have here touched off inlaid with brass". His drawing is very inaccurate, but the heraldry on the armorial shields is recognisably Trillek's.[51] In Browne Willis's early-18th-century plan, the brass is shown on the north-east side of the presbytery, where it is today (Fig. 2.3.17),[52] but this was soon after it had been moved by Bishop Bisse (bp 1713–1721), when he repaved the sanctuary. Notwithstanding, the tomb was still *in situ*, and was rediscovered in 1813. Trillek's crozier, and a papal bull, probably that of his appointment, were found within, as well as his finger ring.[53] The splendid canopy is "the earliest surviving London B full-length brass in the country",[54] even though the outer inscription and much of the engraved metal surround and canopy work is restoration.[55] The bishop is shown "vested in amice, apparelled albe, stole dalmatic, and chasuble, with the maniple on his arm, gloves

and ring on his hand, mitre on his head, and crosier beside him".[56]

Trillek has been accused of cowardice in the face of the plague, in his avoidance of any permanent residence in the city of Hereford.[57] It is true that he resided during the epidemic at his manors in the county and elsewhere, but this was interpreted by William Dohar as "pragmatism over heroism".[58] Certainly, the evidence seems to suggest that he worked tirelessly to replace the depleted beneficed clergy and that he was not hiding away, but limiting the probability of his becoming infected, so that he could be on hand to provide sound advice and leadership to his executants, and recruit and ordain fresh candidates for the ministry.

He was from a small landowning family in Monmouthshire, and had at least one useful family connection – Bishop Adam Orleton being his uncle.[59] He was educated at the University of Paris from 1329 to 1336.[60] He was appointed a canon of Hereford Cathedral in 1327. From then on he steadily acquired a portfolio of benefices in the West-Country and beyond, including one at St Mary's Abbey, Winchester. He is said to have "devoted himself to the administration of his diocese, only leaving its confines for an occasional visit to London or his houses at Prestbury and Goldhill, and practically taking no part in the business of the outside world".[61]

On the available evidence, the state of the cathedral fabric on Trillek's succession was still "work in progress". This would not have come as a great shock, since the new incumbent was conceivably familiar with the cathedral since the age of 9 years old, when his uncle was enthroned (he was born *c.* 1308). In any case, in 1327, during his student years, he was appointed a canon, doubtless at the instigation of Orleton, in the year that the latter was transferred to Worcester. At that time, Trillek would have had no diocesan duties, but he possessed a canonical house and would have worshipped in the cathedral from time to time. He could not have failed to be aware of any progress, or lack of it, in the building works, about which his uncle would have been able to keep him informed. The only hard piece of information to suggest that he had been active in fitting out the building himself is the statement that he was said to have given "*multa bona et plurima ornamenta*" to the church and discharged the duty of this office with activity.[62] In classical Latin, *ornamenta* suggests trappings, and possibly fittings, decoration and embellishment, and in medieval Latin, ornamentation and adornment. Whether or not he was involved in the choice of the executant of the monumental brass on his tomb, it suggests a considerable degree of artistic discrimination on his part, which, equally, applies to the choir furniture (Fig. 2.3.1). A similar artistic ambition is revealed in the innovative handling of the canopy above his *cathedra*.

After the translation of Cantilupe's relics in 1349, there was a revival of interest amongst the laity in the shrine. Given the financial challenge of completing the cathedral's planned building works, any spike in the income from alms would, assuredly, have been welcome. The cathedral's endemic problem of shortage of funds, however, did not abate during Trillek's episcopacy. In 1355 there were still worries about the non-completion of certain portions of the renovation, and "Trillek was offering to try to procure indulgences from all the bishops assembled in parliament towards the fabric".[63] Moreover, Morris pointed out that the chapels of St John the Baptist and St Michael in the south-east transept were not finally completed until 1364, well after Trillek's death.[64]

Any extra income from the shrine in the early 1350s could have funded the completion of the choir furnishings, which would have invigorated the liturgy of the cathedral's recently introduced major feast day on 25 October. The Hereford *Customs* of the mid-13th century stipulate the particular services that the bishop should attend if he is in the county, including Christmas, Ash Wednesday, Maundy Thursday, Good Friday, Easter Eve, as well as the feast of the Assumption of the Virgin.[65] In Trillek's case, and exceptionally, he would have had no difficulty in fulfilling these requirements because, unlike many bishops at the time, he was an assiduous diocesan. The conduct of the other principal and double feasts was the dean's responsibility.[66] "It was also the duty of the dean to pour water on the bishop's hands, and with the precentor to lead him to and from the incensing of the high altar".[67]

There is an account of the consecration and enthronement of Bishop Courtenay at Hereford, Trillek's successor but one, in 1370, which gives a flavour of how a new bishop was inducted in Britain during the High Middle Ages. William Courtenay was the second son of the 2nd Earl of Devon, and was destined to become Lord Chancellor and archbishop of Canterbury. It is worth quoting here briefly from a first-hand account.

> "He was coming through the middle of the city in bare feet,[68] a numerous retinue of people escorting him to the west door of the said church, and was received by the dean, canons and priests with a solemn procession, which proceeded to the presbytery step. There, on bended knee and bowed body for some time, he worshipped before the high altar, certain prayers suitable for the reception of such a prelate being said over him. Then, rising, he kissed the altar, and admitted at the kiss of the mouth (with his mouth) all the canons there present. And afterwards he went to the vestry (*vestibulum*)…".[69]

Courtenay was later enthroned with the following invocation:

> "*auctoritate ecclesie Cantuariensis ego vos induco in corporalem possessionem ipsius ecclesie cum suis juribus et pertinenciis universis et hic vos intronizo. Dominus custodiat introitum tuum et exitum tuum ex hoc nunc et usque in seculum*".[70]

The canonisation of Cantilupe, the remodelling of the nave and presbytery aisles, the pilgrimage cult and the installation of the retrospective episcopal effigies, the stabilisation of the bell tower, the appointment of Bishop Trillek, the lavish furnishing of the new choir with its key provision of a bishop's throne, not to mention the completion of the eastern transepts and the final fitting-out of the Lady Chapel, can be seen to be all part of one overarching extended campaign to consolidate the building, provide much needed facilities for the conduct of the liturgy and boost the institution's profile and income. Taken together, they provide a context for the provision of the timber choir furnishings, particularly, the episcopal throne. The latter's considerable aesthetic quality reflects the excellent academic and social connections of John Trillek, their design being unmistakably *au fait* with early trends in the development of the burgeoning English Perpendicular style, as well as the West-Country and metropolitan-influenced stalls at Gloucester Abbey. The design of the throne itself is of international importance.

Addendum

The use of timber as the medium for the three major surviving West-Country thrones is often emphasised, although stone was the most common choice in Western Europe.

Thrones were usually designed to be *en suite* with a set of clergy stalls, and in Mediterranean countries were often made of the same material. However, probably for climatic reasons, in Britain there is no evidence that choir-stalls were ever made in stone, although there was a documented set as far north as Douai. In terms of style and scale, only at Hereford is there evidence of a true matching in appearance of both components. At Exeter Bishop Stapeldon's relatively modest stalls were designed and built by a different team of craftsmen up to a decade earlier than the far more ambitious throne. At St Davids it is harder to judge, as we have only the slightest knowledge of the design of the 14th-century stalls, but at least it is safe to say that there would have been little conformity in terms of scale, the throne presiding magisterially over proceedings

On the basis of the evidence of Britain's surviving choir-stalls, one could hazard that there was a preponderance in the use of timber in Britain's High-Medieval thrones. Moreover the survival of three timber thrones in these, admittedly, remote West-Country locations suggests that they were to be found elsewhere. The West-Country enjoyed no natural advantages in its soil for the propagation of the best quality oak timber, which is usually considered to have been grown on the clay uplands of East Anglia, as well as other favoured parts of the Midlands and southern England. The West-Country's proximity to the prevailing Atlantic winds, causes "shakes" in the grain, that were observed in the structural study of the Exeter bishop's throne (Appendix III). For the St Davids throne, it is possible that the timber was shipped in from the Baltic, or possibly Ireland. Generally, in much of Britain it was far easier to acquire good quality oak.

In this connection, the relative suitability of timber and stone for constructing an episcopal throne is worth considering. As at Wells and Durham, we find that stone is less adaptable for creating an ambitious lofty three-dimensional monument. To achieve this it is essential to incorporate a self-generated stability, as in the case of the Neville Screen at Durham, with its mainly solid and buttressed lower zone (see Fig. 4.37). Otherwise an aesthetically discrete monument in stone is dependent upon being keyed into an adjacent architectural support system. At Wells this arrangement comes at the price of needing to conform dimensionally to the pre-existing architecture. At Durham, whose canopy is much taller, the price is an almost complete loss of transparency (see Fig. 4.1). Oak with its relative lightness compared to stone and its self-buttressing tensile strength, produced in large part through the technique of framed construction, offers the possibility of creating a robust free-standing three-dimensional structure of considerably greater height and transparency than most equivalents in stone. The episcopal throne builders in the West-Country, particularly at Exeter and St Davids, were well aware of the liberating possibilities of their material.

It is important to remember that oak was selected not for any intrinsic status, but for its utilitarian attributes.[71] In any medieval hierarchy of precious materials, it would have come somewhere near the bottom. It was almost invariably disguised to imitate more costly materials, such as gold, silver and precious textiles, or as a ground for the application of coloured images. These functions are dramatically demonstrated on the Exeter throne by Eddie Sinclair (see Appendix IV, Figs App. 4.1 and App. 4.2, and Fig. 2.1.20). At St Davids, although the figurative elements in the painting scheme have mostly disappeared, the polychromy on the throne's structural members has survived much better. The polychromy on all three of the timber thrones discussed would have instilled in the majority of worshippers a striking out-of body experience.

Notes

1   Browne Willis shows no sub-stalls. We know that there were four dignitaries at Hereford Cathedral, presumably the dean, precentor, chancellor and treasurer, and 28 prebendaries, 12 priest vicars, 4 lay vicars: 48 in total. The seven choristers, an organist, verger, two sextons, a master of the grammar school and usher, could have been accommodated on benches. It is uncertain if there were any sub-stalls.
2   Scott 1879, 290–91.
3   *Ibid.*
4   Whitehead 1995, 183.
5   Scott 1879, 290.
6   Scott signed the contract for the work in 1858, and his responsibilities at the cathedral came to an end in 1863. Whitehead 2000, 276.
7   Originally, the stalls were approximately 48 ft (14.6 m) long, and terminated at the western edge of the east tower piers. In this position,

they did not encroach at all upon the three-bay presbytery.

8 There remains a made-up set of five seats, now at the west end of the cathedral nave, as well as some of the stalls in the choir at All Saints' Church, Hereford, which probably originated in the cathedral.

9 Scott 1879, 290–1.

10 For some of the conflicting evidence in identifying this tomb, see Morris 1974, 26; Leland 1910, 181–2; Godwin 1743, 481; Gough 1786, 18, pl. iii; Marshall 1951, 33–4; Lindley 1995, 113–14, and Thurlby 1995, 15.

11 The fine timber ogee balustrade at the top of the enclosing wall on the south side, which returns for a short way at each end, was unquestionably designed *en suite,* because, even though the architrave may not be ancient, the plinth certainly is. This extra component would have further highlighted the starting point for a review of the episcopal "burials" on a tour of the east end from the south choir aisle.

12 For an earlier discussion of the stalls, and their stylistic relationship to contemporary furniture elsewhere, see Tracy 1987, 30–7.

13 Havergal 1869, 36. This kind of anomaly can be picked up on commissions undertaken around the time of the Black Death, for instance at Gloucester Abbey, see Tracy 1988, 44, *passim.*

14 The upper level of the stall canopy work seems to have been redesigned, and the dean's formerly returned stall is ceiled with a lierne vault inside the coving, and a traceried seat back. This manufacturing discontinuity can be disentangled from a close study of the architectural and ornamental elements.

15 The Hereford woodwork has traditionally been dated to the second half of the 14th century. Bond 1910, I, 29.

16 The so-called "Dean's stall" may not be his original seat, but is one of the three dignitaries' returned stalls that were retained and placed at the south-west end of the 19th-century re-arrangement. The dignitaries' stalls were probably all vaulted, in contrast to the lateral seats, which were simply coved. From the 14 lost dignitaries' and lateral stalls, there is now the made-up group of five lateral stalls, placed at the back of the north nave aisle.

17 For a selection of comparative images from the Hereford choir-stalls, see Tracy 1987, pls 93–107.

18 For a more detailed discussion of the Wells choir-stalls, see Tracy 1987, 25–9. See also *ibid.* for the foliage carving at Hereford and Wells, pl. 102.

19 *Ibid.,* pls 90, 104.

20 For further discussion of the throne's stylistic relationship with the work of the "London"-related English architects, see below. Within the throne enclosure and at each end of the choir-stalls, the nodding ogee arches at Hereford, which front either a straight gable, or a spire, are very similar to this ubiquitous motif at Gloucester. It will be recalled that this formula was an invention of Thomas of Witney, it was used on a large scale on the bishop's throne at Exeter. For a fuller discussion of the stylistic relationship between the Hereford and Gloucester choir furniture, see Tracy 1987, 44–8. For William Ramsey III, see Harvey 1984, 242–5.

21 The flat unadorned lateral side pieces were added when the throne was moved to its current position. For stability, the side wings extend backward as well as forward.

22 Willis 1727–30, II, facing 498.

23 Mackenzie 1844, pl. 17. For William Ramsey III, see Harvey 1984, 242–5.

24 Mackenzie 1844, pl. 4. The Hereford choir-stalls abound with quotations from William Ramsey III's work at St Stephen's, such as the rosette-filled friezes, quatrefoil-pierced and embattled parapets, hexagonal buttresses on the corners of the stall ends, buttresses with blind tracery lights let in with gablets above, and the way that the elevation, particularly on the stall ends, is divided horizontally into separate components.

25 Wilson 1995, 468–70; Harvey 1984, 31.

26 Morris 1978, 30, n. 35; Wilson 1979 unpublished, 161; Heighway and Bryant 2007.

27 For a fuller description of this monument, see Lindley 2003, 165–8.

28 *Ibid.,* 166.

29 For the change of design during the monument's construction, see Morris 1994, 211–12.

30 The high altar ciborium tower at Bad Doberan is somewhat lower than that of the sacrament tower.

31 Gloede 1970, 77.

32 At Hereford the throne superstructure in its original position against a stone pier, would still have suffered some visibility problems because of the immediate proximity of a strong light on either side. At St Davids, excessive back-lighting was not a problem, and at Exeter, the monument is large and dense enough to effectively disperse the light from the south-aisle window, which, in any case, is much smaller than that at Hereford.

33 At Doberan most of the coloured high-lighting seems to be authentic, although it has unquestionably been refreshed.

34 A polychromy analysis should be able to indicate what colour was originally employed as a background. Also it would be interesting to know if there are any signs of colouring on the seat backs.

35 The standard work on the stained glass at Hereford is still Morgan 1979. For details of the restoration of the north-east transept windows, see Iles 2000.

36 Fictive jointed (painted) surfaces are found on the Westminster Abbey sedilia, *c.* 1308.

37 See Chapter 4, 122–5 for further thoughts on throne canopy parallels.

38 It is known that Bishop Robert of Béthune, who presided over the completion of the building, had written to Abbot Suger seeking relics. Lindley 1995, n. 51.

39 Morgan 1982, 145.

40 Finucane 1982, 137–44, esp. 138–42.

41 The Lady Chapel at Hereford is thought to have been completed by the 1230s. Morris 2000, 208.

42 Between Michaelmas 1290 and Michaelmas 1291, the total receipts from Cantilupe's tomb was £178 10s 7d, see Morgan 1982, 147. By the end of the 1320s, the relics of Edward II at Gloucester almost eclipsed the appeal of St Thomas's shrine. Hereford's ambitious building project began with the construction of the inner north nave porch (1288–90), essentially the pilgrims' entrance, and the remodelling of the north and south nave aisles. The north nave aisle leads directly to the north transept, for many years the receptacle of the shrine. On the other hand, the south nave aisle would have directed the pilgrims to the first of the ten historicising bishops' effigies in the presbytery aisles. For a comprehensive account of the 14th-century architectural history of the cathedral, see Morris 1974, and for the effigies, Lindley 1995; Morris 1974.

43 Morris 1974, 26.

44 There was also the lost axial tower at the west end.

45 Morris 2000, 221–2.

46 *Ibid.*, 222, and ns 78, 79.

47 For the Hereford pulpitum and the watercolour by John Carless of its west side in 1833, see Morris 2000, 224–5, col. pl. xi. For the Browne Willis plan, see Willis 1727–30, vol. 2, facing 498, and fig. facing 498.

48 Following a vigorous and successful money-raising campaign headed by Edward II, in *c.* 1320, the shrine was made in London by several craftsmen. For details, see Morgan 1982, 150–1. The subsequent fate of this important monument is unknown.

49 Nor is Trillek mentioned by Marshall 1951 in this capacity.

50 Tracy 1987, xxiii, 30–3.

51 For the drawing and inscription, see Dingley 1867, fig. cxiii.

52 Willis 1727–30, vol. 2, page facing 498, fig. 16.

53 The crozier and bull are conserved in the cathedral library, the ring was stolen in 1838. Parry 1916, xi, and T. Russell, "A Short Description of a Portable Shrine" (1830), unseen.

54 Badham and Norris 1999, 333.

55 Even the bishop's surname is missing.

56 Winnington-Ingram 1956, 16.

57 Dohar 1995, 55–77, esp. 55–60. For John Trillek's career, see Lepine 2012a and Emden 1958, 1906.

58 Dohar 1995. 56.

59 Emden 1958, 1906.

60 With his younger brother Thomas, he received by bequest some land in Oxford, which became known as Trillock's Inn, where he possessed a hall for students, which on his death, Thomas sold to William of Wykeham, for the endowment of New College. Thomas was elected dean of Hereford in 1355, and appointed bishop of Rochester in 1364. Parry 1916, vi, and Lepine 2012b.

61 Emden 1958.

62 Havergal 1869a, 21.

63 Morgan 1982, 151.

64 Morris 1974, 27.

65 Marshall 1951, 62.

66 Bradshaw and Wordsworth 1892–97, II, Pt. 1, 62, and Marshall 1951, 62.

67 Marshall 1951, 62.

68 In 1452–53 John Stanbury was enthroned as bishop of Hereford, and is said to have walked barefoot from St Guthlac's priory to the cathedral. Iles 2000, 321.

69 "… *Ipse quidem per medium civitatis, comitante et obviam sibi veniente numerosa populi multitudine, usque ad dictam ecclesiam nudus pedibus incedens, receptus fuit ad hostium occidentale ipsius ecclesie per decanum, canonicos, et ministros cum processione sollempni, et inde procedens usque ad gradum presbyterii, flexis ibidem genibus et curvato corpore aliquamdiu adoravit ante majus altare, et dictis super ipsum quibusdam oracionibus ad recepcionem talis prelati, ut michi videbatur, congruis, surgens deosculatus est altare et subsequenter admisit ad osculum oris omnes canonicos tunc presentes. Et postea accedens ad vestibulum…*" Capes 1914, 4–5. My thanks to Robert Higham for his suggestions with regards to this approximate translation.

70 *Ibid.*

71 With the rare exceptions, timber was used in the Middle Ages for domestic furniture. Also, it was generally employed as an architectural structural component. On another level, was its use on prestigious commissions as a high-quality ground for panel painting, such as, in England, in the 13th-century painted panels of the Westminster Retable. Binski 1995, 152–64.

CHAPTER 3

THE LINCOLN CATHEDRAL
BISHOP'S CHAIR

3

The Lincoln Cathedral Bishop's Chair

Description and physical analysis

In the chapter house at Lincoln Cathedral is an impressive canopied oak *cathedra*, or chair, with large lions lying on the arms, and a rectangular panel of reticulated quatrefoils under the seat (Figs 3.1–3.4).[1] The handsome coved canopy must have been made for J. L. Pearson, the cathedral's architect from 1870 to 1893, as it was not recorded by Precentor Venables in 1890 (see below).[2] It is of a type commonly used in the 15th century on chairs of estate, where the panels of the coving would have been shaped by steaming. Similar coving was often used on English single-screen choir-stalls during the 14th century, as for instance at Chichester Cathedral and Hereford Cathedral. However, in view of the construction of the original back panel, it is improbable that the Lincoln chair ever had an integral canopy. It probably had a simple backboard, rising to just above head level (Fig. 3.5).

The chair itself is 14th-century, and of primitive joined construction, but incorporates an element of proto-panel-and-frame work. Mason's mitres are used throughout, and the mouldings around the prominent panels are all carved in the solid. An unusual feature is the box construction of the arms, but a comparison with the drawing by S. H. Grimm (Fig. 3.6) indicates that this feature is modern. Evidence for a higher seat back originally, are the two sawn-off tenons at each end of the top rail, as well as the truncated mouldings on the inside (Fig. 3.5). Although the seat is only some 46 cm

(18 in) high, the very considerable seat depth of more than 58.5 cm (23 in) pre-supposes the use of a footstool. The overall dimensions of the chair are: height, 111 cm (43.7 in); width, 189.2 cm (74.6 in); depth, 67.5 cm (26.6 in). Paul Woodfield comments on the construction as follows:

"The chair has been assembled with a series of stub tenons, more a work of carpentry than of joinery. The single stub tenons are secured by single pegs of two differing diameters, the larger, c. 25 mm used for the main structural elements, and c. 15 mm used for ancillary work. As far as can be ascertained, the tenons are never housed, and the only variation is the use of bare-faced soffit tenons for the seat supports, although in many places the tenons are not axial but set to one side. The seat boarding is lodged at each end, presumably on grounds, and each of the five cross boards are pegged to bearers running front to back below. The arms are boxed, using 10mm thick oak boards, nailed presumably to a ground on the internal face of the frame. It cannot be seen how the grounds are fixed without removing the panels, but they are probably also nailed or tacked.

The decorative front panel below the seat has two openwork tiers of quatrefoils enclosed in a slender frame, all carved from a single piece of oak. This is secured to the backing with wrought iron nails with 15 mm diameter heads. No attempt has been made to conceal these.

The lion carving and the top roll and hollow moulding of the arm rests are of one piece of oak, secured to the rear upright of the chair by a tenon, set in a mortise, and pegged in from the side, and at the front, by a mortise set over a short vertical stub tenon worked on the top of the front stanchion of the frame.

The rear panel of the chair is composed of a large single panel of oak, possibly secured in grooves, not

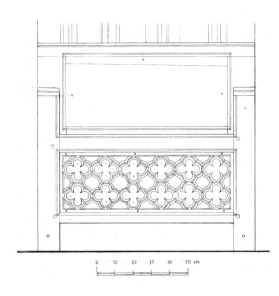

Fig. 3.2 (right) Lincoln Cathedral chapter house. Side view of bishop's throne. Measured drawing. Copyright P. Woodfield.

Fig. 3.3 (far right) Lincoln Cathedral chapter house. Front view of bishop's throne. Copyright P. Woodfield.

Fig. 3.4 (below) Lincoln Cathedral chapter house. Plan view of bishop's throne, including truncated moulding of original superstucture. Copyright P. Woodfield.

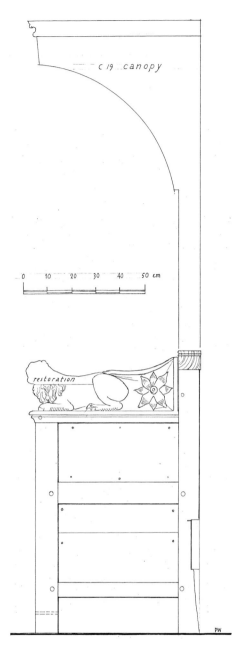

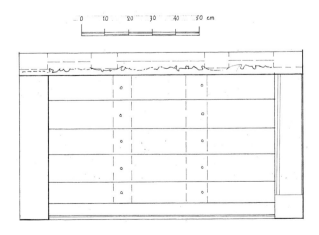

now visible. The top horizontal member carries the edge roll and fillet moulding, which surrounds all panels, and has on its top face slight evidence of the original higher back of the chair. It appears that the carving of the back rising from the top horizontal member consisted of one central and two narrower side fields, divided by vertical elements. The latter are "cushioned". These and the fields between them are intensively moulded or carved. There is no evidence as to whether the vertical elements at the extreme sides of the chair back were similarly carved or moulded. Unfortunately, only the bottom impression of the carving remains, in a rather mutilated state, to some extent due to the creation of a high back in the 19th century, and does not readily correspond to any recognisable moulding series. However, the elements appear to be a series of wide pulvinating or cushioned sections, interspersed with clearly defined beaked mouldings, as is found in stonework from the mid-13th century to the later Decorated period. As the verticals have no mortises, it is difficult to see that it could continue to any significant height, and perhaps simply provided a low decorative back no higher than the top of a mitre.

Simple ergonomics suggest that the seat of the chair is approximately the original height from the ground, although there are on the front of each front post a single dowel hole 80 mm from the floor passing through the post. There are no mortises. One possible explanation for these features is that they are locating points for dowels on a footstool, but this would seem rather difficult to use and is unsatisfactory as an explanation. One further unexplained feature is the pair of corresponding mortises on the inner face of the bottom side rails towards the back of the chair. These pieces may be re-used, but this seems most unlikely in a high status piece of furniture".

It is appropriate in this context to mention Britain's first medieval monumental timber

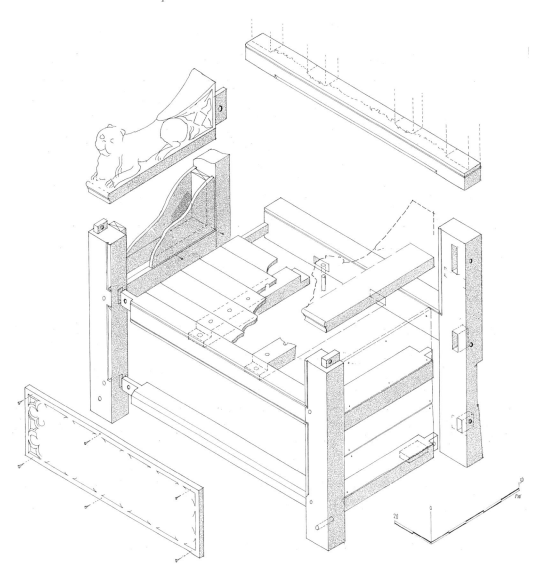

Fig. 3.5 Lincoln Cathedral chapter house. Isometric view of the bishop's throne. Measured drawing. Copyright P. Woodfield.

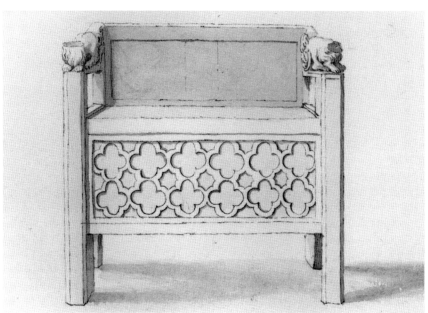

Fig. 3.6 Drawing of the old episcopal chair at Lincoln, Sept. 1784, by S. H. Grimm. British Library Ms Add. 15,541, fol. 123. By permission of the British Library.

S. H. Grimm's drawing, the earliest record of the Lincoln chair, is inscribed "The old episcopal chair at Lincoln. Sept. 1784" (Fig. 3.6).[6] Both lions are shown as decapitated, but the dexter one is turning slightly to the right. In this, the carver may have been indulging in a little artistic licence, so that he could show off better the side view of the animal. The seat back appears disproportionately lower than it does in reality, and he has failed to articulate any of the almost ubiquitous rounded mouldings. The two vertical cuts across the grain of the wood on the seat-back can still be seen today. Grimm does not indicate the split at the top of the seat-back, which may have only developed since. The sides of the arms are shown as open, so, as already mentioned, they must have been boxed in since. In Grimm's day the chair may have still possessed its original seat, as it is shown to be in one piece, as opposed to consisting of a number of narrow butted planks today.

Grimm made another drawing, entitled *Episcopal Chair in the Chapterhouse at Lincoln. August 1784* (Fig. 3.8).[7] This shows a Baroque-style chair, clearly based on the cathedral's medieval throne, with lions lying on the arms, rosettes behind them and water-leaves spreading forwards from the back. From the drawing it seems to be a piece of box construction of few subtleties. The adjacent side appears to consist of butted planks with Classical mouldings attached, to give the appearance of panelling. Curiously this moulding is not completed at the bottom. This must be the bishop's chair still in use under James Essex's late-18th-century lofty throne canopy, although it is hard to explain what it was doing in the chapter house.[8] Perhaps it had been removed there for use by the bishop at the Consistory Court, although there is no evidence for this. The table in front would have been for the use of the clerks, for which two tabourets were provided. A larger one would have been available for a dignitary.

The earliest written contribution on the Lincoln *cathedra* was a brief notice provided by E. Venables in 1890.[9] He tells us that "For a century or more this interesting relic of the past was stowed away, as a useless encumbrance, in the vestibule of the Cathedral Library". He confirmed Grimm's statement that it was "always known as the 'Bishop's Chair'". His accompanying drawings (Fig. 3.9) show the object in at least a partly restored state, again with no sign of the horizontal cracking on the

chair at Westminster Abbey, the "Coronation" or "St Edward's" chair, made between 1297 and 1301 (Fig. 3.7).[3] In that case, up to three significant objects are documented: first a maquette to be cast in bronze, secondly a never-completed full-size bronze chair, and thirdly, the extant autonomous timber specimen. The latter is, surely, too massive to be a model for a bronze version. Whilst by no means resembling the form of a stone throne, it is, nonetheless, a somewhat primitive attempt at timber joinery, a skill that was being developed in southern England during the first decade of the new century on sets of choir-stalls, as notably at Winchester Cathedral, 1308 *et seqq*.[4] The Westminster chair combines a somewhat unstable frame with a series of full-height pegged and butted planks for the seat back. Warwick Rodwell has observed that, "as a stand-alone frame, it would have been flimsy and easily distorted".[5] The boards for the side wings have tracery, front and back, carved in the solid, but applied capitals on the front only now missing. Although the constructional techniques used on the Lincoln chair reflect the considerable distance in date of manufacture, as is noted above, the Lincoln chair is also of a relatively primitive construction for its date.

Fig. 3.8 Drawing of the Episcopal Chair in the Chapterhouse at Lincoln, by S. H, Grimm, August 1784. British Library Ms Add. 15,541, fol. 124. By permission of the British Library.

seat back. His is a much more reliable record than Grimm's, and includes a cross section, which shows some of the construction. He also records that the lions at that date were still in their decapitated state.

A complete restoration seems to have been undertaken by Pearson. This included the replacement of the seat, the boxing-in of the chair arms and the replacement of the lions' heads. He also seems to have provided a desk, which has long since disappeared.[10] Francis Bond, writing in 1910, stated that the lions, which by that date had acquired new heads, were modern, which is only partially correct, since the bodies are medieval.[11]

It is most likely that, initially, the medieval throne at Lincoln was replaced in 1671/72, by the one designed by William Woodruffe, surveyor and draughtsman, who was closely associated with Sir Christopher Wren. Many of the medieval presbytery fittings would have been vandalised during the Civil War, probably after the siege of Lincoln in 1644, and in any case as a result of the abolition of the episcopacy by the Long Parliament in the following year.[12] Any pre-existing throne canopy had probably been damaged also, or even entirely removed.

Discussion

Venables made the suggestion that the chair may have been used for the Plantagenet kings, at the beginning of the 14th century, when they attended meetings of Parliament in the chapter house. He particularly mentioned Edward I's parliament of 1301. He noted that Pearson was of the opinion that the throne was made at the beginning of the 14th century. Twenty

years later Bond recycled the same argument precisely. However, this date is too early, and it will be argued that the chair could not have existed during any of the five sessions of Parliament held at Lincoln during the 14th century, which took place between 1301 and 1327.[13]

Nonetheless Venables did raise an important possibility that the Lincoln chair had a secular, rather than religious, purpose. Admittedly the lions on the arms can easily be shown to have secular connotations. For centuries these beasts have been used as symbols of political power. But they more normally appeared at the foot of a royal throne, as originally on the Westminster "Coronation" chair (Fig. 3.7).[14] Ancient precedents can be cited from Persia, Jordan and Classical Rome.[15] But, in a medieval European and Christian context we would do well to start with the passage from the *Second Book of Chronicles* (*Third book of Kings* in the Vulgate):

> "King Solomon also made a great throne of ivory: and overlaid it with the finest gold. It had six steps: and the top of the throne was round behind: and there were two hands on either side holding the seat: and two lions stood, one at each hand. And twelve little lions stood upon the six steps, on the one side and on the other: there was no such work made in any kingdom".[16]

Since Patristic times the Throne of Solomon had been equated with Christ, but during the High Middle Ages its image was identified with the Virgin. This iconographical development was chronicled by Francis Wormald.[17] The full-blown canonical stereotype of the throne utilises fourteen lions, twelve allocated to each side of the six steps on either side of the seat, and one each side of the base.[18] To

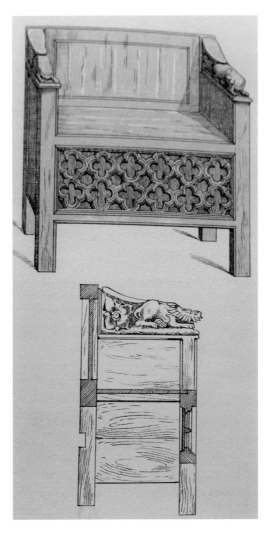

quote the prescription in the 13th-century
Bible Moralisée:[19]

> "Solomon also made a throne of ivory. And there
> were two little lions on the arms of the chair, and
> twelve little lions which between them supported
> the throne, which itself was placed on six steps …
> The throne of Solomon signifies the throne which
> the Father prepared for the Son, that is to say the
> Blessed Virgin. The two little lions represent the Old
> Testament. The twelve little lions the twelve apostles.
> The six steps the six Virtues".[20]

What is interesting is that the image of a
secular object, the throne of an Old Testament
king, has taken on a very special religious
significance. It is not just a royal seat, but the
throne which the Father has prepared for the
Son, namely the Blessed Virgin. These mature
iconographical images are all of the Virgin as
the Throne of Solomon, and the Virgin as the
Sedes Sapientiae.[21]

Moreover, the pair of lions placed on the
chair will have had, on the authority of the *Bible
Moralisée*, a direct relation to the Old and New
Testaments. The Throne of Solomon in a *Bible
Moralisée* in the Bodleian Library, shows lions on
either side of the throne (Fig. 3.10), not standing
or stretching up against it, as in most such cases,
but lying upon it, as at Lincoln.[22] It is difficult
to know how much influence these huge
luxury Bibles, almost certainly commissioned
by Blanche of Castille (1182–1252),[23] would
have had in English artistic circles, although
recensions have been identified in Europe in
such varied media as enamelling and tapestries,
as well as in books.[24] There are annotations in
English in the Bodleian and British Library *Bible
Moralisée* leaves, but until recently these were
thought to have been added by a 15th-century
hand. Patricia Stirneman has recognised that,
in fact, they must have been inserted during
the second half of the 13th century.[25] Lowden
has suggested that the Oxford-Paris-London
Bible must have been presented to Henry III,
either during his visit to Paris in December
1254, or in 1259, to celebrate the Treaty of
Paris.[26] He pointed out that, in spite of it being
in London so early, it seems to have had very
little art historical influence. He also remarks
that these manuscripts would not have been
"generally accessible to artists or used as
models, except when it came to making further
Bibles Moralisées". Nonetheless, in this instance
is it not possible that the young Edward III
might have proudly shown off his copy to
Bishop Burghersh?

The Westminster Abbey St Edward's Chair,
was probably guarded by a pair of seated lions.
In the account of Adam the Goldsmith, which
provides most of the information about the
making of this chair, two small painted and
gilded wooden leopards were mentioned as
having been sent to Master Walter of Durham
to be set on the chair.[27] There was a payment of
13s and 4d to Walter, who was the king's painter
for making them. Wormald believed that these
animals would originally have been located on
the chair arms. He states:

> "The word used for 'side' (in the account) is 'costa',
> and this may well mean the arms, since the remains
> of small wooden blocks, probably used for attaching
> some form of carved decoration, have been found on
> the arms during the recent decoration of the chair.
> This arrangement would have followed that seen in
> the *Bible Moralisée*".[28]

In English heraldry the lion *passant gardant* is a leopard, and that to some extent the two animals were interchangeable.[29]

Although none of the medieval surviving episcopal thrones in Britain features lions, apart from the Lincoln Cathedral chair, there was no shortage of *royal* images of enthroned monarchs resting their feet on the creatures. As late as the mid-19th century, the *interior* seat-back of the Westminster Abbey, St Edward's Chair, still displayed the fragments of a former high-quality painting of a monarch, with a lion at his feet.[30] The great seals of England, of Henry III, Edward II and Edward III, each conform to this type, and in the first two cases, pairs of lions rampant stretch up on either side.[31]

But to return to episcopal thrones, during the Early-Christian period, the appearance of lions, such as at Salerno, may have been a comparative rarity, although there was a clear link in Italy with seats of authority from Classical times (see Figs 1.17 and 1.19).[32] On the 4th-century stone throne at S. Ambrogio, Milan, lions are placed on the chair arms as at Lincoln, and in the *Bible Moralisée* (Figs 1.15; 3.10; 3.11). By the 11th century, they had become a popular attribute, with a rash of examples on the Italian mainland, such as S. Maria-in-Cosmedin, and SS. Nereo and Achilleo, in Rome, and Monte Sant'Angelo, Bari, Calvi, Canosa and Agnani, in the south.[33] The use of lions must have been inspired by a revival of interest in ancient Rome, and the animals were placed in their traditional secular position at the base of the chair, as if bearing its weight.[34] At Lincoln there was an additional reason for featuring lions on a throne, the family's heraldic arms of the occupant, Henry Burghersh, included a lion rampant with forked tail. His throne would have been placed

Fig. 3.10 The Throne of Solomon, from Bible Moralisée, Bodleian Library, MS. Bodl, 270b, fol. 164. The Bodleian Libraries, The University of Oxford.

Fig. 3.11 Lincoln Cathedral chapter house. Detail of carved lion and eight-petalled flower on bishop's throne.

in the Gothic position at the east end on the south side of the choir. It must have remained there until the Civil War.

By 1784, Burghersh's throne was looking somewhat worse for wear, the artist's epithet for, "old episcopal chair", has a slightly disparaging ring to it. Indeed Grimm's drawing is so slap-dash, it hardly makes the most of so venerable a piece of furniture (Fig. 3.6). Perhaps for him, in the circumstances, it was not worth the trouble to make a detailed recording of such an outmoded object. Casting back to the period of the Civil War, a traumatic time for the cathedral, it is probable that the chair was taken to a place of safety during the ultimately successful siege of the city by the Parliamentary army in 1644. Subsequently, the soldiers were permitted to ransack the cathedral, wreaking considerable damage, particularly to the brasses.[35] After the restoration of the monarchy, Wenceslaus Hollar's cathedral plan, dated 1672, omits any evidence for the survival of a bishop's throne in the choir.[36] However, a replacement was provided soon after, designed by Edward Woodruffe.[37] As already mentioned, this was superseded in 1779 by James Essex's extant Gothick *cathedra*.

An attractive feature of the Lincoln chair is the quatrefoil panel at the front (Fig. 3.12). This geometrical motif is commonly used in England in the early 14th century. It is found in a frieze of single quatrefoils on the stone panelling in the choir at Gloucester Abbey, begun after 1337,[38] and on the choir triforium at Beverley Minster of *c*. 1340.[39] On the Lincoln throne the quatrefoils do not enmesh, like parallel rows of cog-wheels, as they do at the base of the choir triforium and cross screen

at Exeter Cathedral, dating from the 1270s.[40] They stand one row on top of another, with the intervening spaces as incurving octofoils, an unusual decorative motif at this time. Parallel, but earlier and more full-bloodedly Decorated in spirit, is the so-called shrine of St Dunstan on the south wall of the sanctuary at Christ Church, Canterbury, of 1304–05 (Fig. 3.13).[41] In that case the incurving hexafoils interlock with "spiked" trefoils, an admirably more developed ornament arrangement.

The splendid carved lions are the largest British examples in wood of the period, but their restored heads are regrettably more Trafalgar Square than Eleanor of Castile.[42] How-ever, perhaps the most stylistically diagnostic elements are the eight-petalled flowers behind these animals. They can be compared with those on the cathedral's pulpitum (Figs 3.11, 3.14), and the four-petalled flowers on the wall of the west chapel of the south-east transept, now the choristers' vestry, and the north wall of the choir aisle. These structures are thought to have been erected in the 1330s, during the tenure of Bishop Burghersh, who held office from 1321 to his death in 1340.[43]

Henry Burghersh (1292–1340), who was of minor aristocratic family, was well educated and became an outstanding royal administrator.[44] At an early age, under the patronage of his maternal uncle, Sir Bartholomew Baddlesmere, he obtained a royal clerkship, and was elevated to the bishopric of Lincoln in his late 20s. This exceptionally early preferment to such a position, in the face of other papal candidates, amongst other factors, was due to the persistent support of Edward II. Within a year, when in June 1321 Burghersh's uncle turned against the king, the young bishop had little choice but to join the opposition, headed by Thomas of Lancaster; then, in the following year he found himself on the wrong side after the Battle of Boroughbridge, and suffered an attempt by the king to remove him from office. His temporalities were confiscated, and his uncle was imprisoned in the tower. However, he was adept at winning his way back into a monarch's favour. He was to serve both Edward II and his son, quickly rising in political rank from Treasurer to Chancellor, the latter promotion at the age of 37. From 1337, he became active in the diplomatic sphere for Edward III, and died on 4 December 1340 at Bruges.

In spite of his interests in politics and

diplomacy, Burghersh was reputed to be an efficient and conscientious diocesan. When necessary he would delegate to a vicar-general, even appointing in later years Simon Islip, a future archbishop of Canterbury. He is thought to have assigned the arrangements for his burial to his brother, Sir Bartholomew Burgh, who founded a chantry for both of them at the altar of St Katherine on the north side of the cathedral retrochoir. The manufacture and installation of the stone fittings, accredited to his period of office, would have been left in the hands of a trusted executant, it seems likely that the carver of the timber throne was a member of the same workshop. As on the base of the tomb he used quatrefoils as decoration, and employed the characteristic Lincoln eight-petalled flower motif on the chair arms, so conspicuously evident on the west side of the pulpitum.

A medieval dating for the throne is corroborated by the paint analysis undertaken by Catherine Hassall.[45] It would have looked very rich with its red background and blue sides. The vermilion, crimson lake and azurite pigments used were all expensive, befitting an object of such importance. Unfortunately no medieval polychrome was found on the front quatrefoil panel. This would certainly have been painted, with some decorative, or even figurative, elements in the quatrefoils themselves. There was no evidence of any gilding, which has presumably worn off.[46]

Conclusion

The chair now in the chapter house at Lincoln Cathedral is almost certainly a medieval episcopal *sedes lignea*. It can be dated to the third decade of the 14th century. Given the size of the tenons embedded in the top of the chair rail, it is not likely to have exceeded about five feet in height. Furthermore, given the make-up of the seat back, the chair is unlikely to have supported a permanent integral canopy. Very probably, as at Canterbury Cathedral, a cloth of estate would have been used for this purpose. Possible evidence for the earlier throne's adoption at the time of the installation of new choir-stalls in the late-14th century, is the curious fact that the terminal sub-stall at the south-east end is undecorated, whilst its counterpart on the north side displays tracery like the others.[47]

Fig. 3.12 Lincoln Cathedral chapter house. Detail of quatrefoil panel on bishop's throne. C. Tracy

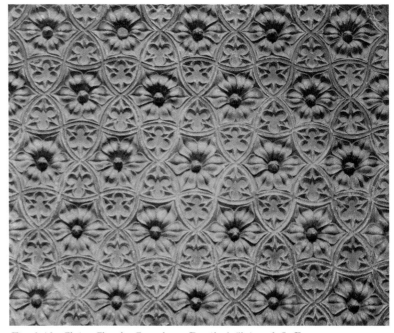

Fig. 3.13 Christ Church, Canterbury. Detail of Shrine of St Dunstan on sanctuary south wall. C. Tracy.

Fig. 3.14 Lincoln Cathedral pulpitum. Eight-petalled ornament detail from west side. C. Tracy.

Fig. 3.15 Illustration of Bishop Beckington of Wells (bp 1443–1465) seated in a throne. Trinity College, Cambridge, MS. R. 14.5, fol. 8 v. The Master and Fellows of Trinity College, Cambridge.

The dating of the chair has been arrived at on the basis of the carving style, and the palette of colours with which it was decorated. It was probably manufactured in the 1330s, on account of the similarity of the flower motif at the back of the arms with those found on a string of interior stone fittings in the cathedral, associated with Bishop Burghersh. It is one of only four surviving medieval timber British episcopal thrones, or chairs, and of strikingly modest proportions. In its scale and form it must have broadly resembled the lost timber throne in the choir at Canterbury Cathedral, and certainly stands apart from the thrones within the large-scale architectural canopied structures found at Exeter, Hereford and St Davids.

It is surprising that the existing throne was not replaced in the 1370s, when the extant choir-stalls were commissioned. Normally, these functional components go together. Unfortunately, due to the paucity of medieval fabric accounts for Lincoln, we have practically no information about the history of any of the medieval choir furniture. However, it is probable that, when the new stalls were commissioned, it was decided to retain the earlier chair in deference to the memory of their distinguished former bishop.

Miscellaneous later *comparanda* at Christ Church, Canterbury, Wells Cathedral and Llandaff Cathedral

As already noted, at Christ Church, Canterbury in the Late Middle Ages, there is written evidence for a wooden (arch)bishop's/prior's chair (*sedes lignea*) located in the Gothic position at the south-east end of the choir-stalls on the south side.[48] It existed independently of the earlier marble throne (*sedes marmorea*), which, after the introduction of the Corona and the shrine to Thomas Becket, was only used during the enthronement ceremony of a new archbishop. Notwithstanding, Phillips stressed the distance in status between the marble throne and the wooden chair. He was tempted to posit the existence of a third chair for the archbishop during the papal and high Mass, although he concluded that there would have been insufficient room for it in the already congested sanctuary, and that the wooden chair, was conveniently enough sited and within easy reach of the high altar.[49] It will be recalled that, upon his accession to the see of Exeter, Bishop Grandisson must have considered the high altar excessively distant from his throne in the choir (Fig. 2.1.2), as he commissioned a new wooden bishop's chair, confusingly titled, *cathedra episcopi*, for use in the sanctuary during the high mass.[50] In the Roman church, a portable faldstool was often used for this purpose.[51] In its liturgical context, it would have been of equal importance as the permanent *cathedra*. At Canterbury, Philips tells us that:

> "In 1540 there is an entry in the cathedral inventory 'One Canopie of silke baudekyn and gold to hang over the bishop'; and again in 1584 – presumably for the same article – 'A Canopy for my Lord Archbishop his seat of Reed Caffay (i.e. damask) spangled with birds of gold', along with 'two long Reed staves for

the archbishop's seat',[52] doubtless to support the canopy".[53]

He suggested that the chair had had no permanent architectural wooden canopy. Moreover, it is unlikely to have incorporated a carved integral seat back.

There is some uncertainty as to when during the Civil War the Canterbury chair was removed from the choir. It is not shown in the well-known view of the east end by Thomas Johnson, painted in 1657.[54] As Phillips tells us:

> "An entry in the 1662 inventory schedules 'Mourning for the Pulpit and for the Archbishop's Seat', which seems to suggests, in view of the short time that had elapsed since 1660, that it had by then been called into service again. A further inventory entry (dated 1689) describes 'the furniture of the archbishop's seat, kept in the vestry', in a fashion which certainly seems to fit it, and also suggests there was a good deal of shabbiness that needed to be covered up! 'One purple pendant vallance with a deep fringe' is presumably the canopy for which 'four gilded supporters' are provided. 'Another (vallance) of the same hanging before the seat' may have served to conceal deficiencies, along with a 'large satin cushion flowed with gold with four gold tassels to lay upon the seat'. Here 'seat' apparently means the desk, for there is 'a large purple velvet cushion with four silk purple tassels to sit on'. 'Two cushions more of purple satin flowed with gold, one long the other square', were presumably for His Grace's chaplains; and 'one watered curtain', we may conclude, protected the whole group of personages from draughts".[55]

This passage emphasises the well-established tradition that colourful and costly textiles and upholstery were deployed to enhance the appearance and comfort of plain wooden and stone thrones. This was being assiduously followed at the metropolitan cathedral.

The Canterbury throne survived until at least 1640, because it is mentioned by the antiquary William Somner, in the following terms:

> "Above these stalls (that is, to the east of the choir-stalls) on the south side of the Quire, stands the Archbishop's wooden seat or chaire, sometime richly gilt and otherwise well set forth, but now nothing specious through age and neglect. It is a close seat made after the fashion of such stalls, and called thence *Faldistoria*".[56]

But he goes on to point out that whereas faldstools were moveable, "this is fixt".[57] This suggests that, although it would have been possible to move it, it would not have lent itself to the procedure.

By the 18th century Canterbury's medieval throne was conclusively usurped, with the setting up of Archbishop Tenison's throne, attributed to Grinling Gibbons. The reference to the use of a canopy over this chair in the late 17th century can be compared to similar accounts from the 16th century, of the use of a "cloth of estate".

The manuscript image of the mid-15th-century bishop's chair, putatively belonging to Bishop Beckington of Wells (bp 1443–1465), is, quite probably, a useful indicator of the general appearance of a portable bishop's chair in the 14th century, and quite possibly a lost corpus of episcopal seats formerly in bishops' palaces (Fig. 3.15). Beckington is seen receiving a book from Dean Thomas Chandler, of Hereford. He sits in a joined high-backed chair, behind which is an embroidered foliate backing with a matching vallanced canopy.[58] The latter certainly looks as if it could with ease have accompanied the chair from place to place. From what we know of the Exeter *cathedra episcopi*, and the Lincoln and Canterbury chairs, they were probably all provided with similar "cloths of estate".

We can reliably surmise that polychromy was an essential adjunct in the decoration of all six of the extant monuments discussed in this book. For the most part it was used purely decoratively, and only at Exeter can we hypothesise, and at St Davids verify, the deployment of figurative painting. There is a strong likelihood that polychromy was employed on most of the thirty lost medieval British thrones.

At Llandaff, the timber episcopal throne was erected, *c.* 1480, by Bishop Marshall (bp 1478–1496), and the medieval choir-stalls were swept away in the neo-Classical reordering by John Wood in 1736. Luckily, an earlier visitation by Browne Willis, and the local antiquary, W. Wotton, in 1719, salvaged for posterity the medieval ground plan (Fig. 3.16).[59] The large polychromed back-board, 6 ft (1.8 m) high by 5 ft (1.5 m) wide, originally placed above

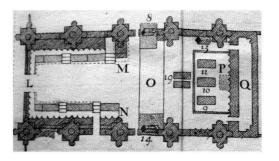

Fig. 3.16 Llandaff Cathedral, Cardiff. Choir ground plan in 1719. The medieval choir-stalls and bishop's throne (marked N). From Willis (1719).

*Fig. 3.17 Llandaff
Cathedral, Cardiff,
bishop's throne. Painted
backboard with
unattributed 'Assumption
of the Virgin'.
H. Harrison.*

*Fig. 3.18 Llandaff
Cathedral, Cardiff,
bishop's throne.
Suggested integration
with back-board.
Hugh Harrison
Conservation.*

LLANDAFF CATHEDRAL, WALES, BISHOP'S THRONE
Sketch showing Conjectural Reconstruction of
Throne around Surviving Painted Panel.
drawn by PETER FERGUSON Dip. Arch (UCL), RIBA. 2014.

the head of the enthroned bishop on the back wall, was preserved from desecration during the Civil War by means of over-painting (Figs 3.17; 3.18).[60] Later, during remodelling of the east end, two cathedral joiners managed to secrete it above Wood's central baldacchino in front of the high altar, where it was rediscovered in the mid-19th century.[61] It consists of a depiction of *The Assumption of the Virgin* in oils, now somewhat compromised by the over-painting, with "lampblack", which was later removed.[62] The polychrome is duller than it would have been, and the gilded passages are lost, revealing the bare wood beneath. The paintwork of the vesica is in poor condition, and many of the sun-rays and most of the roses obliterated, as well as what was already a crown on the Virgin's halo. The originally multi-coloured aerial background is likewise duller, and the sky, with its white cloudlets, has lost the gilding on the stars. The angels in their albs, and their wings are better preserved. Both are skilfully drawn. There are ten angels, six assisting the Virgin's passage to paradise. The two at the top play musical instruments, and at the bottom another swings an incense boat towards the prominent figure of the praying Bishop Marshall on the right, a classic adoring donor figure, who kneels facing respectfully in the direction of the Virgin. Another angel, at bottom left, holds a shield with the combined Marshall and cathedral armorial coats,

The scroll which emanates from the bishop's mouth bears the Leonine hexameter:

"*O Virgo scandens sis Marshall celica pandens*
(*O Maid, that goest up in state, Open to Marshall heaven's gate*)".[63]

Such a level of theological ambition for the embellishment of a British, or even European, bishop's throne is so far unprecedented. Quite apart from enhancing the sacred location of the throne itself, it stresses the donor's desire to imprint his identity thereon, and his intention to do so unequivocally.

Notes

1 This chapter is based on an article by the author published in *Apollo Magazine* in January 2002. I am grateful to the journal for permission to republish it here in expanded form.

2 The dimensions of the modern canopy section are: height, 1295 mm; width 1892 mm; depth 675 mm. For Pearson, see Quiney 1979, 263.

3 Rodwell 2013, 45–75; Percival-Prescott 1957; Binski 2003, 208–9. For more on the Coronation chair, see Chapter 1, n. 102.

4 For the choir-stalls at Winchester Cathedral, see Tracy 1987, chapter iii, pls 54–8.

5 Rodwell 2013, 45, where the author emphasises that the chair gets its rigidity from the full-height boards, which are arranged panel-like on three sides.

6 BL Ms Add. 15,541, fol.123.

7 BL Ms Add. 15,541, fol.124.

8 The missing moulding at the bottom of the chair sides has since been replaced with a plain version, and the front lower panel has been moved about 46 cm towards the back of the seat. This chair is a rather badly constructed amalgam of 17th-century panelling, possibly a 17th-century seat and late 18th-century lions, of poor sculptural quality, on the arms. The panels on the seat back, sides and the apron are most probably re-used wainscotting from the suite of wooden chancel furnishings, designed by William Woodroofe for the cathedral, and executed by the Lincoln joiner, William Evitson, in 1672/3. The contract for this work survives (Lincoln Record Office D&C Ciii/31/1pt1). On constructing the new throne and presbytery furniture Essex removed the fine Wren-style high-altar reredos and altar rails.

9 Venables 1890. Bond also mentioned the *cathedra,* see Bond 1910, 113–14 and pl., opposite 115.

10 See Bond 1910, pl. opposite 115.

11 *Ibid.,* 115.

12 For the violent siege at Lincoln, see Lehmberg 1996, 31–2.

13 Sessions of Parliament were held at Lincoln in 1301 (Edward I), 1312 (Edward II), 1316 (Edward II), 1318 (Edward II), and 1327 (Edward III). See *Parl. Paps,* Vol. LXII (London 1878). pt. 1, 13–54, pt. 3, ix.

14 Rodwell 2013, 100–1; Binski 2003, 213–15.

15 Grabar, 1954a, 34, figs 17 and 18.

16 Douay Bible, 1609, *Third Book of Kings,* Chapter X: 18–20.

17 Wormald 1988.

18 For instance, see Gauthier de Coincy, Throne of Solomon from the *Miracles of the Virgin,* 1325–50, Paris B.N., nouv.acq.fr. 24541, fol. iv. Illustrated in *ibid.,* pl. 53.

19 Oxford, Bodl. MS 270b.

20 "Salomon fecit thronum eburneum. et duos leunculos qui sunt duo brachia throni. et xii leunculos qui totum sustenant thronum et totus thronus dispositer est super sex gradus … Thronus Salomonis signet thronum quem pater filio disposuit scilicet beatam virginem. Duo leunculi. vetus et novum testamentum. leunculi xii. Apostolos. xii. sex gradus sex virtutes".

21 Wormald 1988, 63–4, where it is pointed out that the iconography stems from the *Sermon on the Nativity of the Blessed Virgin,* assigned to Nicholas of Clairvaux, for which see Petrus Damianus, *Sermo xliv in Nativitate S. Mariae, Migne Pat. Lat.,* Vol. CXLIV, cols. 736–40.

22 The Bodl. Oxford, MS 270b, fol. 164. Lions can also be seen on the arms of Solomon's throne in the *Hortus Deliciarum* (Bibliothèque Nationale, Ad. 144a), which is reproduced in Wormald 1988, pl. 54.

23 Lowden has proposed that the Oxford-Paris-London version (Oxford Bodl. MS 270b; London BL Ms Harley 1527; Paris Bib. Nat. MS latin. 11560) was ordered by Blanche of Castille for presentation to Marguerite of Provence, Louis IX's bride. They were married in 1234. See Lowden 2000, I, 183.

24 For instance, on the wall painting in the Bishop's Chapel at Gurk Cathedral, Carinthia. See Wormald 1988. pl. 56.

25 Stirneman 1999. The name John Thwayte is written in the London leaves between fols 60*v*– 65. Also on the last (blank) page in London is written: "ix score leves a(n)d xi and iii witthoute the ferste lef withe Maieste" (with a thorn for the <u>th</u>). (Transcribed from Lowden 2000, I, 185).

26 Lowden 2000, I, 183.

27 Rodwell 2013, 39.

28 Wormald 1988, 67.

29 It is generally asserted that the pair of lions at the foot of the St Edward's Chair, like the four present 16th-century specimens, were probably seated on the ground. However, this is by no means certain. See Rodwell 2013, 142–8.

30 Rodwell 2013, figs 91–7.

31 *Ibid.*, 20, figs 26, 1–3.

32 Nees has claimed that the origin of the lions on the reconstructed throne at Salerno is in the 3rd or 4th century. Nees 1999, 777.

33 For the Early-Medieval south-Italian examples, see Nees 1999, and for more on lions in the Early-Christian period, Chapter 1, 12–15.

34 For a secular English mid-13th-century example, it is worth recording that Henry III ordered his keeper of the works that bronze leopards should be placed beside his throne in the Great Hall at Westminster "of bronze instead of cutting them out of marble". Binski 2003, 214.

35 Lehmberg 1996, 31–2.

36 Dugdale 1673, 257.

37 The surveyor and draughtsman, Edward Woodruffe, had been a close associate of Christopher Wren. He designed the new suite of timber fittings for the cathedral's sanctuary, which the local joiner, William Evitson, carried out. The fine carved altarpiece, and at least sections of the altar rail still survive, the latter in Sleaford Church.

38 Verey 1970, 208; Bony 1979, fig. 324.

39 Bony 1979, fig. 304.

40 *Ibid.*, figs 102 and 103.

41 Prior Eastry's benefaction of the choir and sanctuary furniture at Christ Church, Canterbury, is recorded in Willis 1845. Originally, this decorated stone fragment formed the back of the high altar sedilia.

42 For the lions on the tomb of Queen Eleanor of Castile in Westminster Abbey, and the excellent *comparandum* from the Queen Mary Psalter, *c.* 1310–1320 adduced by Marie Louise Sauerberg in the same volume, see Rodwell 2013, figs 133 and 135.

43 Pevsner and Harris 1989, 113.

44 Bennett 2004.

45 She stated that: "The throne was given a ground consisting of two coats of pure white gesso, and the colours were laid over this. The rear back panel was painted with red using a mixture of vermilion and red lead. This opaque red was then glazed with a thin layer of crimson lake. The side was painted with blue using pure azurite over an undercoat of lead white. The leg may also have been painted blue, as the paint samples include gesso with a thin layer of lead white over the top, as used under the azurite". C. Hassall, *Paint Analysis, Report no. X325,* January 2001. This included colour microscope photographs of the six samples taken. Hassall also noted a later secondary decoration.

46 A sample taken from behind the lion on the outside of the right side, as you face the chair [Sample 4], "shows the original azurite covered with a layer of blue overpaint. The pigments in this blue are lead white, carbon black and indigo. Samples 2 and 3 (from the front lower panel) show a layer of red which either post-dates the indigo scheme, or is contemporary with it, as sample 3 contains a small flake of the (indigo) blue, which must have been caught up by the painter's brush. The red is a mixture of lead white, iron oxide red and red lead. It is resting on a greyish ground of chalk, lead white and carbon black". See *ibid.*

47 The extant choir-stalls at Lincoln Cathedral are recorded as being made during the Treasurership of John of Welbourn (1350–1380). See Muniments of the Dean and Chapter of Lincoln A/1/10. For a critical commentary on the choir-furniture at Lincoln, see Tracy 1987, 49–55, and Allen 2008.

48 Phillips 1949, 30–1. The chair is mentioned in an account of Prior Wodnysbergh's funeral in 1428.

49 *Ibid.*

50 Chapter 2.1, 41.

51 See Chapter 1, 10–11.

52 Somner 1640, 169.

53 Phillips 1949, 31.

54 Johnson's painting is inscribed: "Canterbury Quire as in 1657 … ye prospecte from ye Clock House". This picture was purchased in about 1910 by the architect W. D. Caröe.

55 Phillips 1949, 32.

56 Somner 1640, 169. As Somner admits, *faldistoria* is counter-intuitive, as its medieval meaning was, literally, "fold-stool".

57 Added in the author's own interleaved copy. The Canterbury chair is likely to have been panelled and stall-like.

58 Illustrated in Swanton and Lepine 2000, 69 and fig. 18. The image of the Wells throne is CUL, Trinity College MS. R. 14.5, fol. 8 v.

59 For Wotton's description of the cathedral, see Browne Willis 1719, 1–34, and his discussion of Bishop Marshall's throne, 15–16.

60 See Williamson 1938, 10–20.

61 Williamson 1938, 17–18. In 1935 it was cleaned by Professor E. W. Tristram.

62 For a discussion of a sculpted *Assumption of the Virgin* at Sandford, near Oxford, of a similar date, see C. Tracy, "A forgotten Assumption of the Virgin. The reredos at St Andrew, Sandford-on-Thames, Oxfordshire", *Apollo Magazine* (September 2003), 15–22.

63 Williamson 1938, 19.

CHAPTER 4

THE MEDIEVAL STONE EPISCOPAL THRONES
AT WELLS AND DURHAM CATHEDRALS

4

The medieval stone episcopal thrones at Wells and Durham Cathedrals

Andrew Budge

Introduction

On New Year's Eve 1724, a young representative of the Swedish Department of Mines, Henric Kalmeter, visited Wells as part of his travels in the south-west of England.[1] His journal records his very favourable impressions of the town and his extensive observations on its primary trade: knitted stockings. In fact his journal entry on stockings is considerably longer than that on the cathedral though he does compliment the building by saying it is "very large, long, and of superb build". "Furthermore", he comments, "the bishop's throne is a beautiful work in stone".[2] Perhaps Kalmeter's interest in mining meant that his attention was drawn to the large stone monument but his mention of the throne is relatively rare. Writing a hundred years later, John Britton provided a more typical reaction. Britton urged that the bishop's throne at Wells and other aspects of the choir "deserve minute and detailed attention", but went on to say nothing further on the matter at all.[3] For such a prominent and innovative structure the bishop's throne at Wells has provoked very little comment, academic or otherwise.

The stone throne at Durham has fared better through Christopher Wilson's analysis as part of his consideration of the Neville Screen, the relatively fulsome account of the monument by Pevsner, and the mid-19th-century observations of R. W. Billings.[4] However, despite the unusual designs of these 14th-century stone thrones at Wells and Durham, more interest has been excited by the positioning and functions of the comparatively simple earlier thrones in stone at Canterbury and Norwich.[5] This is, perhaps, due to the greater physical prominence of their central raised positions acting as a focal point for the choir clergy. The Canterbury throne also benefits from the survival of medieval documentary evidence; it forms part of Gervase's famous account of the reconstruction of the cathedral's east end following the fire of 1174, and the chronicle of the monk John Stone in the 15th century places specific emphasis on the enthronements of archbishops Stafford, Kemp and Bourchier.[6] There are extensive surviving records from the 1330s at Wells but these relate primarily to the cathedral's statutes and to the funding of the choir-stalls, with no reference made to the throne.[7] At Durham, the later chronicler of the *Historiæ Dunelmensis* mentions the throne only in passing and the writer of the *Rites of Durham* in the 16th century is simply and succinctly factual on the matter.[8] This relative lack of medieval sources has been mirrored in the dearth of more modern commentary. A further contributory factor in their comparative neglect may be the perception, fostered for example by Francis Bond in his *Wood Carvings in English Churches* of 1910, that the Wells

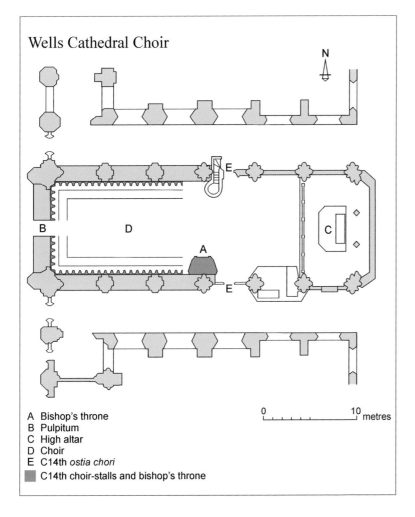

Wells Cathedral Choir

N

B   D

C

A

E

A Bishop's throne
B Pulpitum
C High altar
D Choir
E C14th *ostia chori*
⬛ C14th choir-stalls and bishop's throne

0   10 metres

throne had been substantially, and detrimentally, altered in the 1840s restoration supervised by Anthony Salvin. Bond commented that the throne at Wells "is fifteenth century work and, by a pretty fancy of the 'restorers', its tracery is filled with modern plate glass, and the door is a solid swinging stone!"[9] The bold polychromy of the throne at Durham might also give the (false) impression that the throne and its now gaudily decorated tomb beneath cannot be a wholly original construction but, at least in part, a more modern fabrication.

This chapter seeks to redress this neglect of the thrones at Wells and Durham. It will examine their formal aspects, assess the impact of any restorations and discuss the dating of the structures. It will then go on to explore the contexts, both physical and political, of these distinctive though somewhat large-scale examples of 14th-century micro-architecture.

The Wells throne

The bishop's throne at Wells stands against the middle pier of the southern elevation of the choir and presbytery (Fig. 4.2). The three bays to the west, towards the pulpitum at the crossing, contain the choir-stalls for the canons and vicars choral of the cathedral while the three bays of the presbytery to the east, with their

Fig. 4.2 (above) Wells Cathedral. 14th-century choir ground plan. J. Read.

Fig. 4.3 Wells Cathedral. View of choir with the bishop's throne, from the west. A. Budge.

intense sculptural decoration at the triforium level, provide the rich visual environment for the high altar. The whole is well lit not just from the large clearstorey windows but also from the prominent, seven-light east window above the altar. The throne, at 26 ft (7.9 m), reaches the full height of the choir arcade. Its upper stages are comparatively shallow, leading the throne, at least in its current unpainted state, to meld into its surroundings (Fig. 4.3). It does not have the same degree of prominence and visibility beyond the immediate confines of the choir as the exceedingly tall throne at Exeter.

It comprises three tiers (Fig. 4.4 and Tip-in 4.1). The first is dominated by a single canopy springing from four supports at the back and from side columns placed just in advance of these. The canopy is perhaps the throne's most immediately noticeable feature and is dominated by its flat, front-facing, open-cusped, finial-topped ogee. This encloses a vault of intersecting ribs with foliate bosses and a cusped outer section (Fig. 4.5). Beneath are back panels formed by three blind arches, the outer ones containing particularly subtle multiple cusping. The second tier, resting on the back part of the main canopy, is formed of three niches flanked by crenellated terminals. The central niche is open, square in plan and topped with an ogee arch whilst the niches to either side, by contrast, are canted outwards from the centre, polygonal in plan, enclosed at their backs and topped with nodding ogees (Fig. 4.6). The upper tier, to which we will return in discussing the 1840s restoration, now comprises a central open gable flanked by crenellated blocks. These three tiers stand on a raised stone area three steps above the level of the choir, fronted by polygonal desking with intricate blind panelling.

The throne is constructed predominantly from Bath stone, consistent with its emerging use in the cathedral in the second quarter of the 14th century, together with some use of Doulting, particularly in the desking, and one block of Chilcote stone, at the base of the eastern niche on the second tier.[10] The canopy has been constructed in two sections, joined at the apex, with the bases for the niches and pedestals of the middle tier carved from them. The throne retains evidence of 14th-century construction methods and design, such as black mastic workshop repairs, the use of poured lead dowling joints, and small "spur"

leaves between the crockets. One surprising element is the lack of finishing on the crockets of the main canopy. All other details on the throne have been completed in the round, irrespective of their location. The crockets on the canopy, however, remain un-carved on their inner elevation (Fig. 4.7).

Fig. 4.4 Wells Cathedral. Bishop's throne from the north. A. Budge.

Fig. 4.5 Wells Cathedral. Bishop's throne. Vault of the main throne canopy. A. Budge.

Fig. 4.6 Wells Cathedral. Bishop's throne. East side second tier niche. A. Budge.

Fig. 4.7 Wells Cathedral. Bishop's throne. Crockets of the main canopy, showing the lack of completion of inner faces. A. Budge.

Inspection of the throne reveals little indication of its original polychromy. Traces of dark pigment are retained in the crosses of the crenellated pinnacles, but it would appear that the "scraping" undertaken by Salvin's workmen was particularly effective. Documentation from the work on the choir in the 1840s does, however, shed some light on earlier painting schemes of the throne. Canon Barnard, who made a contemporary record of the restoration, stated that "the Bishop's Throne which was painted in very bad taste and style … was effectively divested of its wretched daubing", and from a letter written in 1894 by J. R. Clayton, Clerk of Works in the 1840s, we learn that prior to the restoration:

> "the throne of the bishop was entirely painted over to represent <u>Green Marble</u>! and that on the panel on the back was a rude representation of a landscape! The paint, being in oil, was extremely tenacious and gave much trouble in its removal. The effect produced by the change was extraordinary".[11]

From what remains it is difficult to determine whether the paint removed from the throne during the restoration in any way reflected an earlier arrangement. However, the possibility that the throne might originally have had a green colour scheme raises an intriguing prospect of a colour-coordinated east end to the cathedral with the green and yellow colours of the east window being reflected in both the throne and in the 14th-century vestments used in the choir (Fig. 4.3). The Wells Consuetudinary elaborates the colours of the vestments to be worn on particular saints days – and green and yellow together are specified for seven specific feasts.[12]

Mention of the restoration carried out by Anthony Salvin demands a more detailed consideration of the extent of changes made to the throne in the 1840s. This is aided by the accounts and chapter minutes of the period and by comparing the recent drawing of the throne (Tip-in 4.1) with two illustrations of the throne made in the 1820s before the restoration took place. These are the engraving of the choir elevation, dated 1823 and first published by Britton in 1824, and the watercolour of the choir by R. W. Essex dated 1826 (Figs 4.8 and 4.9).[13] Salvin was commissioned by the dean and chapter at Wells in 1847 as an experienced advisor for the restoration of the choir, replacing Benjamin Ferrey who had, for a number of years, been progressing the restoration of other parts of the cathedral.[14] The chapter's primary

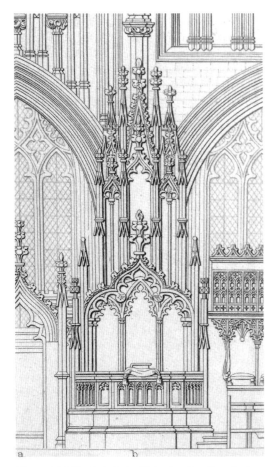

Fig. 4.8 Wells Cathedral. Choir elevation. Detail of an engraving of south side, showing bishop's throne. After Britton (1836, pl. xv). This same engraving was also published in the 1824 edition of this publication.

Fig. 4.9 Wells Cathedral. Detail of choir showing bishop's throne from the west. After watercolour by R. W. Essex, 1826. Wells Archives DC/PL/214.

concern, as in the 1330s, appears to have been the choir-stalls; little attention was paid to the bishop's throne.[15] However, the accounts of the works do show that scaffolding was erected around the throne in early November 1848 and that two carvers spent at least some of their time carving finials and pinnacles for the throne in nine of the weeks between December 1848 and March 1849.[16] They were also working in parallel on replacement parts or repairs for the triforium and for the doorways to the choir, so it is unlikely that there was time to undertake a significant amount of new carving for the throne. Comparison with the 1823 engraving and the 1826 watercolour confirm that any changes made during the restoration were not substantive, though some caution needs to be exercised.[17] Assessment of the current throne, the pre-restoration illustrations and

contemporary accounts suggests that there were two main changes made. The first was to the upper tier of the throne. The pre-restoration illustrations show this whole upper register as a wave-like undulation of decoration with the central, straight-sided, open gable flanked by crenellated bases topped with pinnacles and finials. The current throne has lost these outer pinnacles and finials. The original crenellated bases have been raised on supports of new stone so that the outer elements of the upper tier now terminate rather abruptly and leave the central gable decoration somewhat isolated (Fig. 4.10).

The second substantive alteration relates

Fig. 4.10 Wells Cathedral. Bishop's throne. Detail of top section, showing the insertion of new stone. A. Budge.

Fig. 4.11 Beverley Minster. The Percy tomb from the south side. Conway Library. The Courtauld Institute of Art, London.

to the lower part of the throne. The access to the bishop's seat was changed from the right, western side of the throne to the left, eastern side.[18] This access now includes the "swinging stone door" that so offended Francis Bond. But there are other difficulties. The front of the desking clearly incorporates stone of different types and the carving of the upper parts of the blind arcade at the front is exceptionally crisp (Fig. 4.4). Other changes, perhaps related to the alteration of access from west to east, are also visible. The far western front pinnacle now abuts the main structure of the throne uncomfortably closely, and at the equivalent position on the eastern side there is evidence of the beginnings of an arch between the outer pinnacle and the main structure. Furthermore, Canon Barnard commented on the restoration that "the Bishop's Throne which ... projected unnecessarily forward was ... contracted within narrower, but not less convenient dimensions".[19] This statement is difficult to reconcile with the current geometry of the throne, which, in its five-sided arrangement, is consistent with the 1823 engraving.

So what can we conclude in respect of the restoration? We can be confident that the great majority of the throne is as it was constructed in the 14th century. There have been changes to the top tier, but the original design can be reasonably reproduced. The same cannot be said of the desking area, but it is likely that elements of the original have been re-used in the current arrangement. The throne is now very stark in its bare stone and would have given a different impression when originally painted. Whether the predominant effect of the original polychromy was green, as indicated by the 19th-century commentators, cannot now be ascertained as insufficient original paintwork remains.

The design of the throne at Wells marks a distinct departure from its freestone predecessors. In terms of its scale, the intricacy of its design and its decoration, the Wells throne bears little formal resemblance to the thrones at Canterbury or, looking further afield, Lyon or S. Clemente, Rome.[20] Those thrones all reflect the formal tradition dating back to the positioning of the bishop's seat as part of the synthronon of the early church.[21] The Wells throne is more closely aligned to contemporary micro-architecture with its tiered structure, multiple pinnacles, ogee arches and openwork niches, yet close parallels are not available. The quintessential monument of the Decorated period, the Percy tomb at Beverley Minster, completed in 1340 or shortly after, includes motifs similar to those on the Wells throne such as the nodding ogees. It is, however, an altogether more massive and bold construction, encrusted with detailed decoration to an extent that makes the Wells throne look positively bare by comparison (Fig. 4.11).[22] Similar motifs also appear in the slightly earlier tomb of Edward II at Gloucester completed in the early 1330s – for example, the three-tiered, openwork structure – but here again the differences are marked. The subtle recession of gables with their minute crockets in the upper tier of the royal tomb, and the cusping within the pinnacles, both exhibit a concern with detail and variety not on obvious display at Wells (see Fig. 2.3.13). Nor is the oak throne at Exeter a clear source for the formal elements of the design, even allowing for the difference in materials. The Wells throne, constructed just over 20 years after that at Exeter, is half the height and has much less decoration (compare Fig. 4.4 and Fig. 2.1.1, and Tip-in 2.1.1 [Exeter North elevation] and Tip-in 4.1 [Wells]). The Exeter throne's baldacchino-like canopy, its diagonal buttresses, and its heavily-cocketted gables, find few parallels at Wells. The tiers and spire above Exeter's canopy give that throne its immense verticality. By contrast at Wells the array of niches above the canopy is squat, and the spires and pinnacles (even before Salvin's alterations) appear almost stunted.

Rather than search outside for precedents for the design of the Wells throne, the majority of the formal devices can be seen somewhat closer to hand, in the contemporary work on the refurbishment of the choir and presbytery. This significant integration with the throne's surroundings can best be seen in the triforium of the choir – the three bays to the west of the throne (see Fig. 4.2). Here the triforium utilises many of the motifs found on the throne including the same use of crenellation on the cornice; nodding and flat ogees for the main niches topped with bulky finials and open cusping; and the same use of spur leaf decoration. Furthermore, one of the distinctive features of the throne, its canted niches at the second tier, is mirrored in the triforium. The westernmost bay of the triforium next to the

crossing comprises a combination of niches, one straight-gabled and the others ogee-arched. The decorative scheme becomes richer as it progresses eastwards, culminating in the third bay beneath which is the bishop's throne. Here the triforium is canted out from the piers delineating the bay, and the three central niches are surmounted by nodding, rather than plain, ogee arches (Fig. 4.12). The formal motifs of the throne thus reflect the overall decorative intent of the whole of the refurbished choir, echoing its gradual increase in splendour as it proceeds to the high altar whilst also marking the juncture between the new presbytery and remodelled choir. This sense of integration with the choir might also have been indicated in the overall colour scheme of greens and yellows, exemplified now only by the magnificent east window (Fig. 4.3).

Although no masons' marks are visible on the throne there can be little doubt, given the evident commonality between the features of the refurbished choir and the throne, that the latter was constructed as part of the refurbishment undertaken in the late 1330s. Its overall design can therefore be attributed to William Joy who had been appointed by Bishop Ralph of Shrewsbury shortly after he succeeded to the see in 1329.[23] In formal terms the immediate inspiration for the throne can be found locally. In terms of its rationale and meaning, the net may need to be cast more widely as will be examined below.

Fig. 4.12 Wells Cathedral. Choir triforium, third bay from the west, showing canting and use of nodding ogees. A. Budge.

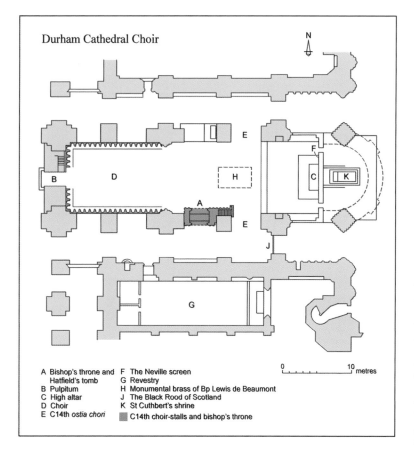

Durham Cathedral Choir

A Bishop's throne and   F The Neville screen
    Hatfield's tomb   G Revestry
B Pulpitum   H Monumental brass of Bp Lewis de Beaumont
C High altar   J The Black Rood of Scotland
D Choir   K St Cuthbert's shrine
E C14th *ostia chori*   ■ C14th choir-stalls and bishop's throne

Fig. 4.13 (above) Durham Cathedral. 14th-century choir ground plan. After W. St John Hope in Fowler 1903. J. Read.

Fig. 4.14 Durham Cathedral. Bishop's tomb and throne from the choir. After Billings (1843, pl. lvi).

The Durham throne

Despite formal differences, the bishop's throne at Wells resides clearly within the group of 14th-century thrones from the south and west of the country that includes Exeter, St Davids and Hereford. The episcopal seat at Durham, erected after 1362 and before 1381 during the episcopate of Thomas Hatfield, however, is often treated as something of an outlier, and not just a geographical one.[24] It is a unique edifice that combines both a throne and the Hatfield tomb; one with few, if any, direct precedents or antecedents (Fig. 4.1). It stands prominently on the south side of the choir, between, to the west, the choir-stalls of the convent and, to the east, the high altar behind which was the shrine of St Cuthbert (Fig. 4.13). The throne merits only an oblique reference in the *Rites of Durham* in a comment whose prime subject is the tomb of Bishop Hatfield underneath, which is described as "betwixt 2 pillars under the bpps seate wch hee did make before hee died".[25] The chronicler of the late medieval bishops of Durham described the throne and tomb as "*sumptuosissime construxit*", a view in accord with the "amazing" and "rather bizarre" descriptions of more recent commentators.[26]

Despite its height, at nearly 40 ft (12.2 m) reaching to the apex of the arcade arches, the throne was probably only visible from the choir or the south choir aisle. It is, effectively, recessed between the immense Romanesque piers to either side. This, together with the pulpitum and other screens extending across the choir aisles and transepts at the eastern and western crossing arches, would have prevented those in the nave from readily seeing the throne.[27] Further, the restrictions at Durham that prevented the laity from entering the eastern end of the cathedral on all but the four feast days of St Cuthbert, when access was granted to the shrine, mean that the primary audience for the throne and tomb was almost certainly the convent within the choir.[28]

Hatfield's monument was saved from the destructive attentions of James Wyatt in the late 18th century. He had wanted to take down both it and the nearby Neville screen and merge them into a single edifice.[29] But an assessment of the extent of any less drastic alterations to the monument is made difficult by the current, vibrant polychromy, covering all surfaces of the

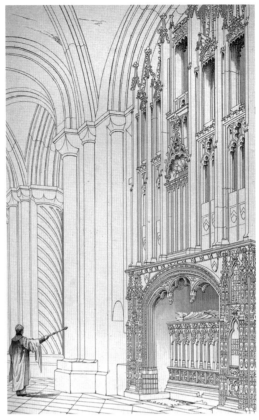

Fig. 4.15 (far left) Durham Cathedral. Bishop's tomb and throne. Photograph with a restored termination to the eastern end. First quarter of the 20th century. Raphael Tuck & Sons.

Fig. 4.16 (left) Durham Cathedral. Bishop's tomb and throne from the south choir aisle. After Billings (1843, pl. lviii).

throne and tomb with the exception of the bishop's effigy.[30] There was originally some form of vertical termination at the eastern end of the steps from the choir. This was, at some stage, sheared off but a facsimile was erected, probably in the late 19th century, before it too was removed to allow a continuation of the balustrade (Figs 4.1; 4.14 and 4.15).[31] The lower steps were altered as part of these changes, but the upper ones appear medieval. Elsewhere, the upside-down angels on the open cusping of the tomb's choir façade are certainly recent, though those on the south choir aisle façade were recorded by Billings in 1843 (Figs 4.14 and 4.16).[32] Otherwise there is no extant evidence that would suggest substantive changes since the 14th century, and comparison with Billings' drawings rules out any major alterations in the last 170 years. Specifically, there is no obvious evidence to support Fowler's suggestion that the tomb may once have projected further to the south and has since been shifted back between the piers of the choir.[33]

Discussion of the throne cannot proceed without first considering the tomb of Bishop Hatfield which both forms its base and, it must be confessed, dominates the structure

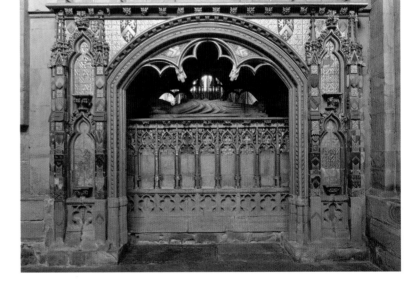

when viewed from either the choir or the south choir aisle. The tomb comprises three main parts: the tomb chest with the effigy of the bishop; its immediate canopy with wall paintings; and the outer façades to both choir and south choir aisle. These façades present a collection of disparate motifs (Fig. 4.17). They include broad segmental open-cusped

Fig. 4.17 Durham Cathedral. Bishop Hatfield's tomb from the south choir aisle. By kind permission of the Dean and Chapter. A. Budge.

Fig. 4.18 (right) Durham Cathedral. Bishop Hatfield's tomb. Detail of "pinched" trefoils, profuse crocketting, foliate decoration and double-cusping on the north face of the tomb chest. By kind permission of the Dean and Chapter. A. Budge.

Fig. 4.20 (far right) Durham Cathedral. Drawing, from the 1780s by John Carter, of the wall painting at the east end of Bishop Hatfield's tomb. BL Ms Add. 29933. By permission of the British Library.

Fig. 4.21 (below) Durham Cathedral. Bishop Hatfield's tomb, east end. Remains of the wall painting. By kind permission of the Dean and Chapter. A. Budge.

Fig. 4.19 Durham Cathedral. Vault of Bishop Hatfield's tomb. By kind permission of the Dean and Chapter. A. Budge.

arches, an almost obsessive use of heraldry, quatrefoils set in squares at the base of the monument, and an array of distinctively "pinched" trefoil ogees. These are combined with motifs associated more, perhaps, with an earlier generation of monuments such as the extensive impressionistic diaper decoration and the profusion of foliate crocketting. The tomb chest recapitulates many of these same motifs, but in an even higher key. The chest's trefoil ogee panels, for example, incorporate cinquefoil double-cusping and foliate decoration (Fig. 4.18). Above the chest is a lierne vault with heavy ribs and large foliate

bosses (Fig. 4.19). Drawings made in the 1780s by John Carter of the wall paintings decorating this space show, at the foot of the effigy, a figure of Christ in a "red garment" displaying his wounds (Fig. 4.20). To the left is an angel, one originally of a pair on either side, holding a sheet bearing, beneath the figure of Christ, a representation of the soul of Bishop Hatfield.[34] Only part of the angel and an outline of the impression of Hatfield's soul are still visible (Fig. 4.21).

The pinched trefoiled ogees that are such a distinctive part of the tomb can be found briefly in three-dimensional form at York in the reredos of the Lady Chapel.[35] But the motif is also found at Beverley Minster in the sedilia canopies dating from the 1330s or 1340s and, indeed, the furnishings of the east end of

Beverley provide a possible inspiration for the Hatfield tomb in other ways.[36] The prominent ribs and deeply undercut, large-scale bosses of the tomb have parallels with those in the eastern interior of the reredos at Beverley, as has already been noted by Wilson (Fig. 4.22).[37] The reredos also contains significant amounts of diaper-work, another significant element of Hatfield's tomb, to both its western and eastern façades, and shares with the tomb the use of quatrefoils in squares to ground the monument.[38] The bands of studded fleurons of the tomb can be found on the soffits of the gables of the Minster sedilia. Further, the apices of the Percy tomb to the north of the reredos comprise representations of, to the north, Christ showing his wounds and, to the south, Christ receiving the soul of the departed (Figs 4.23a–b). These scenes are conflated in the wall painting of the Durham tomb. The connections between the micro-architecture at the east end of Beverley in the second quarter of the 14th century and the primary features of Hatfield's tomb are therefore strong, but they are connections of ideas not of execution. The ribs and bosses at Durham are distinctly heavy-handed in comparison with those at Beverley (Figs 4.19 and 4.22) and the nature of the diaper-work is very different (Figs 4.24 and 4.25). The Hatfield memorial achieves its diaper effect by incising squares of rippled gesso and then creating small scallops around the periphery to generate the impression of a leaf. When well executed and gilded, as for example on the eastern panels of the southern face of the tomb chest, this proves to be an effective technique. In less competent hands it becomes little more than a space-filling exercise, such as on the choir façade. At Beverley the diaper decoration is carried out in more traditional carved stonework, though this is by no means regularly rendered.[39]

The top of the Hatfield tomb provides an extensive platform measuring *c.* 11 × 7 ft (3.35 × 2.13 m) for the bishop's throne, access to which is provided by steep steps from the east of the choir side of the tomb, now enclosed by a 17th-century balustrade (Fig. 4.1). The throne is, essentially, a canopied screen of three vertical divisions. The primary feature of its central element, above the bishop's seat, is a finely-decorated, tall, lierne-vaulted triple canopy with straight-sided crocketted gables (Fig. 4.26). The decoration, now rather

Fig. 4.22 Beverley Minster. Vault of the rear of the high altar reredos. A. Budge.

encrusted with paint, includes downward-pointing grotesques, a splendid animal head emerging from foliage in the central gable and delicate octagonal relief masks at the pendant stops (Fig. 4.27). Trefoiled niches above this canopy act as the base for the upper register that repeats the triple canopy on a smaller scale with supports from flying buttresses. To either side, the lower parts comprise blind trefoiled panels and cusped hexagonal reticulated tracery whilst the upper registers contain an array of open, canopied niches with tall spires reaching almost to the head of the surrounding Romanesque arch. This delicate and detailed arrangement of niches and canopies contrasts stridently

Fig. 4.23 Beverley Minster. Detail of the Percy tomb: a. figure sculpture at the north and b. south apices of the tomb. A. Budge.

Fig. 4.24 (right)
Durham Cathedral.
Diaper work on Bishop
Hatfield's tomb. By kind
permission of the Dean
and Chapter. A. Budge.

Fig. 4.25 (far right)
Beverley Minster. Diaper
work on the east face of
the reredos. A. Budge.

Fig. 4.26 Durham
Cathedral. Main canopy
of the bishop's throne.
By kind permission of
the Dean and Chapter.
A. Budge.

with the plain, unmoulded and distinctly cumbersome vertical buttress supports to which the canopies are attached. The whole is keyed into the Romanesque piers at three separate points at either side. The rear of this screen, facing the south choir aisle, is much simpler: the heavy structure outlined by the buttresses remains, but the three-dimensional canopies are replaced by flat, curved gables and the square-headed, trefoiled panels are given greater prominence (Fig. 4.28). For the throne's screen there are, as Wilson has identified, very clear connections to the architectural details of the east front at York Minster.[40] The similarities between the distinctive square-headed trefoiled panelling and triple canopies of the throne and the York east end are such that the involvement of the same mason(s), or, at the very least, close acquaintance with the York work, can be confidently proposed (Fig. 4.29).[41]

Despite the close physical relationship between throne and tomb, the one placed on top of the other, the two have remarkably few motifs in common. Both do share the use of narrow bands of fleuron decoration, the extensive display of Hatfield's coat of arms, rows of quatrefoils in squares and the inverted dagger motif. But the key visual elements of the tomb, its "pinched" trefoils, heavily encrusted crocketting, diapering and segmental arch, find no counterparts in the throne. Further, the tall spires, flying buttresses and reticulated tracery of the throne screen are not seen on the tomb below. The openwork of the throne is restricted on the tomb to the cusping of the segmental arch. The construction shows none of the cohesion between its upper and lower parts that can be found, for example, in the Stratford tomb at Canterbury Cathedral (see Fig. 2.2.16).[42] Some of the differences can, of course, be attributable to the different nature of the structures – a canopied screen as opposed to a more substantial tomb. But the marked dissimilarities prompt the question as to whether the tomb and throne were the work of a single designer capable of working in two distinct modes, a not unusual skill for the best of 14th-century master-masons, or whether the Hatfield monument was actually

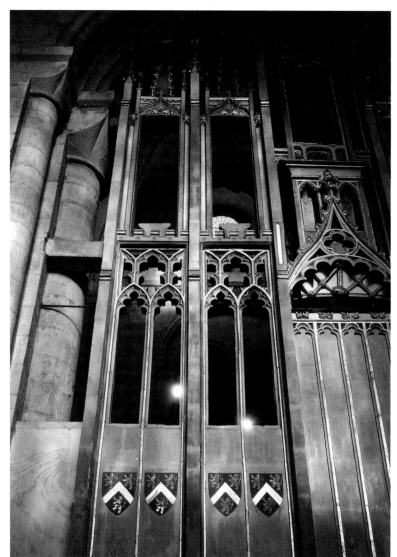

Fig. 4.27 Durham Cathedral. Main canopy of the throne screen. Detail. By kind permission of the Dean and Chapter. A. Budge.

the work of two designers, one for the tomb and one for the throne.[43] Before addressing questions of attribution and dating, two further monuments at Durham need to be briefly examined: the tomb of John, Lord Neville and the Neville screen.

The large freestanding tomb of Lord Neville and his first wife Maud was commissioned in the 1370s (Fig. 4.30).[44] The primary features of its crenellated stone tomb chest are the fine weeper figures, placed under elaborate and distinctive canopies which evoke miniature gatehouses and are separated by heraldic shields carved as if hooked on to the back panel of the niche (Fig. 4.31). The tomb has much in common with the Hatfield throne screen, such as the sloping vaults of the weeper canopies and the squared trefoiled heads to the heraldic

Fig. 4.28 Durham Cathedral. Upper section of the throne screen from the south choir aisle. By kind permission of the Dean and Chapter. A. Budge.

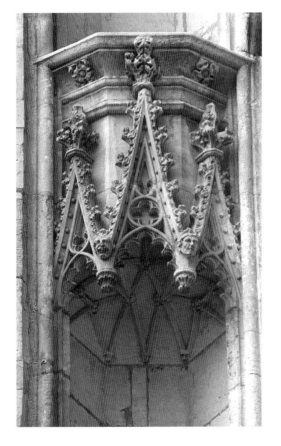

niches, but it is decidedly different, in terms of overall design and detail, from the profusely-diapered, ogee-arched Hatfield tomb.[45]

The Neville screen is arguably the finest extant example of later-14th-century openwork design. It is positioned immediately behind the high altar, was funded by John Neville and Prior John Fossour between 1372 and 1376, carved in London, and then brought to Durham and erected probably in 1380 (Fig. 4.37).[46] There are some similarities between the screen and Hatfield's throne (such as the use of panelled pedestals behind the triple canopies), but the overriding impression is of the gulf in understanding of the possibilities and necessities of openwork design.[47] The throne screen's crude framework and the multiple points at which it is keyed into the adjacent piers (Fig. 4.28) suggest that its designer lacked the experience or confidence to fashion a self-supporting openwork structure in the manner of the Neville screen.

The evidence that might assist in attribution and dating of the monument is both formal and documentary. The observations above have highlighted the distinct differences between the designs of the throne's screen and of the tomb beneath; the former showing close similarities to the canopies on the east end of York, consistently dated to the mid-1360s, whilst the latter exhibits connections to work at Beverley in the second quarter of the 14th century.[48] The formal correspondences between the throne screen and the tomb of John Neville, constructed in the 1370s, suggest that the screen might be similarly dated. The lack of cohesion within the throne screen itself, with the quality of the design and detailing of the canopies standing in marked contrast to the plain, indeed crude, buttresses that provide its framework and support (Figs 4.26 and 4.28), might imply that the York mason was responsible only for the execution of the canopies and other details and did not have responsibility for the screen's overall design. Indeed, the desire for an openwork design for the throne screen, despite the clear lack of requisite experience, might indicate, as Arnold Klukas has proposed, a determination to develop a particular aesthetic within the choir whereby the Romanesque frame was supplemented by furnishings of 14th-century openwork.[49] It might also suggest that the local production of the throne screen was done in the knowledge of the openwork design of the Neville screen being produced in London in the 1370s. These formal considerations encourage a dating for the throne screen in the early 1370s and the possibility that it stood on a tomb completed somewhat earlier.

The documentary evidence places the construction of the monument between 1362, when Bishop Hatfield was granted permission for his tomb by the convent at Durham, and

Fig. 4.31 Durham Cathedral. Detail of the tomb chest of John Neville. By kind permission of the Dean and Chapter. A. Budge.

to the single designer working in multiple modes. There can be little doubt that the canopies and detailing of the throne screen were undertaken by a mason who had worked on the York east end. It is very possible that this mason was subsequently responsible for the tomb of John Neville. Given their disparate designs and detailing, the Hatfield tomb was most likely the work of a different mason or supervising architect, one who drew his inspiration, but probably not his workforce, from the east end of Beverley. That mason could well have been John Lewyn, completing or at least starting the tomb in the mid- to late-1360s, before his incarceration at the hands of the bishop. This leaves outstanding the problem of the overall design and frame for the throne screen. One possibility is that the tomb's architect, proposed here as John Lewyn, designed the framework for the screen but that the canopies and detailing, possibly as a result of the dispute between Hatfield and his master-mason, were subsequently contracted to a mason who had recently worked on the York east end. Another is that the York mason, unused to a requirement for the canopies to be part of an open design rather than backed by a solid wall, made the framework as secure and as robust as possible. The available evidence does not enable a definitive conclusion. However, the disparities between the detailed carving of the canopies and the crudity of the framework would perhaps point to Lewyn having taken responsibility for the handling of the support system.

Contexts

The formal analysis of the throne at Wells concluded that there was little direct comparability in the design of the throne with its immediate and proximate predecessor at Exeter, even allowing for the different construction material. Compared to its West-Country cousin the Wells throne was a product of the refurbishment of the choir undertaken by William Joy, rather than a singular exercise in micro-architectural grandeur. But if the formal correspondences are not strong, the respective reasoning for the erection of large impressive bishops' thrones on the south side of the choir at both Exeter and Wells exhibit marked similarities. This section first examines the arguments, proposed by Veronica

1381, by which date the tomb was said to have been completed in time for Hatfield's funeral.[50] During the majority of this period John Lewyn was the prominent master-mason at Durham and was referred to as "the Bishop's Mason".[51] However, a petition to the king by Lewyn dated 1372 suggests that, for a period in the late 1360s and early 1370s, relations between master-mason and bishop were decidedly strained, to put it mildly.[52] Following a theft, in 1368–9, of goods valued at 2000 marks from the palatine exchequer located in Durham castle on which building work was being undertaken, Hatfield imprisoned the chief suspect, the mason Richard Goldesburgh, together with his master, John Lewyn. In 1372 the master-mason was tried for harbouring Goldesburgh, and subsequently petitioned the king, referring to the evil procurement of the bishop in bringing him to trial and claiming that Hatfield was withholding payments due to Lewyn for previous work.[53] Could this breakdown of relations at a crucial time in the construction of Hatfield's grand monument account for the apparent change in styles between its tomb and throne screen?

These observations do not resolve into a neat solution, but they do suggest alternatives

Fig. 4.32 Wells Cathedral. South transept, showing the tomb of Bishop William of March in the centre. A. Budge.

Sekules, regarding the veneration of bishops at Exeter and finds close correlation with the actions taken at Wells.[54] It then explores the notion of the throne as reliquary and the potential influence of competition on the requirement for a noteworthy seat for a bishop. The "political" motivations found at Wells are then considered in the role that the throne might have played at Durham. Finally, this section examines the apparent necessity of a mutually respectful relationship between bishop and convent or chapter before construction of these imposing thrones could be contemplated.

Veronica Sekules' argument, that the commissioning and nature of the throne at Exeter owes much to the history there of the chapter venerating their bishop, has been set out in Chapter 2.1 but it is worth recapitulating the main points. This history of veneration, Sekules maintained, was exhibited through the moving of the graves of two Norman bishops when the pulpitum was constructed in the 1320s, in the desire of Bishop Bronscombe (bp 1258–1280) to use the Lady Chapel to house the tombs of past bishops, and in the seals of Bishop Quinil (bp 1280–1291) and of the chapter, which imply a close relation between the Exeter bishops and St Peter through their similar poses and setting (see Fig. 2.1.25).[55] As further evidence, the placing of Bishop Stapeldon's tomb to the north of the altar followed a position associated with the venerated bishops at St Paul's, Lincoln and Salisbury.[56] Moreover, the Exeter Ordinals

instructed that the bishop be censed ahead of the choir altars and officiating priests rather than after them, the latter being the more normal order.[57]

This veneration of the bishop finds distinct parallels at Wells. The tombs of seven former bishops were moved from the Saxon cathedral and placed around the choir of the new church, probably in the 1190s, with new effigies being carved for them.[58] In 1324, stimulated by the successful outcome of the campaign by the chapter at Hereford for the canonisation of their former bishop, Thomas Cantilupe, the dean and chapter at Wells presented a petition to the Pope for a similar honour to be bestowed upon one of their former bishops, William of March who had died in 1302.[59] The following year the Archbishop of Canterbury and eight further bishops wrote to the Pope in support of the petition that was again promoted by Bishop Drokensford of Wells in 1329. Although William of March seems to have been an unlikely candidate, the process indicates a desire by the dean and chapter to raise the profile of a holder of their particular episcopal office. Abandonment of the claim for canonisation, upon the death of Bishop Drokensford in May 1329, may have ushered in more pragmatic approaches to venerating their bishop. The sculpturally rich, tri-partite canopy subsequently placed above William of March's tomb in the south transept was one response (Fig. 4.32). The bishop's throne, commissioned in the following decade for Drokensford's successor, Ralph of Shrewsbury, might well have been another.

Veneration of the bishop could also have been indicated through some of the formal aspects of the throne noted above, in particular the canting of its outer parts which gives prominence to that which is in the centre. Canting was used as a decorative device on the triforium of the choir as part of a repertoire of motifs to signal the importance of moving towards the high altar. It had also been seen before as part of church micro-architecture in Prior Eastry's seat in the chapter house at Canterbury Cathedral erected shortly after 1300 (Fig. 1.31).[60] The division of its back wall into three partitions is similar to that at Wells (and Hereford and St Davids) and its early use of gables decorated with crockets and finials to emphasise these divisions is echoed in all three thrones.[61] The use of such a formal device at Canterbury perhaps helped convey the authority of the prior in his chapter house; at Wells it would have been the authority of the bishop in his cathedral.

The enthusiasm to venerate their bishop is but one of a number of connections between Exeter and Wells that might help explain why both institutions constructed a distinctive form of bishop's throne in the early 14th century. These other connections are explored below and include their common relationship with relics and reliquaries, their concerns over the validity of their respective sees, and their sense, shared perhaps also with Hereford and St Davids, of not being in the forefront of the group of English secular cathedrals.

The connections between relics and bishops' thrones go well beyond the impact of the directive of the Fourth Lateran Council of 1215 that required the display of relics and which may well have resulted in the need for a different location for the bishop's throne.[62] On a purely formal basis, there is a striking similarity between the design of reliquaries beginning to emerge in the first half of the 14th century, with their particular combination of tiered designs, open compartments and profuse decoration, and the form of the bishops' thrones, particularly those of wood. The triple compartments of the Reliquary of Charlemagne from the mid-14th century and the Three Spires Reliquary, both from Aachen, find close echoes in the thrones at Hereford and St Davids. Similarly, the tall, tiered and acutely gabled Reliquary of S. Savino at Orvieto bears a close resemblance, if not in scale, with the contemporaneous Exeter throne (Fig. 4.33). The geographical disposition of these examples of micro-architecture makes direct influence unlikely, but the idea of encasing a venerated object in such structures is one that was clearly in vogue at the time of the thrones' construction.

Beyond these formal associations, important thrones had a traditional association with relics. The imperial throne at Aachen includes a compartment for relics behind and beneath the seat of the emperor. The bishop's throne at Norwich is positioned above a niche which opens out onto the ambulatory and which would have been easily accessed during relevant processions.[63] The decoration of this niche signifies a place of importance, one most likely, given its position on processional routes,

Fig. 4.33 Reliquary of S. Savino, Orvieto. Alinari Archives.

to have contained relics of some form. These relics are not connected to the high altar but by a flue rising from the niche, to the bishop's throne directly above. As mentioned in Chapter 1, Eric Fernie uses this evidence to suggest that the throne, in these circumstances, may itself have been considered as a relic.[64]

An association between the bishop's throne and relics seems particularly prevalent where the see had a sparse collection on which to call, and especially where none of those relics was of sufficient importance to warrant the cathedral becoming a major pilgrimage destination. Norwich fell into this category and the attempts by the monks to generate enthusiasm for a number of local saints were only partially successful.[65] Exeter had some relics donated by King Athelstan but none of great importance whilst the relics at Wells could

Fig. 4.34 Relic chests on an altar beam at St Augustine's Canterbury. Trinity Hall MS 1, fol 77r. After Dugdale 1846, 120.

be held aloft by only two vicars choral during the Palm Sunday procession.[66]

Mention of the relics (or lack of them) at Wells might also provide another connection, one that must remain speculative but for which there are tantalising scraps of documentary support. On each side of the cathedral's east end, the westernmost of the three blue lias limestone shafts which mark the division between the refurbished choir and the new presbytery show, just beneath the capitals, evidence of a break, now filled. It is feasible that these visible infills might be the last remaining signs of a beam stretching across the choir. The suggestion that this beam might have been associated with such relics as the cathedral possessed comes from two sources.[67] The first is from the communar's accounts. For every account that has survived, from possibly 1292 to 1537, there is a record of an annual payment of either 6d or 8d for the "bringing down of the relics" "*reliquius deferend*".[68] In the Wells Consuetudinary there is also a reference, in a document itemising the Treasurer's responsibilities, to the number of candles to be lit "on the beam" on various feast days, including the Feast of the Relics.[69] Now of course this could refer to the Rood rather than a beam between the choir and the presbytery, though the Rood is separately specified later in the same document. It is also possible that relics (of William of March or all of the cathedral's repository) were stored in a small room at window level in the south transept, to the side of William of March's tomb and to which permanent access was only provided in the 16th century (Fig. 4.33), and this could be the place from which the relics were "brought down".[70] However, the communar's accounts record the regular payments from a time before the attempted canonisation of former Bishop William and the considerable annual payment of 6d might be considered more appropriate for the taxing, not to say dangerous, task of bringing relics down from a beam some 27 ft (8.3 m) above the choir. The display of relics on a beam in the choir would also be more in tune with the requirements of the Fourth Lateran Council than their storage in the south transept, and would align with Gervase's account of relics being rescued from "the high beam" at Canterbury during the fire of 1174.[71] Gervase later adds further details, explaining that the relic chests were placed on a beam which stretched across the sanctuary between two columns.[72] This positioning of relics on a beam in or around the presbytery was not a singular occurrence. An illustration of the altar screen at St Augustine's, Canterbury, dating from no later than the early 15th century, shows relic chests on a beam above the altar (Fig. 4.34), and at Winchester the bones of Anglo-Saxon kings and bishops were placed in a raised position around the feretory.[73] Any association

Fig. 4.35 Wells Cathedral. Bishop's throne. Detail of break in the blue lias shafts behind the apex. A. Budge.

between the disparate pieces of evidence at Wells must remain conjectural, though the fact that the putative beam's southern end would have been directly over, almost to the point of resting upon, the apex of the bishop's throne merely adds to the temptation to suggest a direct link between the relics and the throne at Wells (Fig. 4.35).

The next connection between Exeter and Wells to be examined here is more political. Exeter, having been established from the two dioceses of Crediton and Cornwall only in the mid-11th century, had reason to assert the cathedral as the rightful location for the see.[74] Both the Saxon Minster and the Romanesque cathedral at Exeter would probably have had the advantage in this respect of an apse within which the bishop's throne could have been prominently displayed, much as at Norwich or the continental examples at Lyon and S. Clemente quoted above.[75] The issue for the chapter at Wells was more complex and contentious, leading it to be fighting on two fronts to establish their cathedral as the rightful seat of the bishop. In the first place Wells had to contend with its immediate neighbour, the rich and powerful Benedictine abbey at Glastonbury. Peter Draper has suggested that the construction of the new cathedral at Wells from about 1180 was a direct response to the building of the Lady Chapel at Glastonbury, and that the plainer elevations at Wells were a deliberate attempt to differentiate the building from its decorative, monastic counterpart.[76] But Wells of course was engaged in a more pressing confrontation, that with the abbey at Bath which, from the late 11th century, had laid claim to be the seat of the bishop.[77] Wells had achieved cathedral status in 909 when the large diocese of Sherborne had been divided into those of Sarum and Wells, but in 1088 Bishop John of Tours moved the see to Bath and proceeded to build a large cathedral priory church there worthy of the see.[78] Little remains of Bishop John's church but construction was underway by 1106, the lower vaults completed by 1122, and the whole finished under Bishop Robert of Lewes (bp 1136–1166). Built on a cathedral scale at over 330 ft (*c.* 100 m) long, the plan resembled those of churches familiar to Bishop John in the Loire Valley, with an apsidal east end with radiating chapels. The likelihood is, therefore, that the bishop's throne whilst at Bath was prominently positioned in the traditional position at the centre of the apse on a raised area over the crypt which probably housed the priory church's known relics.[79] It is perhaps pertinent that, whilst the building at Bath was being finished, Bishop Robert made major changes at Wells which included squaring off the Saxon apse.[80] It is conceivable that this was perceived by the chapter at Wells as a further sign of the emasculation of their church, though it was a form of termination that was to be repeated in the new cathedral built to the north of the Saxon building at the end of the century.

At Norwich the throne, possibly erected for the consecration of Bishop Eborard in 1122, asserted the unity of the see formed from the diocese of North Elmham and Thetford.[81] At Exeter the grandeur of Stapeldon's new throne achieved a similar purpose, harking back to the see's antecedents at Crediton and Cornwall. At Wells the new bishop's throne, placed in the centre of the sumptuous and extended choir, likewise proclaimed the seat of the bishop at Wells, so jealously guarded since its transfer back from Bath in 1245.

At both Exeter and Wells the new bishops' thrones can be seen as emphatic responses to the loss of earlier arrangements of the choir – arrangements in which the architecture of the cathedral naturally reinforced the role of the bishop. Without the earlier theatrical setting provided by a raised platform within an apsidal arcade, each cathedral now provided a magnificent surrounding for their bishop by developing an individual piece of freestanding micro-architecture as a reminder of the past prominence of the throne.

But why, if the 14th-century bishops' thrones were a response, at least in the secular cathedrals, to the changing east ends of gothic church design, do we not have even grander episcopal monuments in the richer cathedrals at Lincoln, York, Salisbury and St Paul's in London?[82] Why might the bishops' thrones of the secular cathedrals in the 14th century be confined to the generally less wealthy sees of Exeter, Wells, St Davids and Hereford? Salisbury, after all, had also been formed out of an earlier divided see and had replaced the apsidal east end of the 11th-century church at Old Sarum with a squared termination, first at Old Sarum in the 12th century and then at Salisbury in the 13th.[83] A possible connection between the chapters commissioning the 14th-century thrones, and a fault-line with their wealthier counterparts, might be found in the rules of canonical life introduced by their bishops at the close of the 11th century. Bishop Leofric (bp 1046–1072), educated in Lotharingia, introduced his own version of the Rule of St Chrodegang at Exeter.[84] Bishop Giso did likewise at Wells and his friend Bishop Walter, also a Lotharingian, probably did so at Hereford.[85] This is not to suggest that the Rule of Chrodegang had a direct bearing on the 14th-century thrones: the rule gave only limited precedence to the bishop compared to other rites.[86] It was discontinued at Wells soon after its introduction, and elsewhere in the 12th century. Rather, it is the fact that the introduction of the rule set these cathedrals apart from the group of Salisbury, Lincoln and York which, in 1090–1, established their own constitutions.[87] This sense of separateness carried over into the continued distinctive liturgies at Exeter and Hereford and might have been a contributing factor in the desire of the cathedrals within this group to honour their bishop with an imposing throne, whereas large

a

b

Fig. 4.36 Chancery seals of the bishops of Durham. Bishop Hatfield: a. obverse; b. reverse; c. Bishop Fordham, reverse. Society of Antiquaries of London. A. Budge and C. Tracy.

c

sees, such as Lincoln, were seemingly satisfied with a much smaller chair.[88]

Thus there are a series of connections between the two West-Country cathedrals that could have contributed to a desire at Wells in the late 1330s to emulate the bishop's throne recently erected at Exeter: their shared veneration for their bishops; the sense that the throne could, in some way, bolster their comparative lack of major relics; the common history of needing to assert the cathedral as the rightful seat of the bishop; and the shared liturgical heritage of some of the more peripheral of the secular cathedrals.[89] Of course Durham, as a monastic institution, was never part of this last debate on the rules of canonical life, nor was it concerned that its relics were insufficiently prestigious. But the convent at Durham did share with both Wells and Exeter the desire to promote the special worth of their bishop, and in Bishop Thomas Hatfield, former royal servant and soldier, they had a man ready and able to assist.[90] The throne in the cathedral can be seen not only as an expression of the particular powers accorded to the bishop but also as a clear declaration of status.

The bishop of Durham was distinguished from the great majority of his episcopal colleagues by the palatinate status of his role: the bishop was not simply the leader of the see but also the centre of government in the region, exercising special judicial powers and minting currency whilst also controlling markets, fairs and hunting rights.[91] That Hatfield was keen to exploit the symbolism of "the throne" can be seen in his redevelopment of the great hall

of Durham castle undertaken shortly after he was raised to the see in 1345.[92] The extremely long hall included not one but two thrones, one at either end, representing his episcopal and his secular roles. This association between throne and power is further emphasised by Hatfield's introduction of a seal used to ratify documents associated with his palatinate role, and therefore in addition to his episcopal "dignity" and "*ad causas*" seals. The design of this new "chancery" seal was not constrained by precedents and Hatfield decided to model it on royal examples. It was circular with its reverse depicting the bishop as a knight on horseback and its obverse showing him seated on a throne (Figs 4.36a–b). Whilst the throne of the seal has little in common with the throne eventually constructed in the cathedral, beyond it being a gabled canopy, the subsequent chancery seals of Hatfield's successors, made after the construction of the throne, do show a marked resemblance.[93] The seals of Bishops Fordham, Skirlaw, Langley and Neville (covering the period 1382–1457) each depict a throne with a triple-gabled canopy surrounded by a structure of openwork niches with saints on pedestals (e.g. Fig. 4.36c). The seemingly free interchange in these seals, whether dignity, *ad causas* or chancery, between the bishop or saints positioned under the canopies of an openwork screen, suggests a desire to blur the distinctions between the two and to promote veneration of whomsoever appears in such a position.

The nature and position of the throne in the cathedral also says much about the relationship between Hatfield and the convent and his predecessors, and his eagerness to assert himself. Bishops of Durham had only been granted permission to be buried within the cathedral since the episcopate of Anthony Bek (bp 1284–1311). But by the time of Thomas Hatfield's election, the prime burial position in front of the high altar was already occupied by the huge brass, measuring nearly 16 × 10 ft (4.9 × 3.0 m), commemorating Bishop Lewis de Beaumont (bp 1318–1333).[94] Such an early use of a brass memorial, and on such a scale, must have been particularly striking and noteworthy. This was certainly the case in the 16th century when the writer of the *Rites of Durham* was effusive in his description of the slab, giving more space to this than to any other episcopal memorial in the cathedral; and still so four centuries later when Fowler declared that "it must have been one of the very finest brasses in the kingdom, or indeed in Europe".[95] Moreover, the iconography chosen by Bishop Lewis, surrounding his own image with depictions of the apostles, was to prove popular with other 14th-century leaders of the church in Durham. Both Bishop Richard de Bury (d. 1345) and Prior John Fossour (d. 1374) were commemorated in the cathedral with their brass images bordered by the Twelve Apostles.[96] With the prime position in the centre of the sanctuary already occupied, the traditionally more prestigious burial position would have been to the north of the high altar.[97] However, at Durham it appears that the prior and convent regarded the north side as their domain whilst the south was the preserve of the bishop, a convention reinforced by the erection of the "Black Rood" of Scotland in the eastern end of the south choir aisle

following its capture at the Battle of Durham in 1346, and the use made by the Bishops of Durham of the vestry situated to the south of the south choir aisle.[98]

Given these circumstances, the co-location by Hatfield of both his tomb and throne on the south side of the choir shows considerable thought. Erecting his tomb underneath a broad, open arch gave it visibility from both the choir and the south choir aisle. Not only did this make a bold statement for pilgrims on the days when they were able to access the shrine of St Cuthbert but also to the convent at Durham due to the specific rituals of the mass. Those saying the mass processed, at its start, from the vestry on the south side of the choir and halted (in the south choir aisle) before entering through the south door to the high altar at the *Gloria Patri*.[99] The procession was thus held precisely beside the south façade of Bishop Hatfield's tomb whilst waiting to conduct the mass. Placing his tomb in this position, together with its associated altar against the pier immediately to the west of the tomb, manned by a single priest, reinforced the bishop's domain to the south of the choir.[100] But more than this, by constructing his throne on top of his own tomb, Hatfield was also able to look down on his predecessor's spectacular brass from, literally and metaphorically, a superior position (Fig. 4.37).

These factors suggest appreciable insight by Hatfield into the impact of the nature and positioning of his double monument. Its commissioning cemented the south choir aisle as the bishop's territory, its position meant that the monastic and lay communities at Durham were constantly reminded of its presence, and the innovative placing of his episcopal seat above the tomb enabled Hatfield to utilise once again the powerful symbolism of the throne whilst seeking a position of advantage over his predecessors.

The picture emerging of Bishop Hatfield and his use of ecclesiastical space might suggest that the relationship between the convent and their soldier bishop was antagonistic, but this was, indeed, far from the case. The 12th century had, it is true, seen fairly acrimonious disputes between the convent and their bishop at Durham.[101] However, an agreement, *Le Convenit*, was agreed by Bishop Poore in 1229 and became "the monastery's basic charter of liberties".[102] There was still scope for

Fig. 4.37 Durham Cathedral. View of the brass matrix of the tomb of Bishop Lewis de Beaumont, the Neville screen and the high altar from the bishop's throne. By kind permission of the Dean and Chapter. A. Budge.

disagreements, such as those between bishop and prior in the episcopate of Anthony Bek, but these were resolved, and despite being obliged "on at least three occasions" to abide by the agreement, Bishop Hatfield appears to have been held in high regard in the diocese.[103] The conduct and outcome of his visitation in 1354 showed a high degree of mutual respect between the bishop and the convent and the chronicler of *Historiæ Dunelmensis* stated that Hatfield was "on friendly terms" with the monks and "maintained peace in the church".[104] This goodwill may well have paved the way for the assent given by the convent for the bishop's tomb and throne in 1362.

In fact, a feature of all the institutions that erected imposing bishops' thrones in the 14th century, whatever their construction material, was the respectful relations between the parties involved, especially when compared to previous or even subsequent eras. It appears that the sanctioning by the dean and chapter, or by the convent, of such a visible sign of the bishop's status, even if they did not commission it, required a very high degree of mutual respect and support and that this was a crucial pre-condition to the erection of these monuments which so dominated the choirs of their respective cathedrals.

At Wells such mutual respect might not have been forthcoming even a decade or so before the commissioning of the throne. Dean Godley and Bishop Drokensford had been in open dispute between 1319 and 1321 on their respective responsibilities, as a result of which the bishop was banned from the new chapter house unless conducting a formal visitation.[105] By Drokensford's death in 1329, however, an accommodation of sorts had clearly been reached; the dean and bishop jointly founded a chantry near the latter's tomb.[106] Drokensford's successor Bishop Ralph of Shrewsbury, in whose episcopate the throne was erected, was, on his death in 1363, accorded a privileged burial position in front of the high altar and, judging by the contributions made beside his tomb, had proved a popular bishop.[107] He had been a canon of Wells before his appointment and contributed to the fabric of the cathedral including the building of the vicars' hall completed in 1348.[108]

The mutually supportive relations between bishop and chapter or convent found at Durham and Wells appear to have been replicated in the other cathedral communities commissioning imposing bishops' thrones in the 14th century. At Exeter the bishop had considerably more power and influence than was the case in other bishoprics, but despite his unusual privileges the Exeter chapter appears to have been very supportive of its bishop.[109] Walter de Stapeldon had been a former precentor at the cathedral before his election as bishop in 1307, by 15 of the 24 canons, and during his episcopate this sense of common purpose was helped, perhaps, by four of the canons being close relatives and three of the dignitaries his personal nominees.[110] The relationships between the bishop and chapter at Hereford had been dire during the episcopate of Bishop Aquablanca (bp 1240–1268), but subsequent bishops successfully recovered this position.[111] Bishop Swinfield (bp 1283–1317) worked closely with the chapter on the canonisation of Thomas Cantilupe, and relations during Bishop Trillek's episcopate were undoubtedly helped by the appointment of his brother Thomas as dean a year after the bishop's election.[112] Any disputes or disagreements at St Davids appear not to have been of a magnitude that warranted extensive documentation. The evidence does therefore show a remarkable degree of equanimity and co-operation between the bishop and chapter or convent at the time of the erection of the thrones. It stands in marked contrast to the relations at some of the other secular cathedrals at the same time, for example at Lincoln, Salisbury, Chichester and Lichfield.[113]

This review of the stone thrones at Wells and Durham has emphasised the formal distinctiveness of their designs; from each other, from the wooden thrones, and indeed from any obvious clear precedents. Their form, rather, was grounded in their immediate environs. In the case of Wells this was to the refurbishment of the choir, and at Durham to a desire for a degree of consistency in the 14th-century additions to the Romanesque fabric. The respective choirs, in their institutional rather than architectural sense, also provided the prime stimuli for the commissioning of these structures. At Wells, as at Exeter, the bishop's throne was an ideal symbol for the chapter to show veneration for the bishop, to bolster their rather sparse relics, to re-assert the church as the centre of the see, and even, perhaps, to sustain the feeling of solidarity with the lesser secular cathedrals in the face of the monasteries and larger, wealthier sees. At Durham, Thomas Hatfield again made use of the potent symbolism of the throne, not just in the cathedral but also in his castle and on his seals. His particular innovation, of placing the throne above his own tomb, enabled him to perpetuate the bishop's dominance of the south side of the cathedral but also to take up a vantage point high above and overlooking the choir.

The 14th-century thrones as a whole do form a coherent group, but their coherence is not based on stylistic affinity but rather on the ability of the thrones, through their scale and visibility, to convey a set of ideas and concepts of particular importance to those that commissioned them. The adaptability of this form resonated throughout the 14th century and produced a number of remarkable monuments.

Notes

1 See Brooke 2001. I am indebted to Anne Crawford, archivist at Wells Cathedral, for bringing the Kalmeter journal to my attention.

2 *Ibid.*, 55–6.

3 Britton 1847, 113.

4 See Wilson 1980, particularly 98–101; Pevsner and Williamson 1983, 199–200, and Billings 1843, 41–2.

5 For discussion of the thrones at Canterbury and Norwich see Phillips 1949; Radford 1959; Reeve 2003 and Fernie 1993, particularly 28–9 and 65–6. They are also briefly discussed in Chapter 1.

6 See Stubbs 1879 and Willis 1845 for Gervase's account and, for commentary, Radford 1959, 127 and Reeve 2003, 131. For the Stone chronicle see Searle 1902, particularly 33–4, 55–6 and 62–3.

7 For the Wells statutes see Watkin 1941. The funding of the Wells choir-stalls is most comprehensively covered in Church 1907.

8 Raine attributed the account of the episcopate of Bishop Hatfield in the *Historia Dunelmensis* to the contemporary chronicler William Chambre, but it is now more likely that this is a continuation of Chambre's history, added in the 16th century. For the account of Hatfield's episcopacy see Raine 1839, cxlviii–cli; for a discussion of its authorship see Piper 2004. For the *Rites of Durham* see Fowler 1903, particularly 19.

9 Bond 1910, II, 110.

10 I am grateful to Jerry Sampson for this petrological analysis. This updates the earlier analyses, where the throne was taken to be primarily constructed of Doulting e.g. Colchester 1987, 126.

11 Canon Barnard's recollections form the basis of Colchester's analysis of the Victorian restoration carried out by Salvin – the quote is reproduced in Colchester 1956, 87. Clayton's comments are found in a letter dated 16 Apr. 1894 preserved in Canon Church's Fabric Record Books in the Wells Archives, reference DC/FAB 2/4 – the quote is reproduced in Greenhaulgh 1982, 186.

12 This observation is from Pfaff 2009, 507–8. The Wells Consuetudinary includes a detailed calendar for the vestments to be used throughout the liturgical year. Most feasts, as was traditional, feature red and/or white vestments but the combination of green and yellow, as noted by Pfaff, is unusually prominent. The feast days so designated include a number of Confessor saints, often associated with green vestments, but do not include all of them. The list includes such prominent saints as Mary Magdalen and St Martin. Authors as diverse as William St John Hope and John Gage have counselled against analysis of the colour symbolism of English medieval liturgical vestments. The choice of colour appears to have been primarily at the behest of the institution, working within the broad guidance emanating from Innocent III at the end of the 12th century. The dean and chapter at Wells therefore would have had a degree of discretion and used this to generate, on 17 feast days throughout the year, a particularly coordinated effect within the choir. For the Wells calendar see Watkin 1941, 130–4. For discussion of colour symbolism and vestments see Hope and Atchley 1918, viii–ix, 3–4 and 151; Gage 1999, 70–1; 2009, 60 and 83–4. For the guidance of Innocent III see Gage 1999, 70.

13 See Britton 1836, pl. xv. The engraving is dated 1823. A copy of the Essex watercolour is held in the Wells archives: DC/PL/214. The ownership of the original is unknown.

14 Colchester 1956, 85.

15 The restoration was thought to present "particular difficulties", probably referring to the problem of the seating arrangements in the choir, specifically the choir-stalls. These generated the most protracted discussions between the chapter and their architect and resulted in the replacement of the damaged 14th-century stalls with new, stone-canopied stalls placed between, rather than in front of, the arches of the three bays of the choir. The extended discussions between Salvin and the

dean and chapter are hinted at in letters from Salvin contained in the Wells Archives (DC/FAB 1/5) and touched on in Colchester 1956.

16   The dates are contained in the Cathedral accounts for the restoration held in the Wells Archives: DC/F 2/52.

17   The engraving, for example, omits the crenellated terminals at the far right and left of the second tier, yet they are clearly visible on the watercolour. The conclusion drawn is that they were omitted in order to simplify the engraving rather than any indication that they are a later addition.

18   The 1823 engraving shows the previous arrangement.

19   Canon Barnard quoted in Colchester 1956, 87.

20   The episcopal thrones erected at Lyon and S. Clemente, Rome in the 12th century followed the earlier traditions of placing a comparatively plain seat on steps in the centre of the apse. See Chapter 1 above and, for Lyon, Bégule 1920, and for S. Clemente, Guidobaldi and Lawlor 1990 and Reeve 2003, 136.

21   See Chapter 1.

22   Matt Woodworth's insightful analysis of the reredos and sedilia at Beverley identifies interesting connections between the micro-architecture at the Minster and that at Exeter. The analysis also proposes that these rarely considered monuments at Beverley be treated alongside the Percy tomb as examples of mid-14th-century craftsmanship. See Woodworth 2011 unpublished, 162-231.

23   Harvey 1982, 86.

24   The range of dates reflects the assent given by the convent for the construction of the throne and tomb in 1362: Raine 1839, cxxxvii–cxxxviii, and the assertion in the *Rites of Durham* that the throne was completed before Bishop Hatfield died: Fowler 1903, 19. The dating of the throne is discussed in more detail below.

25   Fowler 1903, 19.

26   The comment comes as part of the chronicler's description of Hatfield's burial, itself reflecting comments in the Episcopal Register for 1381: Raine 1839, 139 and cxlviii–cli. The other quotes are from Park 1993, 64 and Wilson 1980, 98.

27   See St John Hope's reconstruction of the medieval plan of the cathedral in *Rites of Durham*, Fowler 1903.

28   For the restrictions see Klukas 1995, 73.

29   For Wyatt's intentions see Billings 1843, 15.

30   Britnell 2012, 48 reports restoration of the monument in 1700 and repainting in 1772. The reports of the Friends of Durham Cathedral from the 1930s, specifically 1933-4, 1936-7 and 1938-9, also make regular

reference to work on restoring the colours of the monument.

31   Evidence of the attempted reconstruction of this eastern termination, since removed, can still be seen in the stonework inside the current balustrade. I am grateful to Norman Emery for drawing to my attention the existence of photographs similar to that in Fig. 4.15. This undated photograph can, on the basis of the history of the publisher Raphael Tuck (and that of Walter Scott, the publisher of a similar photograph also showing the eastern termination), be reasonably dated to the first quarter of the 20th century. The Billings engraving of the choir façade (Fig. 4.14), published in 1843, does not show this eastern termination.

32   See Billings 1843, pls lvi–lviii.

33   Fowler 1903, 211.

34   BL Ms Add. 29933.

35   An observation made by Wilson 1980, 98–9. The recent detailed archaeological investigation of the east end of York Minster by Alexander Holton confirms that the ogee-arched canopies, integrated now into the reredos designed by G. F. Bodley in 1905, survive from the third quarter of the 14th century. See Holton 2010 unpublished, 210.

36   Woodworth 2011 unpublished, particularly 162–231, provides a detailed examination of both the reredos and sedilia at Beverley.

37   Wilson 1980, 98.

38   The western façade of the Beverley reredos has often been regarded as a predominantly early-19th-century work. However, Woodworth's detailed analysis has shown that the reconstruction carried out by William Comins between 1824 and 1826 was remarkably faithful to the original. See Woodworth 2011 unpublished, 168–72.

39   The contrasting techniques, and the variable results at both Durham and Beverley, give weight to Woodworth's observation that creating diaper-work, despite its popularity in England, was not an easily-mastered skill. See Woodworth 2011 unpublished, 187.

40   Wilson 1980, 98–100.

41   The combination of trefoiled panels behind canopies as a general design concept has earlier precedents, such as the triforium of the choir at Wells Cathedral built in the 1330s, but the closeness of the designs at York and Durham is marked.

42   For a detailed discussion of the Stratford tomb, and in particular the interrelationship of its various parts, see Wilson 1995, 468–70.

43   A recent advocate of the idea of 'multiple modes' has been Wilson – see particularly Wilson 1990, 191–204. Examples of 14th-

century master-masons working in multiple modes include Michael of Canterbury's work on St Stephen's Chapel, Westminster and, on the basis of stylistic similarity, the gatehouse of St Augustine's Abbey, Canterbury. The use of contrasting styles in the same building campaign can also be seen at the Ely Octagon and the Wells east end.

44 For the dates of commissioning of the Neville tomb see Tuck 2004. The tomb was placed between the southern piers of the third bay west of the crossing – see St John Hope's reconstruction of the medieval plan of the cathedral in Fowler 1903. John Neville was only the second lay-person permitted burial within the cathedral. The first was his father, Ralph Neville, whose tomb was originally placed in front of the Jesus altar in the nave, but was moved to the bay to the east of John Neville's tomb as part of the establishment of the Neville Chapel in the south aisle of the nave in 1416. The chapel has since been demolished. See Fowler 1903, 244.

45 See also Wilson 1980, 100.

46 Wilson 1980 remains the primary reference on the screen. Billings 1843, 42 notes that the erection of the screen occupied seven masons for a year.

47 A view shared by Billings who considered Wyatt's plans to mix elements of the Neville screen and Hatfield's throne screen into a new construction as "utterly beyond comprehension": Billings 1843, 15.

48 For York see Brown 2003, 144–64 whose dating for the main construction period of the east front is broadly confirmed by Holton's examination: Holton 2010 unpublished, 180–95. Holton identifies that many of the relevant image canopies were restored in the 19th century but there appears to be sufficient surviving material, and enough care evinced in the restorations, that we can be confident that the current canopy designs are very close to the 14th-century originals.

49 Klukas 1995, 78 stresses the desire for a common overall aesthetic despite there being an apparent lack of coordination in the various works commissioned at Durham. Such an aesthetic would certainly have complemented the regularly patterned yet delicate rose window of the Chapel of the Nine Altars which had, since its erection in the third quarter of the 13th century, dominated the view to the east. The construction of the choir-stalls with elaborate canopies was another separate commission in the latter part of the 14th century; see Curry 1993, 37–8.

50 See n. 24 above.

51 The first record we have of Lewyn is in 1364,

two years after assent was given for the throne and tomb, when he was sent to a Scottish dependency of Durham. See Harvey 1984, 181–4 for Lewyn's role at Durham.

52 National Archives: SC 8/58/2854.

53 The episode is related in Liddy 2012, 40. Set against this, Hatfield is recorded as having granted a wardship to Lewyn in 1370–1. Harvey 1984, 181.

54 For the veneration of the bishops at Exeter see Sekules 1991a.

55 *Ibid.*, 175–8.

56 *Ibid.*, 176.

57 *Ibid.*

58 Draper 1995, 121 and Rodwell 1982, 16–18. The similar erection of historicising monuments to ten former bishops at another cathedral with a 14th-century bishop's throne, Hereford, is discussed in Chapter 2.3.

59 The fullest accounts of the proposed canonisation of William of March are in Colchester 1987 and Draper 1981.

60 See also the discussion of the prior's seat in Chapter 1.

61 The device might also be in operation in the easternmost tomb on the south side of the church of St Thomas the Martyr, Winchelsea constructed in the first quarter of the 14th century.

62 The Fourth Lateran Council's requirement of churches to exhibit their relics brought them out from their previous positions, beneath the altar table or in the crypt, to be displayed on the altar top. The conventional argument is that congestion on the altar table precipitated their subsequent move to a pedestal behind the altar, which then constrained the access to the bishop's throne in the same area, resulting in the need to find a new location for the throne, at least for day-to-day purposes: see Radford 1959, 129. See also Chapter 1.

63 For a comprehensive and forensic examination of the evidence for the position of the medieval bishop's throne at Norwich Cathedral see Crook forthcoming. See also Chapter 1; Fernie 1993, 66 and Radford 1959, 119.

64 Fernie 1993, 66.

65 See Shinners 1988, particularly 133.

66 The lack of important relics forms a key part of Sekules' argument in relation to the Exeter throne: see Sekules 1991, 178. For the lack of relics at Wells see Colchester 1987, 106.

67 I am again indebted to Anne Crawford, archivist at Wells Cathedral, for her support in identifying these sources and the references to the subsequent published discussions.

68 The earliest communar's account held in the Wells archives is for 1327 (DC/ F 1/1). The

1292 account, recently identified for what it is by Robert Dunning, is in the Somerset Heritage Centre (DD/CC/B 131909/16).

69   The Wells Consuetudinary, and specifically the reference to the beam, is published in Watkin 1941, 6.

70   For discussion of the potential locations for Wells' relics see Spurrell 2002a; 2002b.

71   Stubbs 1879, 4.

72   *Ibid.*, 13.

73   An illustration (Fig. 4.34), now in the collection of Trinity Hall, Cambridge, shows relic chests positioned on a beam above an altar screen at St Augustine's Abbey, Canterbury. The beam is seemingly supported at either end by two columns, an arrangement matching Gervase's description of the relic beam in Prior Conrad's choir at Christ Church, Canterbury. The bones of Anglo-Saxon kings and bishops at Winchester were placed in a raised position around the high altar by Bishop Henry of Blois in 1154 and later, when the Romanesque apse was replaced, moved on top of the screen behind the altar or to beams either side of the feretory. For St Augustine's see Trinity Hall, MS 1, fol 77r, reproduced in Dugdale 1846, 120. For its dating see Binski and Panayotova 2005, 254–5. For Winchester see Crook 2003, 60–3.

74   Bishop Leofric united the sees of Crediton and Cornwall at Exeter in 1050: see Bishop and Prideaux 1922, 22–3.

75   For the likely configuration of the east end of the Saxon Minster see Bishop and Prideaux 1922, 25. For the various contributions regarding the east end of Exeter's Romanesque cathedral, concluding that some form of apsidal termination was used, see Thurlby 1991.

76   Draper 1995, 122–3.

77   Rodwell 1982 sets out persuasive evidence for the longevity of the rivalry with Bath.

78   The most comprehensive review of John of Tours' priory church at Bath is Davenport 1996 from which the material on Bath is taken.

79   Davenport 1996, 22–3.

80   Rodwell 1982, 12.

81   John Crook makes a convincing argument, in his forthcoming paper for the BAA Conference Transactions at Norwich in 2012, that the current height and position of the throne dates from the mid-12th century rather than 1122. It is likely, however, that some form of throne was positioned in the apse at the time of Bishop Eborard's consecration. See Crook forthcoming and Fernie 1993, 66.

82   It is possible that problems of survival have

clouded the picture here but the existence of a prominent throne in any of these locations might have been expected to elicit at least some mention from the various chroniclers over the following centuries.

83   Fernie 2000, 153 and 172.

84   Barlow 1972, 2 and 11.

85   Walter, Giso and Archbishop Aeldred of York travelled together to Rome in 1061 and Aeldred subsequently introduced the Rule to York: see Bannister 1924, 25. See also Church 1894, 5–6 and Klukas 1981, 30.

86   The Exeter Ordinals introduced by Bishop Grandisson (bp 1327–1369) probably encapsulated the distinctive Exeter Use based, in part, on the Rule of Chrodegang. It included the censing of the bishop immediately after the high altar, ahead of the more normal order: see Sekules 1991, 176.

87   The bishops of Salisbury, York and Lincoln set up secular organisations for their cathedrals, probably based on their common experience of arrangements in Normandy: see Edwards 1949, 12–13 and Bannister 1924, 26.

88   The Uses at Exeter and Hereford are discussed at length in Pfaff 2009, respectively at 388–411 and 463–79. Pfaff also analyses the Wells liturgy as based on the Sarum Consuetudinary "modified to suit the needs of Wells": Pfaff 2009, 507. Dix warns however against placing too much emphasis on the separate Uses as "they are only local dialects, some of them hardly more than 'accents'" of the standard rites: see Dix 1945, 585 and also Bannister 1924, 149–51. For the Lincoln chair see Chapter 3.

89   The veneration shown at Exeter and Wells is also seen at Hereford with the erection, in the choir aisles in the early 14th century, of monuments to ten former bishops. See Chapter 2.3.

90   For biographies of Thomas Hatfield see Haines 2004 and the various contributions in Bash 2012, particularly Prestwich 2012; Ormrod 2012 and Liddy 2012.

91   Fraser 1959 identifies the primary powers and responsibilities of the bishop in his palatinate role.

92   For the redevelopment of the hall and its thrones see Goodall 2011, 300–1.

93   The depiction of the throne on Hatfield's chancery seal has greater affinity to the earlier dignity seal of Anthony Bek, and its architecture is more reminiscent of the prior's seat in the chapter house at Canterbury. For illustrations and discussion of the seals see Blair 1922, particularly pls ii, iii, and v.

94   Anthony Bek had been buried on the north side of the Chapel of the Nine Altars. His

successor, Richard Kellawe, a former sub-prior of Durham, reverted to the tradition of being buried in the chapter house. Robert Graystones, briefly elected bishop in 1333 after the death of Lewis de Beaumont, was another monk of Durham buried in the chapter house. Richard de Bury (bp 1333–1345) was buried in the south of the Chapel of the Nine Altars. According to the *Rites of Durham* Lewis de Beaumont's brass was prepared before his death in 1333: Fowler 1903, 15.

95 For the detailed medieval description of the memorial see Fowler 1903, 14–15. The quote is from Fowler 1890, 37.

96 Fowler 1890, 38 and 42–3.

97 This was, for example, the location of Bishop Stapeldon's tomb at Exeter but was also the burial position of the venerated bishops at St Paul's, Lincoln and Salisbury: Sekules 1991, 176.

98 I am grateful to John Goodall for this interpretation of the material in the *Rites of Durham*. The vestry on the south side of the cathedral choir was said to have contained an altar used by the bishop for the saying of mass during the consecration of priests, though in Hatfield's case this was not a regular occurrence: he conducted only two of the 103 ordinations of his episcopate in the church himself. It does appear, however, that Hatfield was generally resident in his diocese. For the Black Rood see Fowler 1903, 216; for the vestry and its altar see Fowler 1903, 19 and 212; for Hatfield's ordinations see Haines 2004; and for his record of residence see Liddy 2012, 42–3.

99 The processional route is recorded in the *Rites of Durham*: see Fowler 1903, 8.

100 The "little altar" attached to the tomb, referred to in the *Rites of Durham*, was probably positioned where the pier masonry has been cut away to the west of the tomb: see Fowler 1903, 211.

101 Crosby 1994, 147.

102 *Ibid.*, 150.

103 Harbottle 1958, 83 and, for the quote, Neville 2000, 224.

104 See Harbottle 1958 for a full account of the visitation particularly 97. The account of the chronicler is in Raine 1839, 137–9. The translations of the quotes are from Harbottle 1958, 83.

105 Church 1894, 304–5 and 344 and Colchester 1987, 18–19 and 156.

106 Church 1894, 312.

107 For approval of Shrewsbury, based at least in part on contributions to the money-box by his tomb, see Colchester 1987, 21 and for his original burial site see Britton 1847, 40–1.

108 Colchester 1987, 21.

109 For example, all canons and dignitaries swore an oath to the bishop, he was able to approve the election of the dean, the position of sub-dean was in his gift, he could visit the cathedral chapter, and all statutes, regardless of subject matter, had to be approved by him. See Edwards 1949, 117–22 and Buck 1983, 55. For the sense of approval, see Crosby 1994, 277.

110 See Buck 1983, 27–31 and 56–8 and, for details of Stapeldon's election, 38.

111 This state of affairs even resulted in the murder of the bishop's agent: see Bannister 1924, 46–9 and 142–4.

112 For Thomas Trillek see Rawlinson 1717, 224.

113 See Edwards 1949, 130.

Appendix I

Significant items connected with the manufacture of Exeter Cathedral's bishop's throne

(representative extracts from accounts of the fabric rolls)

N.B. The printed original entries are in plain text, with italicised Latin in brackets. For brevity, not all of the original Latin quoted in the printed version, is given here. Erskine's comments are provided separately in italics, and Tracy's in bracketted italics.

1309–10
Christmas Term
Cost of Glass and the Stalls (*custus vitri et stallorum*)
In wages of Master John de Glaston' removing the stalls (*removent' stall'*) for 14 weeks 52s 6d, 3s 9d a week.

1312–13
Midsummer Term (25 June–25 September)

Cost of Timber for the Bishop's Throne (*Custus meremii ad sedem episcopi*)

In wages of Master Thomas de Winton being at Norton and Chudleigh (*Chuddelea*) for the purpose of looking over timber (*ad providend' merem' et circa merem' prosternend'*) for one week 3s. (*This probably covers the cost of finding suitable oak trees for conversion*). In wages of William de Membiri carpenter for 3 days 13s ½d. And Richard de Brugges 10½d. And J. de la Wichie 9d. And R. Prodomme 9d. And 2 sawyers 8d. In wages of the said Master Thomas for another week 3s. And William de Membiri carpenter 2s 3d. And Robert Grosp and John Loch 3s 8d. And Richard de Briggis Walter Unfrey and Alexander de Holcomb

5s. 3d, 21d. each. And Thomas Ata Wichie 19d. And J. Prodomme and J. Schere 3s. And 2 sawyers 2s. 6d. And 2 sawyers 2s 3d. And one sawyer 15d. And 2 sawyers 20d.

Week 3 In wages of Master Thomas 3s. And Robert de Galmeton carpenter 2s 2d. And J. Loch 22d. And 2 sawyers 2s 6d. And 2 sawyers 2s 2d.

Week 4 In wages of Master Thomas 3s. And 2 sawyers 2s 6d. For carrying timber to the water at Norton and submerging it (*In merem' apud Norton ad aquam cariand' et mergend'*) 10d. Paid to the same Master Thomas for his expenses in returning home (*in recessu eius versus patriam suam*) 5s.

Week 5 In wages of W. de Membiri 2s 3d. And Robert de Galmeton for the said week 13d. And Benedict Scrogeyn 12d. And Robert Crop 11d. And in one man felling timber (*prosternent' merem'*) for 2½ days 12½d.

Week 6 In wages of William de Menbiri 2s 3d. And Benedict Scrogyn 20 d. And R. Prodomme 18d.

Week 7 In wages of W. de Menbiri 2s 3d. And Crop Penung' 22d. And 8 labourers at Norton for hauling the timber out of the mill-pool there (*ad merem' ibidem de stagno molendini extraend'*) 4s 6d each. For carrying all the timber from Norton to Exeter *in grosso* 36s 2d.

Week 8   For 2 sawyers at Chudleigh 2s 8d. For raising a certain great tree-trunk for sawing there (*In quodam magno ligno ibidem levand' ad secatur'*) 5d. In one carpenter for sawing 2 tree-trunks (*ad ij ligna quarand'*) 2s. And one carpenter for various weeks 12d. For carrying certain planks (*tabulis*) to the water 1d. For 2 sawyers for half a week 15d.

Week 9   In 2 sawyers for one week 2s 2d.

Weeks 10, 11 In 2 sawyers 4s 6d.

Week 12   In 2 sawyers 2s 6d. And in 2 sawyers 2s 3d. And in 2 sawyers for various week 14½d.
              Total £6 12s 8½d

1316–17 (*After a period of 4 years, the manufacture of the throne and canopy must have been complete*)

Midsummer Term

Cost of the bishop's throne (*Custus sedis episcopi*). Paid to Robert de Galmeton and his associate for making the bishop's throne at task (*pro factura sedis episcopi ad tascam*) £4. [Crossed out: And to Nicholas the painter for images 11s].

1317–18
Christmas Term
Week 9   Cost of images for the bishop's throne (*imag' ad sedem episcopi*). For carving 6 images for the bishop's throne (*In vj imagin' talliand' pro sede episcopi*) 32s.

1319–20
Midsummer Term
Week 9   For 2½ lbs of white lead (*albo plumbo*) 10d for the images of the bishop's throne (*pro imaginibus sedis episcopi*).

1323–24
Michaelmas Term
Week 5   For writing 250 letters around the bishops throne (*In ii c et di. literis scribendis circa sedem episcopi*) 5d.

Week 10   Ironwork about the bishop's throne 15s 2d.

Week 11   For additional (*ad huc*) ironwork about the bishop's throne 3s 7d.

1328–29
Christmas Term
Week 13   2 great (*gross'*) "nall" and 20 small "nall" bought for the lord bishop's chair (*cathedra domini episcopi*) 2d.

Week 14   For the part of the lord bishop's chair which is put out to task (*in cathedra episcopi pro parte data ad tascham*) 12s 1d.

Midsummer Term
Week 3   In wages of a smith for making 2 bars, 4 "clomp", 4 staples and 4 hinges for the lord bishop's chair from the smith's own iron 2s. (*for a "cloth of estate"?*).

1329–30
Michaelmas Term
Week 12   "*Reng*" bought for the chair of the lord bishop 4d.

Easter Term
Week 2   One ox-hide (*cor' bovino*) bought for lord bishop's chair 3s.

Week 3   In cloth (*panno*) bought for the lord bishop's chair 12d. (*for a "cloth of estate"?*).

Week 10   For fretting (*frett'*) the bishop's chair 2s.

(*For "frettenda", read diapering/ornament/embroidery. Possibly carved decoration, as in the lozenge work on the buttresses of the bishop's throne, or referring to the embroidering of a "cloth of estate". Freeman's suggestion of "scraping", as in cleaning a stone throne, is not tenable*).

1330–31
Michaelmas Term
Week 12   One bar (*barra*) for the lord bishop's chair 6d. *ditto, for a "cloth of estate"?*

1347
Expenses for cleaning the reredos of the high altar, the bishop's chair (*mundant' retrodors' maior' altar' cathedr' episcopi passionar'*) 5s. Also Note 3, Erskine 1983, p. 278, *passionar':* uncertain reading, almost illegible. It may perhaps refer to a sculptured panel representing the Passion on or near the high altar?

Sources: Erskine 1981; 1983. I am indebted to Christopher Paterson for his suggested editorial emendations.

Appendix II

Significant records connected with the manufacture of the remainder of the Exeter Cathedral choir furnishings by Thomas of Witney's "High Altar team" et al., 1316–1326

Representative extracts from the general and high altar accounts of the Fabric Rolls.

N.B. The printed original entries are in plain text, with the italicised Latin in brackets. For brevity, not all of the original Latin, quoted in the printed version, is given here. Paterson's comments are provided separately in bracketted italics.

1309–10
Christmas Term

Week 15?   In wages of Master John of Glaston' removing the stalls (*removent' stall'*) for 14 weeks 52s 6d, 3s 9d a week.

1316–17 High Altar Accounts

Cost of Caen stone (*petr' de Kain*). One boatload of stones in which are contained 162 "gobbets" and 108 coins bought inclusive (*una naviata petrarum in qua continebantur clxij gobetti et cviij koynge in grosso empto*) £6 13s 4d. 40 loads (*chargr'*) of the said stones carried from Topsham to Exeter 26s 8d, 8d a load. Total £8 by one tally from himself (*de se*).

Week 12   20 Welsh boards bought for moulds (*xx bordis Walens' ad moldis emptis*) 4s 10d.

Week 22   the feast of all Saints [1 November] and the time changes In wages. And 4 carters 3s 10d. And one labourer in the said quarry [Beer] 12½d. And 2 labourers there 14½d, 7 ¼ d each. Fodder of 11 cart horses for this week 7 quarters 1 ½ bushels one peck, that is, to

each horse for a day and a night half one bushel one peck. Total 15s 3d, except the purchase of oats.

Week 24   In wages [14s 9d] In one labourer in Beer quarry 15d. In two labourers there 16d. For a dayn of land leased as well as the digging of stones (*In j terre locata tam petrarum fod'*) 12d. In 2 boys (*garcionibus*) assisting in digging stone for one day 2½d. In one turner (*turnero*) for 3 days 12d. And 4 carters 3s 10d. Fodder of 11 horses [as above] Total 19s 7½d.

Week 27   2 chains bought for the high-altar table (*ij cathenis ad summam tabulam emptis*) 5s 6d.

Week 35   For 25 Irish boards (*bordis Ybern'*) bought for the requirements of the altar-table (*ad necessaria tabulae*) 5s.

Week 57   For 100 large stones carted from Beer quarry to the sea 3s 6d.

Week 58   Paid for 18 cart-loads of stone from Beer quarry to Blackdown (*usque la Blakedoune*) 45s.

1316–17
Michaelmas Term

Weeks 3–7   (*Galmeton busy making centering, with the "other" carpenter, for the construction of the "high roof" (ad summam coperuram). This was the crossing or the eastern bay of the nave. Also "3000 great lath nails" purchased for the same purpose).*

Week 9 One iron bolt for mending the dean's lectern in the quire (*bolto ferreo ad descam decani in choro emendendo*) 1d. (*This may have been merely a security emendation*).

Weeks 10, 13, 14 *(Galmeton making more centerings).*

Midsummer Term

Week 11 One key for the gate which is against the bishop's gate (*In j clave ad portam qua est contra porta episcopi*).

1317–18
Midsummer Term

Week 14 Purchase of marble for the galleries (*marmor' ad aluras*) between the great altar and the choir (*inter magnum altarem et chorum*) etc., £10 8s. (*The next entry mentions 6 great capitals, 32 pairs of capitals, 6 large corbels*).

1318–19
Easter Term

Week 5 Ironwork viz. hooks (*gumfis*) and other requirements for 'la pulpyte' 16d.

Week 9 For making a lectern (*desca*) before (*coram*) Master William Kylkenny in the quire 4d.

(Following the death of Dean Andrew Kilkenny in 1302, his brother William, and others, appropriated the benefice of St Petroc, West Anstey, as a vicarage to the dean and chapter. At the same time a chantry of St Andrew (now St Andrew's Chapel) was founded, and endowed with St Petroc's rectoral tithes.[1] The institution was set up to pray for the souls of Andrew, and three deceased family members, William, formerly bishop of Ely, Henry, formerly archdeacon of Chichester, and Henry, Rector of Bridestowe. The roll entry indicates that the death of Canon William, Andrew's brother, had already taken place, as William was already buried, not in the chantry, but in the choir aisle. William was a rich canon, commemorated in five of the cathedral's later obit lists.[2] The lectern referred to could have been the one, known to be from the cathedral and still surviving in St Thomas's Church. That example is only single-sided, and is, therefore, unlikely to have been the probably larger and double sided lectern, that would have been required for use in the choir.)

Midsummer Term

Week 1 Cost of marble. He reckons for 4 columns with bases sub-bases and capitals (*in iiij columnis cum basis subbasis capitrall'*) £5 6s 8d. Item for 243 feet of marble steps for 'la pulpytte' £4 10s 3 d, 4½d a foot. Item for 2 altars with marble frontals with other fittings 26s 8d. … Item released to William Canoun

£4 by order of the lord dean and chapter out of courtesy (*ex cutialitate*). Total 51s 7d.

(The earliest entry for the construction of the extant pulpitum, recording a payment of an instalment for the Purbeck marble required for the four major columns on the west side, as well as the substructure of plinths and bases (in fact, there are four sets of Purbeck marble columns on both the east and west sides).

1318–19 High Altar Accounts
Easter Term

Weeks 5, 6 Item. To John de Bannebiri for 3 vaults carrying the canopy of the high altar at task 100s.

(This appears to be is the first entry to signal the start of the high altar [pulpitum] building campaign).

Week 14 For making 3 great iron bars 4 pulleys (*poleyes*) 2 iron rods (*virgis ferr'*) 2 hinges (*vertivellis*)and sharpening for the high (*maiorem*) altar 19s 7d.

1319-20
Michaelmas Term

Week 7 Paid to Crokkernewill' (*a smith*) for 500 lbs of iron for making large bars for "la Pulpitte" 15s 5d.

(It is worth noting that Scott found iron bars embedded in the structure of the pulpitum).

Easter Term

Week 11 For making 2 great bars for "La Pulepytte" weighing 400 lbs 12s 4d.

Midsummer Term

Week 8 … To William Frensch for making 3 new reliquaries. Timber for the same 3s. 6 boards and 150 'spykes' for the same 2s 3d. 7 quarters of lime 2s 11d.

Week 9 For making 4 hinges for 'la pulpite' 2s. … 15 boards bought 3s 1d.

(This was the year of the greatest activity in the quarries, in aid of extracting the stone needed for the reredos and carting it to the cathedral. As for the oak used for the throne, the material was provided pro bono at the expense of the bishop.

The total expenditure in 1319–20 on the High Altar Accounts was £34 6s 3¼d, including the cost of carts/repairs, barge-hire, carters, quarry labour and costs allocated per rata the number of workers [between the two teams of masons] of stabling, horse shoes, and oats. The total wages of the craftsmen in the "high altar team" that year were £45 9s 4d. The cost of iron used was £4 8s 8d).

1320–21
Midsummer

Week 14   1500 gold [foils] 57s 5d. 100 lbs of white lead ("blame plum") 17s 2½d. 25 lbs of red lead ("rogeplum") 5s 2½d. For their carriage from Winchester (*Winton*) to Exeter 2s 6d. One lb of "cinopele" 6s 8d. For sacks for the same 3d.

1320–21 High Altar Accounts
Michaelmas Term

Week 1   4 iron bars for the altar 15s 10d, that is for iron and for making them.

Christmas Term

Week 12   One lb of azure bought in London by the lord [bishop?] 3s 6d. One lb of indigo of Baghdad (inde baudas) 18d. 4 lbs of verdigris 2s 4d. 4 lbs of vermilion 2s 8d. 5 lbs of white varnish 5s ¾d. 3 quarters of cinople 4s 9d. For 1000 gold [foils] 38s 4d. 6 lbs of white lead 18d.

Easter Term

Week 6   For 500 gold [foils] 19s 2d. 300 silver [foils] 18d. Half a lb of azure 3s. Sharpening and ironwork for the high (*maior*') altar 18d.

1321–22

(From the "Tablature"/high altar account for this year, it is clear that painting and "image" making activity had reached fever pitch (Erskine 1981, 143–6). Some 11,300 sheets of gold foil were consumed alone, 12 dishes were bought "for colours", possibly indicating the approximate number of executants employed, and equipment for lettering, and a marble stone for grinding colours. Some 45 separate images are mentioned, and painting activity continued unabated throughout the year. Twenty-one pieces of fabric were bought from London for 106s 6d).

1323–24
Michaelmas Term

Week 1   2 locks for 2 doors of the great altar 4s.

Easter Term

Week 4   In 2 carvers (ymaginator') 3s 5d.

Week 7   Iron hinges hooks and bolts for the doors of "la polpytte" 10s.

Midsummer Term

Week 4   For payment made to the carver from London for carving images (*In solucione facta ymaginator' de Londonia pro imaginibus talliandis*) by order of the Treasurer 39s.

Cost of images and marble (*custus ymag' et marrimor*) For 45 images. For 11 panels with a Judgement? And one image in a corner (*xj panel' cum Jud' et j imag' in angulo*) for "la pollepytte" £7 17s 6d.

(This carver, perhaps the craftsman from London commissioned in Week 4, was the executant of the heads for the stone vault of the pulpitum, the 45, presumably high-relief historiated images in the 11 panels along the front of the parapets, and of the corner image, and, possibly six figures in each of the two end panels. The nine small images which follow may well have been associated with the nave altars, "juxta le pulpytte") (see 1324–25, Michaelmas Term, Weeks 11 and 12, below).

1324–25
Michaelmas Term

Week 7   For making hooks hinges locks and other ironwork for the interclose (*interclausis*) near "la Pulpytte" 3s 8d.

(Parclose screenwork and locks around the nave altars).

Week 8   2000 tiles for "la Pulpytte" 16s.

(In 1836 Britton noted that the pulpitum's foundation, identified in 1818, consisted in part of glazed tiles some 6 inches below plinth level. Also Scott recorded a tiled floor, removed by him in the 1870s, in the loft above. A good number of Witney's tiles are still in place in the pulpitum loft).

Week 11   For making ironwork carrying the great Cross (*In factura ferrament portant' magnam crucem*) 12s 4d. Item 12 images in the 2 furthest panels in "la Polpitte" 42s.

Week 12   For cutting 9 small images near (*iuxta*) "la Pulpitte" 15s.

1325–26
Michaelmas Term

Week 3   For 24 iron rods for the enclosure by "la Pulpytte" 20s.

Christmas Term

Week 12   And of 4s for 4 locks 4 hinges and hooks for "la Pulpitte".

Midsummer Term

Week 10   Size bought for the Cross 5d.

Week 14   Colours for the great Cross One lb of azure 9s. 6 lbs of "tenabr" and 6 lbs of verdygrys' 10s 4d. 1000 gold foils 36s 8d. 1000 silver foils 5s. 3 lbs white varnish 2s.

(Completion of the painted rood, which was fixed from the side walls of the choir with an embedded iron rod).

1330–31
Michaelmas Term
Week 11   In a smith for ironwork around the eagle (*ferrament circa aquilem*) in "le Polpit" made from the smith's iron 4s 6d.

(This seems to be a finishing touch to the pulpitum, which had been on the go since Easter 1319).

Source: Erskine 1981; Erskine 1983, and Paterson.

Notes
1   J. Killen, West Anstey, http:exmoorencyclopedia.org.uk/contents-list/56-w/1050-west-anstey.html.
2   Lepine and Orme 2003, 47, 317, 320, 324, 328, 333. The authors also published the executors of Andrew Kilkenny, see ibid., 132–3, 171–202, 251, 272–311.

Appendix III

The construction and assembly of the Bishops' Thrones at Exeter and St Davids

Hugh Harrison and Peter Ferguson

Exeter

The results of a detailed examination of the joinery construction of the spectacular early-14th-century bishop's throne at Exeter are an important addition to our comparatively sparse knowledge of the timber furniture of this period. Only a few monumental examples of British church furniture survive, notably the choir-stalls at Winchester Cathedral. Screens are rare, but there are some timber roofs and doors of this date. Roof structures have their own technology, and most of the other surviving pieces, being in some way attached to the walls of their host building, are not structurally independent.

Exeter's bishop's throne is a monumental, yet completely independent, timber structure, whose design partially explores the particular characteristics of timber, yet is also anchored to what can be achieved with stone construction (Tip-ins 2.1.1, 2.1.2). The novelty of the design required a wide range of techniques, so the finished result is a text-book guide to those available before the ubiquitous frame swept all previous construction techniques away. These traditional techniques informed this design, something that would have been almost impossible once the frame became universal. The term frame applies to a type of construction particularly suited to timber, that of using long, often slim, timbers to form a square or rectangular shape jointed at the corners and reinforced by cross rails. The form was strong, used little material, and could be made solid with thin internal panels. Its shortcomings were that it was two-dimensional and weak if the sides were shaped (as the grain of the timber was cut through by the curves). If limited to frame construction how would they have made the great nodding ogee arches, one of the

glories of the Exeter throne design? With the exception of the central tower, which could be a later insertion, there is not a single horizontal member except the ridge beams of the central vault.

The basis of the design was a canopy of honour over the head of the bishop, created by four corner posts linked by tall gable ends emerging from the heavy ogee arches, which span between the corner posts. Perhaps the high-point of the design are the tripods which crash down through the junction of the ogee and the outer single foil of the main arches to stand above the main arch cusp angels. These front tripod posts, together with the single back post, form a triangular shape on plan. They ascend higher and higher to form a tabernacle, formerly over a figure, standing on the massive finial that terminates the gables (see Fig. 2.1.9). These are found on the north, east and west sides, and an empty mortise on the ridge beam of the centre joint might be an indication of an original intention to have a similar tripod on the south side.

As well as designing an enclosure that enhanced the throne and the status of the bishop, Thomas of Witney must have envisaged this extraordinary display of figures at high level. They were quite out of human reach and faced north, east and west. They were also free-standing, so could be seen from all sides, and occupied a space where no other structure existed. In many ways, their presence dictated the monument's entire design.

There is cumulative evidence that the extant central tower and spire were an afterthought, although incorporated within the same building campaign. Due to the loss of some of the vital cathedral fabric accounts for the period of construction, there is no archival reference to a change of plan. A conjectural reconstruction drawing of the original design is included in the main text (Fig. 2.1.10).

Heretofore, Thomas of Witney's work had mostly been in stone. Understanding the throne's construction tells us that the complete design must have been drawn out full-size before carrying out the search for suitable timber in the bishop's woods. The evidence for this is the different sizes of timber used in the same repeat components. The first principle was to find the biggest single piece from which the component could be made whether in length, for a post, or in width, for a gable, and then smaller pieces were added on as necessary to achieve the exact required size (this is quite different from current practice, where modern glues enable large components to be built up from usually fairly similar-sized pieces). Thus the four corner posts of the throne are jointed at different heights, showing that the four longest pieces were first selected and then added to as required to make up the full height.

Throughout the structure one finds little corners or projections added to a main component, which was otherwise big enough. This can be compared to stone construction, where there was rarely a shortage of material so the design could be subdivided into blocks of suitable size according to the characteristics of the stone. This method of construction explains why the throne must have been fully drawn before the trees were felled, as they needed to know the specific sizes of components to select specific trees.

This freedom from the constraints of conforming to a frame by building with solid blocks of timber, characterises the Exeter throne's contribution to timber construction and to the reputation of Thomas of Witney for realising the possibilities that solid construction offered. He would have found that, after mostly designing and building in stone, doing the same in timber was not so different.

Just as the timber construction mirrored stone construction, so in many ways does the design. The architecture is of a stone building so that the corner posts are built like buttresses, as are all the posts with their off-sets and pinnacles. But unlike stone construction, the use of timber enabled Thomas of Witney to build without incurring major outward thrusts from gables and tripod tabernacle canopies. Even the vaulted canopy over the throne would have produced little outward thrust. Here Thomas of Witney was able to use mortise and tenon joints secured with pins to contain these thrusts. The throne is thus a piece of pure design built without constraint to current practices, sometimes following tradition sometimes breaking new ground.

It is rare to have such accurate accounts for work of this date, so to know that the throne was completed in just 4 years (1313–1317) reveals really interesting work practices. The outset of this journey, and where the timber was cut and immersed in ponds has already been described. Even if the material had been cut to thickness before being immersed, much of it would have been 6 in (150 mm) thick. Conventionally, 1 inch per year should be allowed for seasoning, so obviously as the throne was completed in 4 years the timber must have been used green and wet. It is now generally assumed that in the Middle Ages all timber was used green, because, in that state, it is easier to carve. In some circumstances this is so, but in others, cutting and carving green oak is more difficult, as all the tools inevitably rust and sweat from hands mixed with the active tannin, thus turning the surface of the oak black when handled. It can also result in the rapid and uneven seasoning of the timber, when it is pierced and shaped to expose some areas of end grain to the air, but not others, resulting in a higher migration of moisture unequally from within the timber. The uneven movement of moisture results in some parts of a component drying out and other parts retaining the original high moisture content. This leads to splitting and twisting. Thus the attempted conversion of oak green can result in so many other major problems.

As already mentioned, when the Exeter throne was scaffolded for the survey in 2012, allowing unrestricted access to all parts, one of today's experienced gothic carvers was asked how long the carving would take to complete.[1] A complete listed assessment produced a figure of just over 27 years work for one man based on the current 40-hour week. As the components are mostly cut from solid boards, the joiners would have previously had to cut the shape of the component and then create all the different levels found in each component, in the same manner as working stone. To this should be added all the jointing and possibly reworking of joints as the timber moved during the drying out process, together with all the pinning-on of additional small components where the original piece was not quite big enough. Also to be allowed is the construction time on site, so the total of the joinery would probably equal the carving time, producing a figure of 54 years work for one man. As the throne was completed in 4 years, this equates to 13 men working full-time over that period. It is noteworthy that so many really skilled men were apparently available, and one assumes that most would have had to relocate to carry out the work.

A change in design

When the conjectural design for the throne is studied, it looks complete as a display of figures at high level and a canopy for the bishop at ground level. When the present structure is studied, so much seems lost in a crowded jumble of woodwork, which is undeniably awesome in its height. Whereas the conjectural design impresses from its balanced proportions and its clarity of purpose, the finished design is mostly about height. When the conjectural design is compared with the later sedilia also by Thomas of Witney (Fig. 2.1.12), one recognises many similar features.

This cannot be said for the tower and spire. Allied to the concept that these components may not have been part of the original design, there are several physical signs of alteration to the structure. It must be emphasised that all the points set out below can be explained by simple errors, either by the craftsman himself, poor instruction or changes in construction order. It is just that when there is so much perfection in all other aspects of the throne it is difficult to accept errors as being simple.

It seems that a major change in design took place while the throne was still in the course of construction. Evidence from the woodwork itself suggests that the central tower, the spire and the central vault at its present height were not part of the original design. There is no archival evidence for this, and the constructional data may not seem conclusive, yet, cumulatively, it does create an extraordinarily strong case. The details are as follows:

- The inner tripod posts are fully carved and were originally polychromed, suggesting that they were meant to be seen, but are now completely hidden by the central tower and battlemented side boards. In the "original" design they would have been seen through the corners between the gables.
- The fully carved and polychromed inner tripod posts have been cut off at the present height of the ridge of the vault. This clearly secondary intervention suggests that the central vault was once lower, as the post is now cut off directly underneath a buttress setback, an architectural feature which would never have been replicated, and one that could have been moved upwards quite easily if the centre vault had always intended to be the present height.
- It is interesting to see that the diagonal vault ribs are secured up to the diagonal cross beams, with vertical struts jointed at each end with mortise and tenon joints. This could be in response to the vault being raised and the ribs now being in two lengths, with their stiffness therefore compromised.
- The bottom rails for the tower tracery were obviously inserted after the tripods were constructed, since they cut through the back tripod posts, clearly suggesting a change of design. In addition, the cornice of the lower stage of the tower completely cuts through the front tripod post so that the pinnacle becomes a separate piece and was fixed on top of the cornice as though the post continued up through it.
- The carving on the inside face of the gable crockets is roughed out. This could be an acknowledgement of a change, realising that it was unnecessary to complete when the tower was added, and therefore mostly obscured the back faces of the gables. On the other hand, it could be considered acceptable, knowing that the inside faces of the gables were fully visible, but at such a height that finished carving was quite unnecessary.
- There is an empty mortise in the ridge beam of the centre vault for an inner tripod post on the south side (this mortise could of course have been an oversight in construction and was simply not needed).
- Blocks are pinned to the inner faces of the corner posts at the level of the top of the battlemented side boards. On one of these blocks a tracery light and canopy is roughed out. The tracery and canopy were not completed presumably because they would not have been seen once the design had changed. The other three were never started.
- The conjectural drawing shows that above the springing of the centre vault, all the superstructure is centred on the gables, and that apart from the corner posts there was no visual obstruction in the corners between the gables to see the back of the opposite gables and up to the tabernacles. To insert the two diagonal beams as roughly finished baulks of timber diagonally across the throne they would have been very noticeable at the corners, both because of their size and finish (Fig. 2.1.11). In addition, as the corner posts are jointed to the main arches at much the same height there was little need for diagonal bracing at this point.

When the new tower and spire were added, the original structure would have needed strengthening, and the insertion of the diagonal beams would have been the natural way of achieving this. They also provide the structure to carry the tower, an aspect not allowed for when the vault was built, although, on the other hand, it must be recognised that the vault was nonetheless incredibly carefully designed to take the inner tripod posts. The very spacing of the bosses below the vault and the actual size of the tripods are interlinked by the fact that the bosses were carved in the solid ridge beam to provide the strength to carry the inner tripod posts.

One curious feature is that the mortises for the tower corner posts extend beyond the posts. If this was for a bigger tower, they must have realised that the tracery rail and cornice would encroach even further through the inner tripod posts. Or were they cut for some quite different additional structure behind the gables, or was this just another mistake?

- It is conjectured that the battlemented side boards were indeed a later intervention as they have no specific housing in the main structure and are merely nailed to the edge of the corner post and the edge of the adjacent gable. It is suggested that they were added to hide the diagonal beams etc.
- The upper stage of the tower is built on the lower stage in a somewhat naïve manner, with no provision for vertical linkage between the two stages. Corner

blocks are planted across the corners of the lower stage cornice. Into these brackets are tenoned the posts for the upper stage. Of course, the latter has to be parallel with the lower stage, in order that the tabernacle faces the front of the throne so that the major central figure also faces front.

- One feels that the sophistication of the two dimensional triangles of the gables interacting with the three dimensional tripods set on the three sides of a square is compromised by the addition of the tower. If the tower and spire had been planned from the beginning, would not Master Thomas have set the lower stage on the diagonal (as a diamond within the square), and might he have used the inner tripod posts as the corner posts for the internal structure required to support the tower tabernacle and spire above?

- Another aspect that sets the tower design and construction apart from the rest of the throne is that the architecture is close to standard frame construction, with four corner posts linked by a lower rail and top rail with cornice. Also the mullions of the tracery run out on a standard chamfer on the bottom rail, whilst the top rail is jointed at the corners with quite complicated masons' mitres. The only variation from standard frame construction is that the tracery is not contained in grooves but fitted with oak pins to a matching chamfer mould on the posts and top rail. Like the cornice on the south fence at dado height, which has failed due to subsequent shrinkage, this tracery has split throughout as the wide panels are pinned each side preventing the panels from contracting as they dry out.

The anomalies in the design and the construction described above, together with the areas of roughed-out carving not completed and of completed carving that cannot be seen, and the addition of the battlemented side-boards all make compelling evidence for a sudden late change of design. Once this evidence is accepted the magnificence of the original monument can be appreciated. It would have been a highly successful interpretation of the original brief – the provision of a grand canopy above the bishop, with minimal visual interruption of his throne. The bishop would have been honoured by the richly carved canopy above him, inhabited by recognisably important figures adding to his own importance. Although the change of design and the addition of the tower did provide a magnificent central location for one highly important figure, the denseness of woodwork detracts considerably from the original free-form of the design. The addition of such grandeur to the throne detracts from the impact of the other (now missing) figures. However, despite this the present throne remains one of the most spectacular and important examples of British High-Medieval woodwork.

Captions and notes on the Exeter appendix figures

Fig. App. 3.1a. Exeter Cathedral. Plan through fence screen below dado level.

This drawing is included to provide a plan at ground level to enable the reader to understand the structure at the base of the throne with that above. All the structure except the corner posts is 19th century.

The north-east and south-west bases for the corner clusters of shafts above the fence are circular, whereas the north-west and south-east bases are octagonal. This alternating feature is not repeated in the amulets halfway up the clusters of shafts, nor on the capitals to the shafts, nor is it likely to have been repeated on the original lower shafts below the bases. This variation of circular and octagonal bases must be a decorative detail and illustrates the desire for a variety of decoration over architectural consistency. Interestingly, if fences were not part of the original construction this alternating feature would have had significant visual impact.

Fig. App. 3.1b. Exeter Cathedral. Plan taken through corner posts above dado rail.

The cornice at dado height on the south fence, and on the corner posts, is carved out of pieces of timber with vertical grain which are fixed to a 19th-century internal rail in the case of the south fence, and to the corner posts with oak pins. This construction technique is typical throughout the throne whereby lesser features are added to major components in order to achieve the most economic use of the timber. Although, in this instance, the use of horizontal grain may have been more practical, the joiners methodically followed their standard technique of applying minor components in the same grain direction as the host piece. With the introduction of heating into the cathedral the technique of making the horizontal cornice for the south fence from a number of pieces of vertically grained timber has shown its shortcomings. Each component has contracted, leaving substantial gaps, as are recorded on the drawing. Although environmental conditions varied far less at the time of construction, it would be hard to believe that there would be no shrinkage of such wide blocks of wood over such a length of continuous ornament. This raises the question of whether the joiners understood and allowed for the expansion and contraction of oak in differing conditions of humidity. From the further splitting of the tower tracery panels, there is some evidence that if they did understand the problems, they did not allow for them. We should remember that, as all the timber would have been heavily painted, its response to varying environmental conditions would have been slower and less.

Fig. App. 3.2a. Exeter Cathedral. Mirrored plan taken through lower canopy showing vault in elevation.

The complex jointing of the main ogee arches to the

corner posts is well thought out, and probably the strongest solution. Considering the length of the joint, and the incorporation of the inside face of the post as slanting shoulders to the tenon, the work was certainly not labour saving. It involved fitting heavy baulks of timber each side of the post to shoot the joint.

Note the enclosed hollow moulds of the ribs.

Fig. App. 3.2b. Exeter Cathedral. Plan taken through main gables above vault ribs showing jointing.

The vault shows many interesting constructional techniques:

- The centre boss and the centre north boss on the north–south ridge rib are carved in the solid out of the ridge rib. Although this may seem to be an extremely wasteful use of timber, the process of carving back the substantial beam to the small profile of the ridge rib, that leaves the rib big enough to carry the centre boss, demands that it is not weakened by the cutting of mortises out of it for the tenons of the intersecting ribs. It should also be remembered that a huge mortise is cut out of the top surface of the north boss for the tenon of the inner tripod post that stands on this boss.
- The same principle is found on the short east–west ridge ribs. Here like the north boss on the main ridge rib, the bosses on the east/west ridge beams have substantial mortises cut out of the sides of the tenons of the tierceron ribs, and a mortise is taken from the top face for the inner tripod posts.
- The ends of the ridge ribs become part of a multi-component joint, where they are continued by extension pieces into the gable fronts. These complex joints have a dual function. The extensions are made big enough from which to carve the half bosses, and they connect the two halves of the gable end panels. As the extensions are only pinned together, their strength in holding the joint in the gable end panels is negligible and there is a slip tenon in the joint of the latter just above, so their structural contribution is very little. Maybe we are attributing too many functions to these elements, and they are merely typical add-on pieces from which to carve the bosses.
- Note that the fronts of the tripods are slightly wider than the sides.
- The gable fronts are held together with slip tenons. This makes no allowance for shrinkage, and one or two have split close to their joint with the corner posts.
- Apart from the finial and the pinnacle shafts, which are separate pieces, the entire projecting hood on the south side is made from one block of timber 2 × 1 × 3 ft (610 × 305 × 915 mm).

Fig. App. 3.3. Exeter Cathedral. Relationship between inner tripod posts and central tower.

This clearly shows how the inner tripod posts have been cut off just above the ridge beam of the centre vault. When they were cut they were complete and carved. This is either a mistake or evidence that the central tower was inserted during or after the construction of the throne. Further evidence of the tower being an addition can be seen where the cornice and tracery bottom rail, on the north side, cut right through the inner tripod post of the north (front) tripod. This tripod is very slightly bigger than the east and west tripods, so the left hand and centre details of this drawing show the cornice and bottom rail interfering less with the inner tripod posts on the other two sides.

Fig. App. 3.4a. Exeter Cathedral. Plan of central tower through middle stage vaulted canopy over St Peter.

This plan view is interesting as it shows the corner blocks to which the upper stage of the tower and spire are fixed. The footprint of the upper stages is really very small at 2 ft 6 in × 2 ft 6 in (760 × 760 mm) onto which is seated a structure 26 ft (7.925 m) high with no other support. It literally stands on the corner blocks with double tenons 3 in (75 mm) long into each corner block. The blocks themselves are poorly fixed with just one oak pin at each end of each block. The latter are recessed a very short distance below the top edges of the cornice, which will provide some stability but not much.

The blocks themselves are roughly shaped, and are not a matched set. The design and workmanship of this important junction between two major components is so different from all the other work that one cannot avoid wondering if this is an indication of different craftsmen being involved in the insertion of the tower as a last minute intervention.

Note the use of conventional masons mitre joints on the cornice of the tower, basically a standard frame construction, which has not changed to this day. These are the only mason's mitre joints on the throne.

Fig. App. 3.4b. Mirrored plan taken through central and tripod towers showing vaults.

- The central tower tracery panels are chamfered on their outside edges, and pinned to the sides of the posts. With the later advent of heating, the panels have shrunk, and, as they are fixed on each side and therefore cannot shrink, they have subsequently split. The advantage of pinning the panels in this way is that they could be fitted after the tower had been built. In all later construction, tracery panels are held in grooves in the main frame.
- The tracery on these panels is considered to be a trade-mark design of Thomas of Witney, and is found on the timber gates to the side compartments of the pulpitum and in the window fenestration of the cathedral.

Fig. App. 3. 5. Mid-sectional perspective of vault showing back face of north gable front.

The vault is very tall for its width, with the ribs rising almost vertically for a considerable portion of their height. It has been conjectured elsewhere that the vault has been raised. If this occurred during construction, the ribs could have been retained from the original height vault and lengthened. However, as there is not much other evidence of such a major intervention, this suggestion should be regarded as highly conjectural.

Figs App. 3.6a–b. South and north gable front constructions.
These drawings highlight the construction of the gable fronts and the ogee arches, and show the typical construction discussed above, where smaller pieces were added on to major components to make them complete. These drawings also demonstrate "cumulative" construction. In later construction with frames and panels, large solid areas can be made up with additional framing and panels. With the construction used for the throne, large solid areas of wood are built up by fitting one piece next to another. Most frequently, adjacent timbers were held together with loose tenons, which are tenon-shaped pieces let into mortises opposite each other in the edge of each timber. These are pinned as in a conventional mortise and tenon joint. On both Fig. App. 3.6a and b, these loose tenons can be seen to have been frequently used on every joint.

Another technique used was to reinforce joints by using oak pins rather in the manner of a modern steel nail. These can be seen fixing the tops of the crocket boards (B) together on the left drawing of Fig. App. 3.6a, also the hood (F) on the south elevation to the gable end as well as on Fig. App. 3.6a. A further example is the fixing of the carved sill of the niche on the south elevation (G), where two pins are driven diagonally through the sill into the gable end behind. These pins are oak dowels, that are carved back to a slim taper, and are often left with slight arrises which grip the hole, hence "square peg in a round hole". The pins are driven as hard as possible so that the arrises actually bite into the timber of the hole.

A third form of reinforcement can be seen where the pinnacle shafts either side of the hood to the niche on the south elevation (G) are made in three sections, which are reinforced with dowels in the centre of the shafts. These dowels are cylindrical and may have had pointed ends, and are a tight fit, but they are not driven so hard that they grip the hole in which they are fitted.

All these techniques join two pieces of wood, and if the loose tenons are draw-boarded (the holes in the tenons are very slightly offset to those in the mortises, so that as the pin is driven, it tightens the joint), they will provide a tight joint, but all of these techniques would be more long lasting if the joint was also glued. It is known that glue was used in the mid-14th century at St Stephen's, Westminster, but there is nothing documented earlier than this.[2] No investigations have been carried out at Exeter to see if there is evidence for its use on the throne.

The use should be noted of stub tenons. These are tenons formed in the solid component, over which an open ended mortise on an adjacent component fits and is pinned. They are well illustrated in Fig. App. 3.6b, where the gable end panels (D) are jointed at their bottom ends to the main ogee arches (F). It is a curious hybrid joint, but perfectly logical if one is making an object in solid construction rather than a frame construction.

Fig. App. 3.7. Composite construction details of principal corner posts.
This drawing records the many components added to make the posts. It shows a whole array of techniques for making them, from the largest pieces available as the main element, but also those attaching to the smaller pieces to make up the size. Note the long thin pieces attached to the face of the posts with in one case eight pins. Note also the addition of pinnacle gables as solid elements to one side of the crocketted tops to pinnacles as a regular technique for both of the top two pinnacles. Note that on the south-west the added piece to the top pinnacle post has sixteen pins.

Where sides have been added to posts, the pins are shown as internal dowels; they are actually pins driven from the front surface of the post, but are cut off level with the face of the recessed panel which is not shown on the drawing.

Note also the frequent use of stub tenons explained in the text on Figs App. 3.6a–b.

Fig. App. 3.8. Tripod-tower construction plans showing jointing.
Of note is that all the joints of the vault ribs are made with pins driven diagonally or crossing each other to lock their fixing of the joint. The perimeter ribs are pinned to the centre rib, but have no connection with the posts supporting the centre ribs; also the centre ribs are connected with quite different joints in the centre of each vault.

The tall canopy ribs are fixed at the top with vee joints and cross pins.

Fig. App. 3.9. Construction details through parts of central tower.
In the same way that the upper stage of the tower is poorly fixed to the lower, the spire joint with the top tabernacle could easily come adrift. The drawing shows the joint in the top right hand corner, and it will be seen from the section and Plan at D–D, that the spire ribs merely sit on very shallow platforms cut out of the inside faces of the top posts. They are secured with single diagonal pins. Any slight lean on the spire and the pins would have snapped, and there would be nothing to stop the spire from falling. Equally, any warp or twist to the posts, free standing at this point, could have created sufficient deflection to have removed the seating for the ribs, so the weight of the spire would be dependent on partially withdrawn pins.

Note the cross pinning of the spire ribs in Plan B–B is similar to that in the tall ribs to the tripod tabernacles, see Fig. App. 3.8.

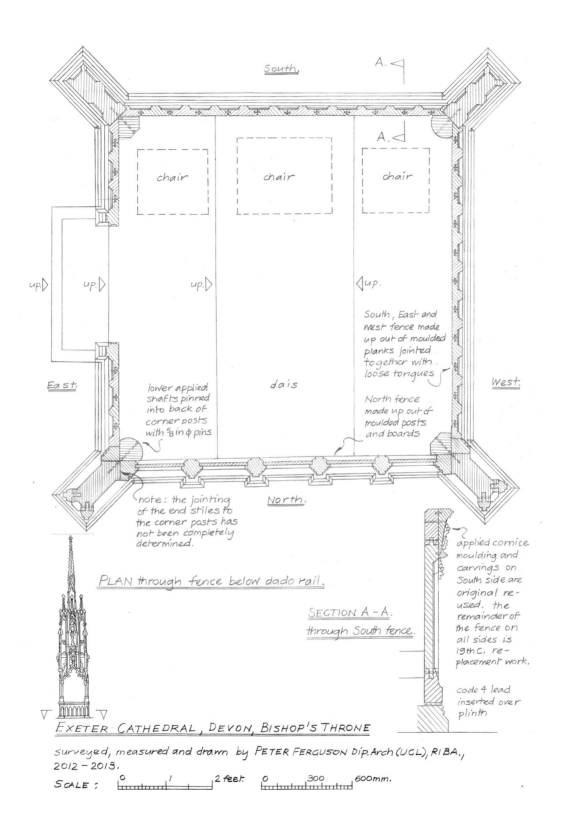

South.

A.

A.

chair   chair   chair

up. up. up. up.

South, East and
West fence made
up out of moulded
planks jointed
together with
loose tongues

East.

West.

lower applied
shafts pinned
into back of
corner posts
with ⅝ in ⌀ pins

dais

North fence
made up out of
moulded posts
and boards

note: the jointing
of the end stiles to
the corner posts has
not been completely
determined.

North.

PLAN through fence below dado rail.

SECTION A - A.
through South fence.

applied cornice
moulding and
carvings on
South side are
original re-
used. the
remainder of
the fence on
all sides is
19th C. re-
placement work.

code 4 lead
inserted over
plinth

EXETER CATHEDRAL, DEVON, BISHOP'S THRONE

surveyed, measured and drawn by PETER FERGUSON Dip. Arch (UCL), RIBA.,
2012 – 2013.

SCALE: 0   1   2 feet.   0   300   600mm.

Fig. App. 3.1a Exeter Cathedral bishop's throne. Plan and section through fence below dado rail. P. Ferguson.

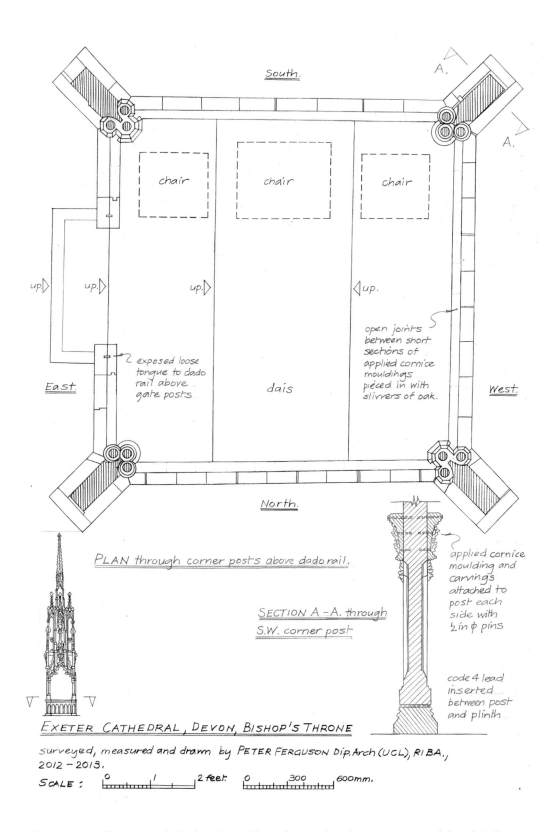

South.

A.

A.

chair   chair   chair

up.   up.   up.   ⟨up.

open joints
between short
sections of
applied cornice
mouldings
pieced in with
slivers of oak.

exposed loose
tongue to dado
rail above
gate posts

East.   dais   West.

North.

PLAN through corner posts above dado rail.

SECTION A-A. through
S.W. corner post

applied cornice
moulding and
carvings
attached to
post each
side with
½ in φ pins

code 4 lead
inserted
between post
and plinth

EXETER CATHEDRAL, DEVON, BISHOP'S THRONE

surveyed, measured and drawn by PETER FERGUSON Dip.Arch (UCL), R.I.B.A.,
2012 – 2013.

SCALE :   0   1   2 feet.   0   300   600mm.

Fig. App. 3.1b Exeter Cathedral bishop's throne. Plan and section through corner posts above dado rail. P. Ferguson.

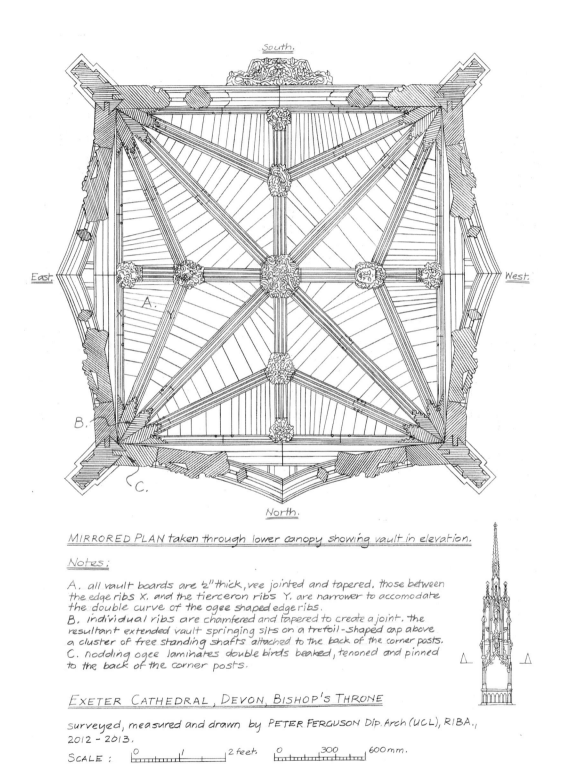

South.

East.

A.

B.

C.

West.

North.

MIRRORED PLAN taken through lower canopy showing vault in elevation.

Notes:

A. all vault boards are ½" thick, vee jointed and tapered. those between the edge ribs X. and the tierceron ribs Y. are narrower to accomodate the double curve of the ogee shaped edge ribs.
B. individual ribs are chamfered and tapered to create a joint. the resultant extended vault springing sits on a trefoil-shaped cap above a cluster of free standing shafts attached to the back of the corner posts.
C. nodding ogee laminates double birds beaked, tenoned and pinned to the back of the corner posts.

EXETER CATHEDRAL, DEVON, BISHOP'S THRONE

surveyed, measured and drawn by PETER FERGUSON Dip. Arch (UCL), RIBA., 2012 - 2013.

SCALE: 0 1 2 feet.   0 300 600mm.

Fig. App. 3.2a Exeter Cathedral bishop's throne. Mirrored plan taken through lower canopy showing vault in elevation. P. Ferguson.

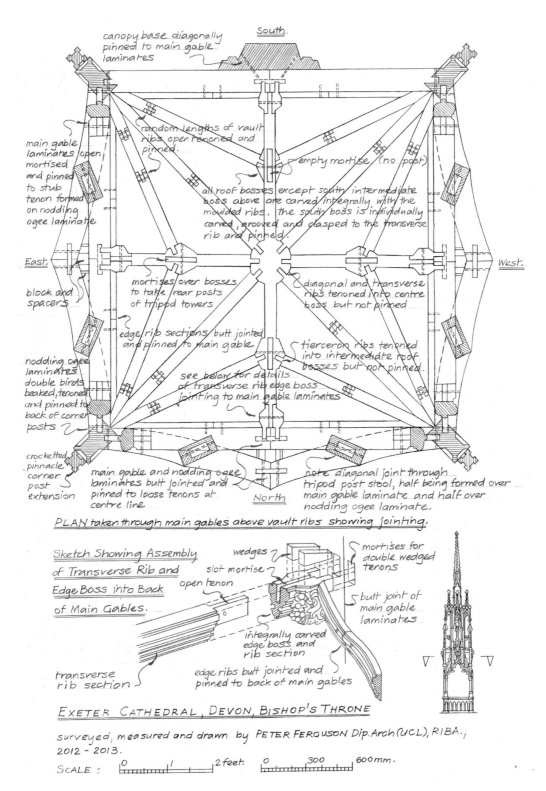

canopy base diagonally pinned to main gable laminates

random lengths of vault ribs open tenoned and pinned.

empty mortise (no post)

main gable laminates open, mortised and pinned to stub tenon formed on nodding ogee laminate

all roof bosses except south intermediate boss above are carved integrally with the moulded ribs. the south boss is individually carved, grooved and clasped to the transverse rib and pinned.

East.   West.

block and spacers

mortises over bosses to take rear posts of tripod towers

diagonal and transverse ribs tenoned into centre boss but not pinned

edge rib sections butt jointed and pinned to main gable

tierceron ribs tenoned into intermediate roof bosses but not pinned.

nodding ogee laminates double birds beaked, tenoned and pinned to back of corner posts

see below for details of transverse rib edge boss jointing to main gable laminates

crocketted pinnacle corner post extension

main gable and nodding ogee laminates butt jointed and pinned to loose tenons at centre line

note diagonal joint through tripod post stool, half being formed over main gable laminate and half over nodding ogee laminate.

North.

PLAN taken through main gables above vault ribs showing jointing.

Sketch Showing Assembly of Transverse Rib and Edge Boss into Back of Main Gables.

wedges

slot mortise

open tenon

mortises for double wedged tenons

butt joint of main gable laminates

integrally carved edge boss and rib section

transverse rib section

edge ribs butt jointed and pinned to back of main gables

EXETER CATHEDRAL, DEVON, BISHOP'S THRONE

surveyed, measured and drawn by PETER FERGUSON Dip.Arch (UCL), RIBA., 2012 - 2013.

SCALE :   0   1   2 feet.   0   300   600mm.

Fig. App. 3.2b Exeter Cathedral bishop's throne. Plan taken through main gables above vault ribs showing jointing. P. Ferguson.

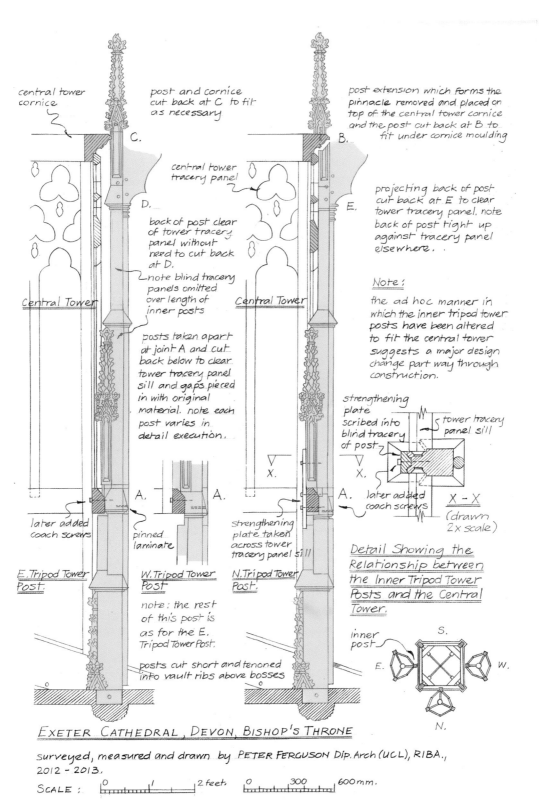

central tower cornice

post and cornice cut back at C to fit as necessary

post extension which forms the pinnacle removed and placed on top of the central tower cornice and the post cut back at B to fit under cornice moulding

C.

B.

central tower tracery panel

D.

E.

projecting back of post cut back at E to clear tower tracery panel. note back of post tight up against tracery panel elsewhere.

back of post clear of tower tracery panel without need to cut back at D.

note blind tracery panels omitted over length of inner posts

Central Tower

Central Tower

Note:

the ad hoc manner in which the inner tripod tower posts have been altered to fit the central tower suggests a major design change part way through construction.

posts taken apart at joint A and cut back below to clear tower tracery panel sill and gaps pieced in with original material. note each post varies in detail execution.

strengthening plate scribed into blind tracery of post

tower tracery panel sill

X.

X.

X - X

(drawn 2× scale)

A.

A.

A.

later added coach screws

later added coach screws

pinned laminate

strengthening plate taken across tower tracery sill

Detail Showing the Relationship between the Inner Tripod Tower Posts and the Central Tower.

E. Tripod Tower Post.

W. Tripod Tower Post

N. Tripod Tower Post.

inner post

S.

note: the rest of this post is as for the E. Tripod Tower Post.

E.

W.

posts cut short and tenoned into vault ribs above bosses

N.

EXETER CATHEDRAL, DEVON, BISHOP'S THRONE

surveyed, measured and drawn by PETER FERGUSON Dip. Arch (UCL), RIBA., 2012 - 2013.

SCALE :   0   1   2 feet.   0   300   600 mm.

Fig. App. 3.3 Exeter Cathedral bishop's throne. Detail showing relationship between inner tripod towers and central tower. P. Ferguson.

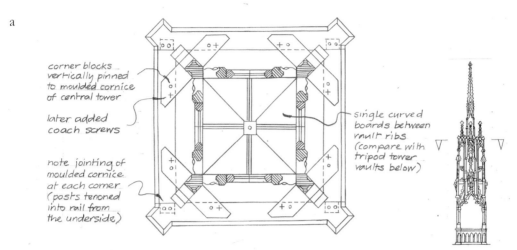

a

corner blocks vertically pinned to moulded cornice of central tower

later added coach screws

note jointing of moulded cornice at each corner (posts tenoned into rail from the underside)

single curved boards between vault ribs (compare with tripod tower vaults below)

PLAN of central tower taken through middle stage vaulted canopy over St. Peter.

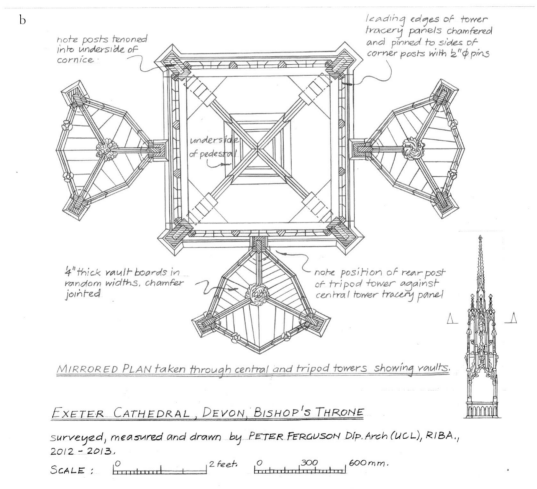

b

note posts tenoned into underside of cornice.

leading edges of tower tracery panels chamfered and pinned to sides of corner posts with ½"ø pins

underside of pedestal

4" thick vault boards in random widths, chamfer jointed

note position of rear post of tripod tower against central tower tracery panel

MIRRORED PLAN taken through central and tripod towers showing vaults.

EXETER CATHEDRAL, DEVON, BISHOP'S THRONE

surveyed, measured and drawn by PETER FERGUSON Dip. Arch (UCL), RIBA., 2012 - 2013.

SCALE: 0   2 feet.   0   300   600 mm.

Fig. App. 3.4a Exeter Cathedral bishop's throne. Plan of central tower taken through middle stage vaulted canopy over St. Peter. P. Ferguson. b Exeter Cathedral bishop's throne. Mirrored plan taken through central and tripod towers showing vaults. P. Ferguson.

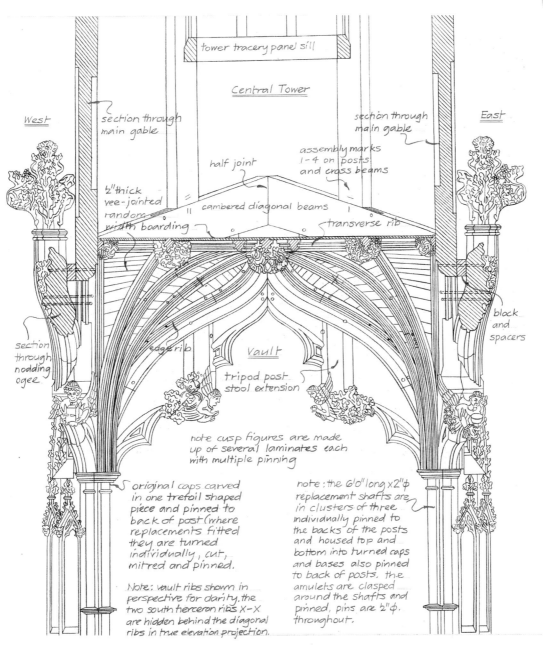

tower tracery panel sill

Central Tower

West

section through main gable

section through main gable

East

half joint

assembly marks 1-4 on posts and cross beams

½" thick vee-jointed random width boarding

cambered diagonal beams

transverse rib

block and spacers

section through nodding ogee

edge rib

Vault

tripod post stool extension

note cusp figures are made up of several laminates each with multiple pinning

original caps carved in one trefoil shaped piece and pinned to back of post (where replacements fitted they are turned individually, cut, mitred and pinned.

Note: vault ribs shown in perspective for clarity, the two south tierceron ribs X-X are hidden behind the diagonal ribs in true elevation projection.

note: the 6'0" long x 2"φ replacement shafts are in clusters of three individually pinned to the backs of the posts and housed top and bottom into turned caps and bases also pinned to back of posts. the amulets are clasped around the shafts and pinned, pins are ½"φ throughout.

Mid-Sectional Perspective of the Vault showing Back Face of North Gable Front.

EXETER CATHEDRAL, DEVON, BISHOP'S THRONE

surveyed, measured and drawn by PETER FERGUSON Dip. Arch (UCL), RIBA., 2012 - 2013.

SCALE: 0 — 1 — 2 feet. 0 — 300 — 600mm.

Fig. App. 3.5 Exeter Cathedral bishop's throne. Mid-sectional perspective of the vault showing back face of north gable front.

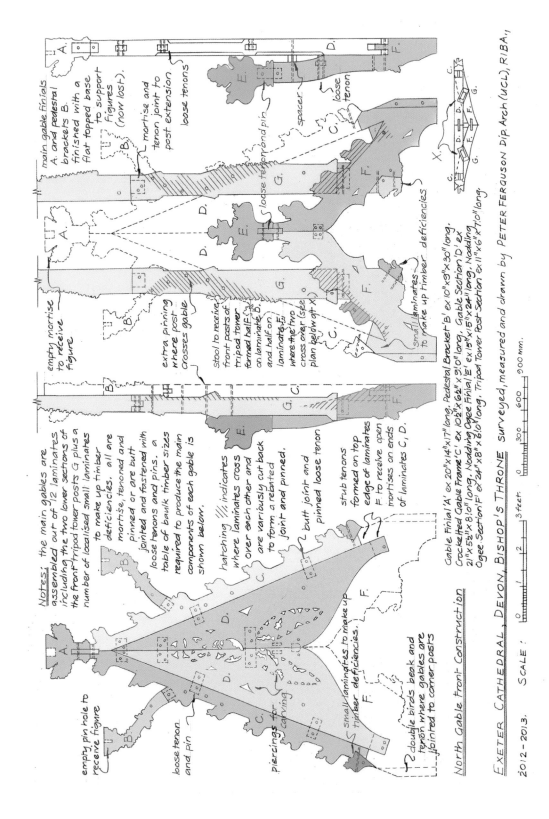

Notes: the main gables are assembled out of 12 laminates including the two lower sectors of the front tripod tower posts G plus a number of localised small laminates to make up timber deficiencies, all are mortise, tenoned and pinned or are butt jointed and fastened with loose tenons and pins. a table of baulk timber sizes required to produce the main components of each gable is shown below.

hatching ///, indicates where laminates cross over each other and are variously cut back to form a rebated joint and pinned.

empty pin hole to receive figure

loose tenon and pin

piercings for carving

2 double birds beak and tenon where gables are jointed to corner posts

main gable finials A. and pedestal brackets B. finished with a flat topped base to support figures B. (now lost).

empty mortise to receive figure

extra pinning where post crosses gable

mortise and tenon joint to post extension

loose tenons

loose tenon and pin

spacer

loose tenon

Stool to receive front posts of tripod tower formed half on laminate D. and half on laminate E. where the two cross over (see plan below at X.)

small laminates to make up timber deficiencies

small laminates to make up timber deficiencies

stub tenons formed on top edge of laminates F. to receive open mortises on ends of laminates C, D.

butt joint and pinned loose tenon

North Gable Front Construction

Gable Finial 'A' ex 20"x14"x17" long, Pedestal Bracket 'B' ex 10"x9"x30" long, Crocketted Gable Frame 'C' ex 10½"x62" x 3'.0" long, Gable Section 'D' ex 21"x5½"x 8'.0" long, Nodding Ogee Finial 'E' ex 15"x15"x24" long, Nodding Ogee Section 'F' ex 24"x8" x 6'.0" long, Tripod Tower Post Section ex 11"x6" x 7'.0" long.

2012 - 2013.   SCALE !   0   1   2   3 feet

0   300   600   900 mm.

EXETER CATHEDRAL, DEVON, BISHOP'S THRONE surveyed, measured and drawn by PETER FERGUSON Dip Arch (UCL), RIBA.,

Fig. App. 3.6a Exeter Cathedral bishop's throne. North gable front construction. Tripod posts are coloured green.

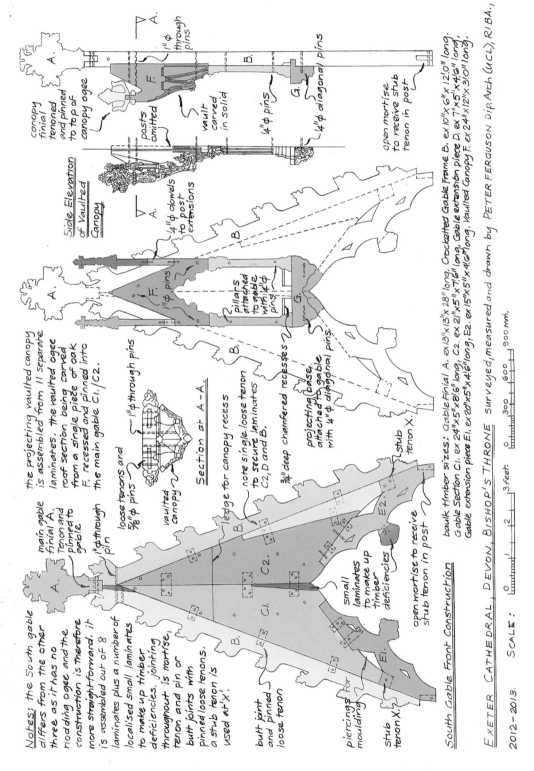

Fig. App. 3.6b Exeter Cathedral bishop's throne. South gable front construction.

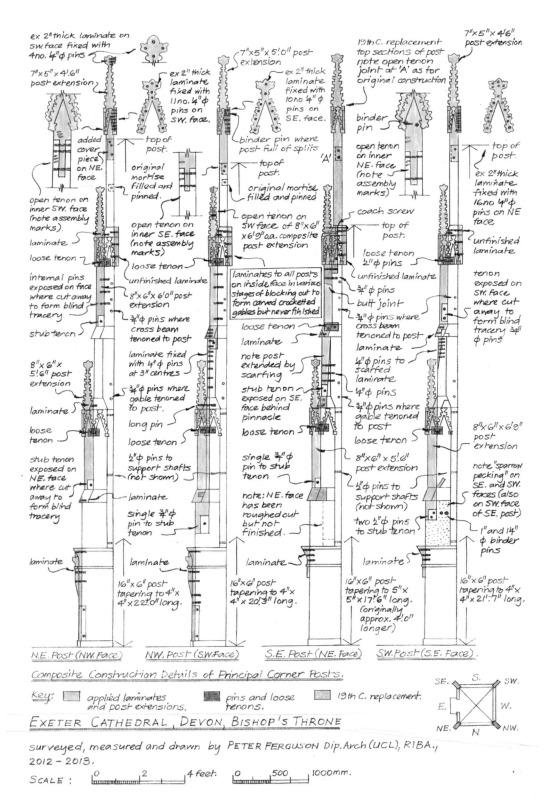

Fig. App. 3.7 Exeter Cathedral bishop's throne. Composite construction details of principal corner posts. P. Ferguson.

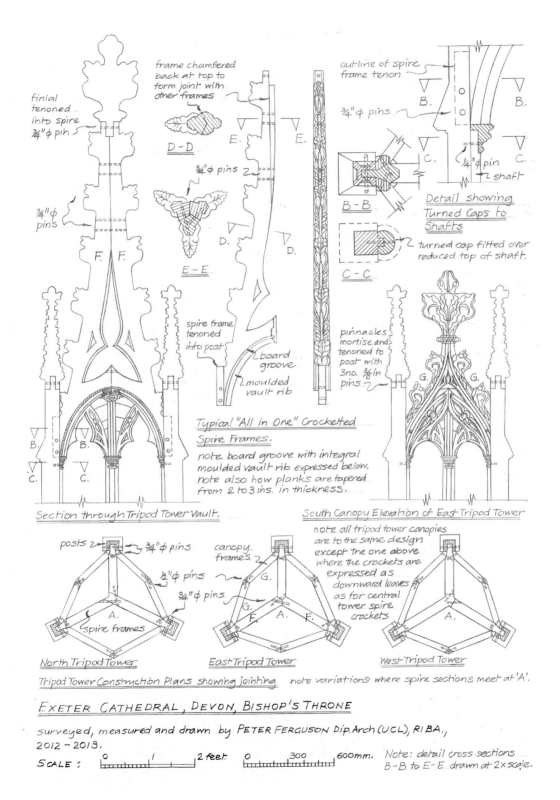

Fig. App. 3.8. Exeter Cathedral bishop's throne. Tripod tower construction plans showing jointing. P. Ferguson.

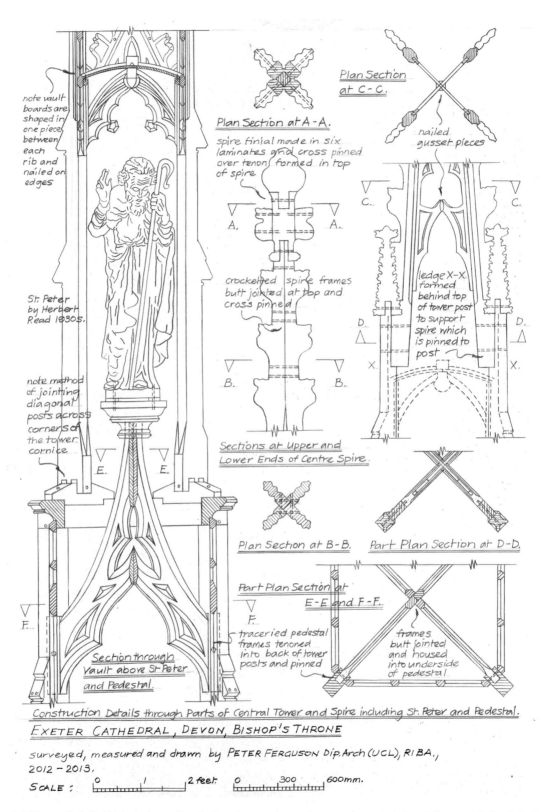

note vault
boards are
shaped in
one piece
between
each
rib and
nailed on
edges

St. Peter
by Herbert
Read 1930s.

note method
of jointing
diagonal
posts across
corners of
the tower
cornice

Section through
Vault above St. Peter
and Pedestal.

Plan Section at A-A.

spire finial made in six
laminates and cross pinned
over tenon formed in top
of spire

crocketted spire frames
butt jointed at top and
cross pinned

Sections at Upper and
Lower Ends of Centre Spire.

Plan Section at B-B.

Part Plan Section at
E-E and F-F.

traceried pedestal
frames tenoned
into back of tower
posts and pinned

Plan Section
at C-C.

nailed
gusset pieces

ledge X-X
formed
behind top
of tower post
to support
spire which
is pinned to
post

Part Plan Section at D-D.

frames
butt jointed
and housed
into underside
of pedestal.

Construction Details through Parts of Central Tower and Spire including St. Peter and Pedestal.

EXETER CATHEDRAL, DEVON, BISHOP'S THRONE

surveyed, measured and drawn by PETER FERGUSON Dip. Arch (UCL), RIBA.,
2012 – 2013.

SCALE: 0   1   2 feet.   0   300   600mm.

Fig. App. 3.9 Exeter Cathedral bishop's throne. Details through parts of central tower and spire including St Peter and Pedestal. P. Ferguson.

St Davids

The bishop's throne at St Davids Cathedral dates from *c.* 1340, some 30 years later than that of Exeter (Fig. App. 3.10; Tip-ins 2.2.1, 2.2.2, 2.2.3). Though only just over half the height of Exeter's throne at 27 ft 7 in (8.25 m) (including its stone platform), it is nonetheless an impressive structure and would have been comparable in scale to Exeter's throne had the latter been completed without the secondary central tower and spire.[3] The design concept however, is markedly different from the Exeter approach where the bishop's seat itself was an independent piece of furniture made prominent by being set under a huge canopy. At St Davids, the bishop's seat is an integral part of the complete structure and its seat back rail and arm rests are part of the structural frame. This also applies to the supporting chaplains' seats which take on an importance of their own, expressed as part of the throne's overall design concept, an option not considered at Exeter. The St Davids throne would have been a better candidate for building in stone than that at Exeter, as in essence it is only three sided (yet the decision to build in timber is not readily understood).

The transition from solid to framed construction

The Welsh throne has all the indications of a framed structure with its four back posts linked by mortise and tenon jointed rails, both at the base and at vault springing height. No pins were found on any of these horizontals, though the mortises and tenons were accessible for measurement. The pins were hidden in the front by the vaults and the seat boards whilst at the rear they were covered by a later applied Victorian panel. By inference pins must be present, otherwise, the joints would have opened up or come apart, and pinning is consistent where other mortise and tenon joints occur on the structure.

As at Exeter no evidence was found pointing to the use of glue to reinforce the joints. However it seems likely that glue was used, particularly where mitred joints occur, because on the vaulted canopy gables the butt joints, cut on the mitre, are only held together by cross pinning in one direction. The framed construction is continued with the jointing of the front posts to the bishop's chair where the moulded arm rails are mortised, tenoned and pinned to the front and back posts in a curious mixture of mason's mitres and sinkings, thus doubling up as a mid-rail as does the moulded seat back rail to the bishop's chair which is tenoned into the back posts, but off-set and detached from the back panelling. Another curiosity is the jointing of the very similar chaplains' seat back rails which are roughly chamfered to the line of the back post mouldings with no attempt at scribing and are merely once pinned through to the posts at each end.

We therefore have a perfectly formed frame. Yet we still have evidence of the earlier technique of solid construction, as seen at Exeter, particularly in the traceried vault rails, which are each formed from one large piece of timber[4] and the four back posts, which are also made in one piece.[5] Of solid construction, these posts are extraordinarily complex with joints on at least three of the four sides. This means that, in the first place, the carpenters had to set out, in vertical terms, where the carving was placed, but to leave "full" all the areas where joints were positioned, because, in the time taken to carve all the foliage and mouldings, the post would have certainly shrunk or expanded as it was emerging from the huge original baulk. The faces of the joints would have been "shot" when construction began.

Considering the weight of the posts, manoeuvring them to fit in the same plane, as well as the woodwork intersecting at right or oblique angles in the case of the vaults, the risk of damage occurring to the crockets would have been high. This may indicate that carving could have been roughed out and then completed after assembly. As no running of mouldings with a carpenter's plane was possible, these would no doubt have been carved as well. The reduction in size of the original baulk from top to bottom would have created so much potential for unequal loss of moisture that the posts would have needed to be well seasoned before work started. The timber would also have had to have been of high quality, that is, slow grown with long straight grain, and largely free of knots, splits or sapwood. It is unlikely that such trees would have been readily available locally given the topography and climatic exposure of West Wales. Dendrochronology has not been attempted to establish its origin, but the Baltic seems a possibility, as the timber could have conveniently been brought in by sea.

What one has to remember is that these posts had to remain perfect in their geometry on all four sides to accommodate the joints connecting the other components on three of the sides. Should the posts have shrunk in width, it would have affected the joints on either side. Brett Wright, an experienced professional ecclesiastical joiner, has suggested that to make these posts all in one, he would have first squared up the baulk timber well oversized, in this case at about 12 × 10 in (305 × 254 mm), left it for a month or two allowing it to move whilst he got out the components which were to be jointed to it. He would then have re-squared it, and cut in all the jointing before carrying out primary assembly. The foliage meanwhile would have been roughed out ready to carve before final assembly.

Evidence of alteration to the throne since completion

Unlike Exeter's throne, St Davids is not a completely free standing structure, though it could have been if the smaller east and west front posts had been taken down to ground level and not tenoned into the two chaplains' seat boards. Evidence remaining on the east and west back posts, which differ from each other in detail, particularly in the jointing, suggests that the throne may have been designed integrally with a return high level screen to the east and the original choir stalls to the west[6] and possibly all in conjunction with a fence. The east back post has a high level redundant joint with an empty mortise for a cornice or head beam whilst the west back post has a redundant vertical slot just above the top of the fence for a 15 × 1½ in (381 × 38 mm) thick panel, both of which extend northwards at right-angles to the throne's back screen. As now configured, the throne is attached to the largely reconstructed fence[7] and, albeit crudely, to the chancel screen suggesting that the screen and the throne have at some time been moved.

The construction described

Each of the three seats has a vaulted canopy planned as half a hexagon with three gabled fronts. In the case of the chaplains' seats, the gables are mitred and pinned at the front and tenoned into the back posts, the tenons being cut at an angle. The canopy for the bishop's chair is altogether much larger and projected forward onto the two front posts, into which the half hexagon three gabled front is tenoned. Unlike at Exeter where the vaults (excluding the central spire) are fully framed and boarded between ribs, St Davids is a hybrid being almost a prototype for timber vault construction. The realisation of the geometry is not fully resolved in its construction. The vaults over the two chaplains' seats revert to the earlier solid construction with no ribs. Each of the spandrels are carved to their correct curves out of the solid and finished approximately 1 inch (25 mm) thick, butt-jointed to each other and edge-dowelled. The vault above the bishop's chair is more complex. The spandrel panels are still carved from solid, but are edge-nailed to the top of the moulded ribs. The ribs are scribed at their springing and diagonally pinned singularly to the inner face of the canopy, whilst at the top they come together centrally, being chamfered to fit and pinned to the underside of the cross beam above the vault. The joint is covered by a shallow carved boss,[8] centre-nailed up into the cross beam. The two front spandrels are not divided by a rib but revert to a butt-joint and edge-dowelling.

The structure is continued above the vault in the case of the chaplains' seats by matching three-sided lofty enclosed spires.

The spire frames are tapered, curved and carved with graduated crockets and are of large cross section at the bases, they are half jointed and pinned over the back of the front gable and the traceried arch rail at the rear. The two back frames where they converge at the top are diagonally half jointed together whilst the front frame meets them at right-angles on plan being scribed and pinned at the centre point of the half joint. Single radially split boards are cut, bevelled and nailed between the spire frames at the front with a similar board being nailed over the rear face of the back frames. The carved finial at the top of the spires is

halved over the top of the frames flush with the back board and attached by the same pin which secures the three spire frames.

The structure over the bishop's seat is designed as a three tier tower surmounted by an open spire. An examination of each tier in section suggests a certain paucity of framed structure, relying heavily on edge-nailed infill boards without full intermediate horizontal railing. As with the spires over the chaplains' seats, the boards are not fitted to the frames in rebates or grooves but are chamfered and scribed to abut the posts. Most of the boards are radially split with each panel formed out of two boards. These are butt-jointed and edge-dowelled to the front (north) of the throne, and are vee-jointed at the back (south) suggesting that the throne was made as though it was to have an unseen back. Yet we know it was always seen because it had contemporary paintings on the back.

The front panel boards to the lowest tier are fitted directly to the corner posts and each pierced by two small plain lancet openings. The intermediate tier is fitted with a traceried arch sub-frame the head of which is mortised and tenoned into the corner posts and the back sub-frame fitted with nailed closed boarding. The top tier on plan presents a curious form of construction relying entirely upon nailed boarding to enclose the frame. Four boards are chamfered to fit diagonally across the opening and are nailed to the posts. They meet somewhat haphazardly in the middle and are connected to each other by diagonal nailing. Three additional boards are chamfered on their vertical leading edges to fit between the diagonal boards on the east, north and west elevations, being deep set behind the corner posts. The back board to the south is edge-nailed to the face of the back corner posts.

Above the top tier, the central tower is crowned by a tall four-sided open-crocketted spire, its frames being pinned from the underside to the covering boards placed behind the projecting ogee gable fronts. Following the precedent set by the earlier solid construction used elsewhere, one might have expected the gables to have been made in one piece. They are, however, made in two halves inclusive of the finial and are butt jointed at the centre and pinned across the angled joints so formed. As with the centre spire, the four corner posts of each of the tiers are tenoned into covering boards or bearers spanning each level interchange.

Extent of decay and restoration

The corner posts are all carried up well beyond the structure they support and are finished with tall crocketted pinnacles. Elegant swan-necked flying buttresses support the intermediate tier of the central tower. These are tapered and crocketted, and mortised and tenoned into the corner posts at top and bottom. They reflect the design of the ogee gables above and below, all of which combine to produce a well-balanced profile on a grand scale, corresponding in

degree to the high office of bishop. When first completed, the throne must have looked magnificent, as evidence shows that the structure was fully polychromed. At the lower level, the throne seems to have been scrubbed clean during Gilbert Scott's late-19th-century restoration, only minute fragments of paint surviving, but enough to indicate that against a background colour of red and to a lesser extent green, the decoration included gold leaf and delicately executed figure painting behind the three seats beneath the vault. In addition there were the upper six panels of the central tower and also the south facing back boards. By Scott's time, the throne was in a state of some decay and neglect, and much of the timber and carving was damaged by exposure to the elements from the leaking choir and presbytery roofs. Gilbert Scott repaired and renewed possibly up to a third of the structure from top to bottom including much high level carved work and the majority of the surrounding fence.

There is very little to suggest that many repairs were carried out in the intervening centuries since the throne was completed, with the exception of accommodation work when the original choir stalls were replaced and the throne moved. The obviously altered relationship between the presbytery screen and the throne still remains unsolved, but the meeting of the two structures at the south east corner must rank amongst the poorest executed alteration jobs undertaken in such a prominent location in a cathedral.

Fig. App. 3.10. Elevations and sections through outer back post east. This drawing highlights the complex task of making each of the back posts out of one piece of timber.

Notes

1. See Chapter 2.1, 32 and n. 23.
2. Tracy 1987, appendix ii.
3. The height to the top of Exeter's tripod towers is 34 ft 3 in (11.273 m).
4. The posts are 10½ × 8 in (267 × 203 mm) × up to 15 ft (4.6 m) long, finished size.
5. 18 × 5 × 39 in (407 × 127 × 990 mm) for the chaplains' seats, 25 × 3 × 48 in (635 × 76 × 1219 mm) for the bishop's seat.
6. The present choir stalls were added in the late-15th century.
7. By George Gilbert Scott.
8. A 19th-century replacement.

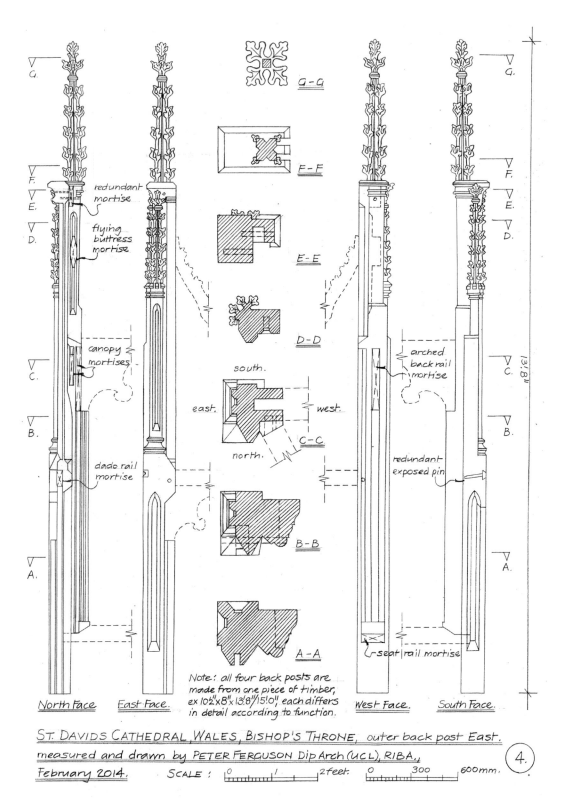

G-G

F-F

E-E

D-D

C-C

south.

east.   west.

north.

B-B

A-A

redundant mortise

flying buttress mortise

canopy mortises

dado rail mortise

arched back rail mortise

redundant exposed pin

seat rail mortise

North Face   East Face.

West Face.   South Face.

Note: all four back posts are made from one piece of timber, ex 10'2" x 8" x 13'8"/15'0", each differs in detail according to function.

ST. DAVIDS CATHEDRAL, WALES, BISHOP'S THRONE, outer back post East. measured and drawn by PETER FERGUSON Dip Arch (UCL), RIBA., February 2014.   SCALE :   0   1   2 feet.   0   300   600mm.

④

Fig. App. 3.10 St Davids Cathedral. Construction details of east back post. P. Ferguson

Appendix IV

The medieval polychromy scheme of the Exeter Cathedral bishop's throne: a summary

Eddie Sinclair

Introduction

The throne today is, to all intents and purposes, an unpainted oak structure. To the medieval craftsman who made it, this would have appeared unfinished. At that time surfaces, whether of wood, stone, metal or plaster, were habitually disguised with layers of paint and gilt. It was the intention of the present survey to search for the remains of colour.[1]

Close examination revealed that the throne was once aglow with polychromy, but its surfaces have, evidently, been the subject of many interventions over the past 700 years (see Fig. 2.1.20). Sadly, it was subjected to a highly efficient programme of stripping under George Gilbert Scott, when most of the paint was removed; presumably, it suffered further inevitable removal of surface coatings when it was dismantled in 1941, and later reconstructed by Herbert Read.

Inspection of the 14th-century choir vault above the throne has shown that Scott's recreation of the polychromy on its ribs and bosses is darker, duller and heavier than the original medieval scheme, and lacks its subtlety, richness and vitality. On the other hand, it does recognise the importance of colour and, to some extent, is more authentic than the present appearance of the throne.

Background summary

- The oak throne of 1313–1324 and the documentation relating to it has been fully discussed above.[2]
- Some of the early furnishings in the cathedral were repainted in the medieval period.
- In 1669, the Duke of Tuscany's secretary referred to the throne as "a marble tabernacle".[3] It may have been repainted in the 17th century, or the remark may have been a misinterpretation of the medieval scheme.[4]
- Under Dean Milles, in the early 1780s, the whole interior of the cathedral was colour-washed with the application of a buff yellow for walls and brown wash for the columns. The throne may have been cleaned at this time and/or given this wash.[5]
- In the 1870s, Scott stripped the throne, uncovering traces of white and gold.[6]
- It was dismantled by Herbert Read in 1941, and reassembled in 1947.
- It was cleaned and waxed in 1967, 1973 and 1982.

Inspection

Detailed inspection of all the surfaces of the throne was carried out with 6× hand-lenses and with strong daylight illumination, with the eyes close to the wood surface. In spite of the excellence of the scaffold, poles obstructed various portions of the monument, preventing their close examination. A total of 85 paint samples was taken for analysis, as well as the two comparative samples each from the sedilia and Bishop Stapeldon's tomb. All remnants of paint and possible paint deposits were plotted on detailed photographs. Samples were examined under a microscope before being sent away for analysis. The methodological techniques employed are described in the full report. The following pages document some of the discoveries made during the survey.

Summary of findings

Paint

Fragments of paint were found on all levels of the throne, even on the interior. Higher up, paint traces become less frequent although fragments of bright colour were also found (Fig. App. 4.1). Red, green and white are the most frequently surviving colours.

Analysis, by Catherine Hassall, identified:

- Two medieval paint schemes.
- Polished-looking deposits of lead white paint. It is unclear whether these represent the original preparation layers or a later marbling scheme.
- Many different surface coatings, such as brown distemper, graining schemes and staining, reflecting later changes.
- Traces of a 20th-century green were found in several locations.

There are not many uncarved parts of the throne. Such surfaces, along with large sweeps of mouldings, are likely to have been decorated with devices such as sheets of tin-relief imitating beaten metal or textiles.[7] The painter would have used such techniques to transform wood into the appearance of a more costly medium.[8]

Although there are no clues as to how the flat surfaces such as the crenellated boards may have been painted, a device such as a fictive masonry pattern may have provided a backdrop for more ornate decoration.[9]

Analysis of original scheme

Analysis was carried out by Catherine Hassall, who examined paint samples under low magnification, then mounted part of each specimen in cold-setting polyester resin, before cutting a cross section for examination at high magnification in halogen and UV fluorescent light. Material from the coloured layers was dispersed on glass slides and the pigments identified by polarised light microscopy.

Ground

On all levels, both inside and outside, the same preparatory layers were applied.

The first coat, a layer of white chalk-based gesso, was present in all the samples; it varied in thickness and in some areas was just a smear. It was followed by a thick white ground consisting of more than one coat of lead white oil paint.[10] In most samples three layers were found but in some places only two appear. A little red lead was added to the under-layers of the ground, whilst the final coat was pure white.[11]

The samples from the sedilia, and one from Stapeldon's tomb also displayed this sequence of the preparatory layers, with a white gesso, followed by a white oil containing a little red lead. This careful degree of preparation indicates a high level of craftsmanship and care, with an eye for longevity. The preparation of the timber with layers of white oil paint echoed that used in the wooden vaults of the cathedral transepts, which were painted to match the adjacent stone vaults.

Paint layers

Most of the samples showed a single coat of coloured paint on the white ground layers, but the greens and blues were also given undercoats. A green glaze was painted over a grey undercoat of lead white, mixed with charcoal black. The artificial copper green, which *may* be part of the original scheme (see full report), was also painted over a lead white and charcoal black mixture. In most of the other samples, which had two layers, one of the colours appeared to be "tailing off", suggesting that we are probably seeing an overlap, rather than interactive layers.

Samples taken from crockets show vermilion over black; this too may be an overlap. However, it is unclear how the black and red relate to each other, as both appear to be from one scheme. Perhaps the corners of the crockets were given extra definition at this height, and touches of black were used to enhance or outline the shadows, which were then given a brush-over with the red in the usual manner, leaving a black edge visible in places. There is no evidence of an original varnish.

Pigments

Although paint deposits were for the most part extremely fragmentary, apart from the white, the indications are that the same materials were used over the whole height of the throne, giving a general palette of red, green, black and white, with yellow appearing lower down.[12] Of the blues, indigo and azurite were only found at ground level, though a bluey-grey mix is seen frequently (see below). It is likely that these costly colours were used elsewhere but no traces have been found; they may have been confined to sculptures destroyed at the Reformation, or used in the vaulting, which has been well stripped.

Analysis revealed that in the medieval period the throne was decorated with the following pigments, although it is not always clear to which scheme these belong (see below): vermilion, red lead, red ochre, orpiment, yellow ochre, iron oxide brown (not definitely original), charcoal black, lead white, copper green glaze, verdigris, artificial copper carbonate green/blue, indigo, azurite and gold.[13]

Organic pigments may have been used but these will have faded and are no longer detectable. The discovery of many traces of artificial copper greens indicates that this colour played an important role. It appears to have been used to paint selected mouldings, as well as the many crockets that adorn the posts, canopies, pinnacles and spire. The orpiment is probably from the first scheme,[14] whereas the yellow ochre and gold, overlying it in the cross-

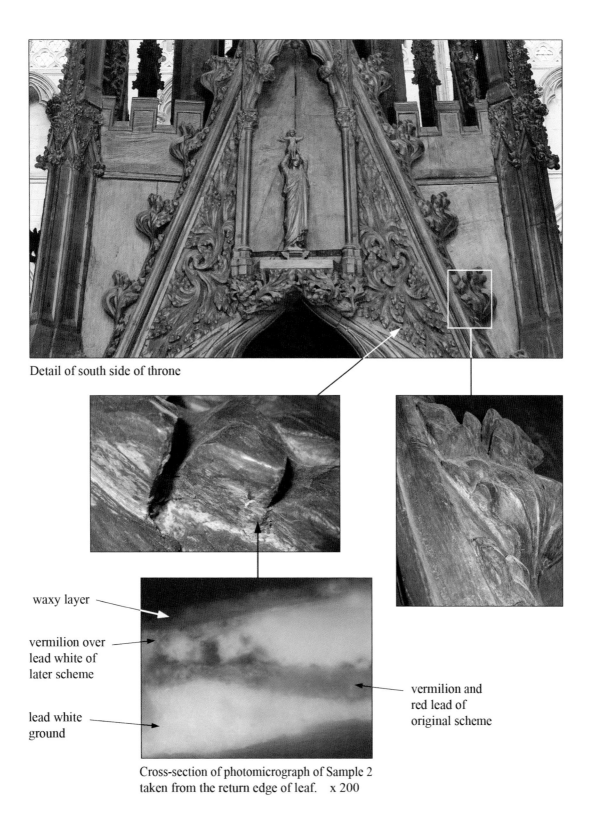

Detail of south side of throne

waxy layer

vermilion over
lead white of
later scheme

lead white
ground

vermilion and
red lead of
original scheme

Cross-section of photomicrograph of Sample 2
taken from the return edge of leaf.   x 200

Fig. App. 4.1 Exeter Cathedral, bishop's throne. Examples of the most frequent survival of a bright red, found throughout the monument on the return edges of leaves, crockets and many mouldings. Analysis revealed two medieval red schemes. The vermilion is mixed with a little red lead, and in two locations there is also the addition of lead white. Analysis E. Sinclair and Catherine Hassall. E. Sinclair.

sections, could be from a subsequent decoration (see "Later decoration" below). Orpiment is a problematic pigment and further evidence may have been missed.

Mixed colours:

- The bright red used on the crockets was vermilion mixed with a small amount of red lead, used to eke out the more costly vermilion as well as to brighten it.
- The flesh tone on the figurative boss above the seated bishop's head was a mix of lead white and vermilion. Pink was also noted under orpiment and the artificial copper carbonate, but it is not clear if this is an undercoat or part of the original scheme.
- A grey-brown, which may be the remains of a faded colour, consisting of lead white, black and a brown translucent organic pigment. Since this occurs on its own, it may have been an intended colour, but it could have been an undercoat for a layer of blue or green, since lost.
- Grey consisting of lead white and charcoal black. In places this could be an undercoat for the copper-green glaze. Elsewhere a paler grey, with less black in the mix might be an undercoat for a lost blue.

Medium

Although no medium analysis was carried out, there are indications that it was oil. There are many references in the fabric accounts to the purchase of oil.[15] The presence of small amounts of red lead mixed with the carbon black suggests that oil is the binder; as carbon black dries poorly in oil, it needs metallic pigments to catalyse the process.

The orpiment (sulphide of arsenic) is richly bound in a medium that has now turned a brownish colour. This has protected this problematic pigment and explains why the bright yellow has not discoloured. Normally where orpiment survives, not only does it turn brown but it causes other colours to deteriorate.

Glue was probably used with the chalk in the first ground layer and it is likely to have been used with the artificial copper-carbonate green, which tends to be dark in oil.

Later decoration

Unfortunately, within the limited space of this appendix, it has not been possible to précis the author's comments in this regard. They can be accessed in the copy of the full report at the Exeter Cathedral Library.

The present appearance of the throne

Nowadays the woodwork of the throne appears dull and sadly lacking in lustre. The thick beeswax with which it has been coated several times since the 1960s remains sticky, with considerable debris and harmful dust embedded in the coating. In places this has become opaque, leaving the wood looking grey and deadened. However, cleaning tests

in a number of locations showed that removal of the wax would be problematic and probably unrealistic; the use of solvents on a large scale would present a safety hazard and would probably produce imperfect results. By 2012 the throne was extremely dusty, and before the survey could begin, a week was spent dusting with brushes and a vacuum. A total of *c.* 5 kg of surface dust was removed from the throne. Since it was last vacuumed in 1982, this has accumulated in the last 30 years.

At the very least, the wax should be buffed and reconstituted, which will help the surface to resist the dust for a time, and greatly improve the appearance. It will, however, require periodic housekeeping.

Conclusions

Whilst it is unfortunate that so little early paint survives on the throne, this survey has revealed some tantalising glimpses of how richly decorated it once was. Paint analysis goes one step further in identifying different decorative schemes and a rich bright medieval palette.

Through looking at all the evidence, it becomes possible to envisage a throne clad in a forest of green foliage, defined by brilliant red, crisp white and gold (Fig. App. 4.2). Apart from the angels bearing instruments of the papal mass, it was inhabited by painted carved beasts, bishops and statues of saints. Its most important east face was clad in dense symbolic vine leaves and grapes, and must have been particularly richly painted. Clearly visible from the aisle, the south aspect displays the finely carved painted heads, traditionally regarded as those of Bishop Stapeldon and Edward II, looking down on the passer-by. They are mounted on an inhabited niche to create an hierarchical tableau.

From his vantage point, within the throne, the bishop looked up to an ornate vault with gilded bosses, sumptuous bunches of grapes and one sole figurative foliate head. He was surrounded by swooping angels emerging from gilded foliage or the clouds of heaven, presenting him with the instruments of the papal mass. If the vault is a secondary insertion, initially, the bishop would have looked up into the secret space of the painted inner structure, inhabited, as elsewhere, with carved heads of beasts gazing down on him alone. At this level, the presence of azurite on the corner posts indicates that the scheme was painted in the costly colours of the choir vault.

The throne is thus entirely fitting for the context in which it is sited. Gold and azure bosses and corbels, spanned by decorated ribs, create a peerless canopy of honour; and to either side were the magnificent high altar and pulpitum.

From the west end of the cathedral, visitors would glimpse in the distance, beyond the lavish stone pulpitum, a pinnacle of green, red and white soaring to the vault, enclosing, most probably, the life-size figure of St Peter. The

Fig. App. 4.2 Exeter Cathedral, bishop's throne. Coloured reconstruction detail of central high vault and spire. It is based on the throne survey and paint analysis, as well as information from other medieval decorative schemes, both within the cathedral and elsewhere. The main structure has been painted to look like white marble. There are many traces of lead white oil paint from the medieval schemes, as well as later decoration, that could relate to such a scheme. The account of the visit of the Duke of Tuscany in 1669, in which the throne is described as a "marble tabernacle", could refer to a 17th century scheme or be a reference to the misunderstood remnants of the medieval decorations. This is one interpretation of the fragmentary evidence. It indicates the use of gilded punched tin-relief decoration on surfaces depicted as white here. Where the medieval white survives it could belong to preparatory layers for this sophisticated technique. Both reconstructions (see also Fig. 2.1.20) need to be viewed as presenting differing possibilities. Notice Scott's 19th-century colour scheme for the high vault. Analysis E. Sinclair and Catherine Hassall. E. Sinclair.

patron saint would thus be appearing at the same height as the carved rood group of the pulpitum. Such effects were not accidental, but indicate that, although each element had its own liturgical function, the individual components worked together to create a theatrical ensemble.

Notes

1 For the full report, see Sinclair 2012 unpublished.

2 I am grateful to Diane Walker for the many references to the throne's post-medieval documentation quoted here.

3 For the Duke of Tuscany's visit, see Chapter 2.1, 42.

4 At Westminster Abbey the 1953 examination and analysis of the oak Coronation Chair identified two decorative schemes, the earliest of which rendered the chair "as an ivory throne". This was, however, based on a misunderstanding of the exposed white preparatory layers. Recent analysis reveals that the Coronation Chair was in fact from the outset decorated to look as if it were made of gold. M. L. Sauerberg, "The Polychromy of the Coronation Chair: a detailed study", in Rodwell 2013, 78–9. Remnants of white paint on the bishop's throne relate to both preparatory layers and decoration for the medieval schemes, as well as later repaints and it is not possible to distinguish between them.

5 A letter dated 24 August 1764, from Dean Jeremiah Milles to his predecessor, Dean Lyttleton, refers to an undertaking by the bishop to have the throne "new cleaned repaired painted and sanded" (BL Ms Stowe 754, f. 137). It is not clear if this was carried out. Presumably as part of this, in 1763 he presented an "Estimate of painting and sanding the Bishop's Throne". This included requiring quantities of turpentine for cleaning ("for water will not clean it"). There is also reference to the fact that "it is now varnished, and the dust very full and cannot be got out without going to the very woodwork". James Meffin Exeter D&C 4695.

6 Several references, not all of which can be believed, describe the throne being "cleaned and scraped" (H. Besley & Son, *The Handbook of Exeter c.* 1880, 27, and Freeman 1888, 100) or plunged "into the necessary bath", from which it "came forth in so fine a condition that all idea of reviving the colouring of which traces were found was well rejected". Scott described the throne as being "cleansed of its paint and varnish, but where it had been decorated in colour this was preserved and restored" (Scott 1879, 23, and Worth 1878, 26); this latter presumably refers to the paintings of bishops on the corner posts (Scott 1879, 345–9). The cathedral's stone walls with their yellow-wash and wooden tower vaults were stripped under his direction.

7 Adjacent to the throne, the contemporary Knights' Effigies in the south quire aisle retain remnants of tin-relief, in the chain mail and on the back wall.

8 The late-13th-century wooden Coronation Chair at Westminster Abbey was once "completely covered with finely-punched gilding and a variety of applied decorative glasswork techniques, and so was entirely reminiscent of ecclesiastical goldsmiths' work." M. L. Sauerberg, "The polychromy of the Coronation Chair: a detailed study", in Rodwell 2013, 77.

9 The Westminster Abbey sedilia, also of oak, retains its extensive 1307 decoration, which includes the use of a painted white and red fictive masonry pattern, mirroring that used on the 1290's tomb of Edmund Crouchback opposite. L. Wrapson, "The materials and techniques of the *c.* 1307 Westminster Abbey sedilia", in Nadolny 2006, 118.

10 Purchases for lead white feature frequently in the fabric accounts. In Michaelmas 1323, for example, 55 lb (*c.* 25 kg) of lead white are purchased in week 2 and in week 5 when mention is made of writing letters around the throne 30 lb (*c.* 14 kg) is documented. Erskine 1981, 146.

11 Paint analysis was in its infancy during the period when the bosses were undergoing conservation. However, a look at cross-sections from the quire bosses (now covered with 19th-century paint), indicated a similar technique. A chalk gesso layer was usually followed by two layers of oil-based lead white, with a little red lead. This was occasionally followed by an extra layer of lead white, usually under the azurite (Hulbert 1998, 35). The painting of these bosses is recorded in the summers of 1302 and 1309 in the fabric accounts, see Erskine 1981, 24, 48.

12 Orpiment particles were observed in one vermilion sample higher up on Level 6, though they could be the result of a dirty brush rather than a deliberate addition.

13 Silver foils are listed in week 3, Michaelmas 1323–24 (Erskine 1981, 147). However, no silver was found on the throne and if it was used it is unlikely to have survived the stripping processes.

14 The entry of the purchase of 1½ lb of what could be orpiment in the fabric accounts for Michaelmas 1323, is followed by other references that clearly relate to the bishop's throne ("For writing 250 letters around the bishop's throne 5d." as well as references to candles for the painter, many gallons of oil and several references "for ironwork about the bishop's throne").

The actual reference in the fabric accounts here is to the purchase of "1½ lb of arnamentum" at a cost of 7s 4d. Whilst Erskine 1981, 146, translates this as a black colouring "atramentum", this item is in fact more expensive than vermilion, whilst black colouring materials are cheap. It is likely that the scribe of the accounts might have muddled the more costly auripigmentum (orpiment) with arnamentum Sinclair 1991, 124.

Analysis revealed that orpiment was used on the west front image screen on crowns and headdresses of the middle and upper register figures.

15 In the fabric accounts of Michaelmas 1323, "11 gallons [50 litres] of oil for the painter, at a cost of 10s 2d". are itemised in week 9. Erskine 1981, 147.

Appendix V

Chudleigh, Norton and the carriage of timber for Exeter Cathedral's bishop's throne

John Allan

In selecting timber for the bishop's throne from the dean and chapter's estate at Norton and from the bishop's own manor of Chudleigh, the Exeter chapter were drawing on the most important sources of timber used at the cathedral throughout the late-13th- and 14th-century building programme.[1] Both were substantial properties; the palace at Chudleigh was the most favoured seat of Exeter's late medieval bishops,[2] whilst the cluster of buildings at Norton included a manor house with hall and chamber, a chapel, and farm buildings including dovecotes, a mill and fishponds.[3] Various entries mention specifically that the timber was actually felled at the manors, rather than being gathered from a wider area; for example, three carpenters were paid 6s 6d for felling trees at Norton in 1318–19, and in 1324–5 four sawyers received 6s for their labours in Norton wood.[4] Sometimes the cathedral supplied the craftsmen working on these estates with equipment from Exeter, as in 1324–5, when 6d was paid for the hire of a horse making two journeys to Norton for carrying carpenters' tools.[5]

Whilst none of the entries for Norton or Chudleigh mentions the initial removal of bark from trees, this commonplace initial procedure in preparing timber is reflected in an entry relating to a neighbouring place: in 1323–4 the cathedral received 7s from tree-bark it sold at Langford, a place in the Creedy valley close to Norton.[6] Neither do the rolls describe the secondary removal of the outer limbs of the trees, but an unusual record of that process may be noted in John Grandisson's letter of 1338 to the bailiff and provost of Chudleigh. It records his gift of 12 oaks to the cathedral; the timber was to be employed in the fabric but the twigs and branches were to be carried to the bishop's house at Chudleigh for use in winter.[7] The

letter is also relevant to an understanding of the throne in a different regard: it states that the timber was to be selected according to the advice of the clerk Thomas of Doulcote and of Master Thomas the mason – i.e. Thomas Witney, the cathedral's master-mason in 1338. This offers a parallel to the initial payment to Thomas Witney in 1312–13 for examining timbers for the bishop's throne;[8] it shows that the employment of Witney for this purpose in 1312–13 was not an isolated or exceptional arrangement; in 1338 he was almost certainly advising on the selection of timbers for the nave roof.

The cathedral's practices in the next stages of preparing timber varied at these two manors. The record of "raising a certain great tree-trunk for sawing at Chudleigh" for the bishop's throne in 1312–13[9] forms part of the plentiful evidence that timber was commonly sawn on the estates. For example, all the 37 horses hired to carry timber from Chudleigh to Exeter in a single fortnight in 1337 carried boards (no doubt sawn), whilst in 1340–1 an assistant was paid 10d for helping raise timber for sawing at Norton, and 2s 6d was paid for sawing 400 ft (122 m) of wood.[10] Not uncommonly, however, great tree-trunks in unsawn state were carted into the city, showing that the entry recording the carriage of all the timber designated for the throne in 1312–13 from Norton to Exeter "*in grosso*"[11] is not exceptional. Great tree-trunks were transported from Chudleigh in 1306–7 and 1320–1, from Norton in 1317–18 and 1318–19, and from Winscott, a farm neighbouring Norton, in 1324–5.[12] The absence of similar entries relating to timber drawn from the more distant estates which supplied the cathedral may show that this practice was feasible only when short hauls were entailed.

Horses were much used for carrying sawn timber from Chudleigh; rather than using its own estate animals, the chapter commonly hired them from other people, and sometimes on an impressive scale. In a six-week spell in 1331–2 up to 31 horses were hired each week to carry boards.[13] Carts were also in regular use for the carriage of heavy materials to the cathedral, and over the same period in 1331–2 some 16 wagons of timber were also dispatched to the cathedral. Carriage from Norton was more commonly of cartloads of timber, and we may presume that carts were essential for carrying large tree-trunks. In the two instances of 1317–18 and 1318–19 quoted above, the cost of carrying such trunks from Norton to Exeter was 2s – the same as an entire cartload of wood. The carts used in 1331–2 were hired, but the cathedral evidently had its own vehicles, since references to the buying and repairing of carts feature commonly in the rolls; they mention their wheels, wheel-plates, ironwork, axles, shafts, saddles and harnesses, lard and tallow, the carters and their boys, and even candles for work in the dark.[14]

The cathedral's general practice of using horses and carts for these journeys seems to have differed from that of much of rural Devon. Even as late as the end of the 18th century, few Devon roads were capable of taking wheeled vehicles of any sort, as a number of horrified visitors pointed out, and it was later still that some parishes saw their first carts.[15] Large and heavy objects such as the monolithic granite piers of Devon church arcades must have travelled long distances far from roads suitable for wagons; in these circumstances sledges were probably used.

The carriage of timber from Chudleigh to Norton

The probable course taken by the timber felled at Chudleigh and sent on to Norton can be described with some confidence. Norton lies almost due north of Chudleigh. The terrain between the two is so steep and difficult that there is no convenient direct route, even today; a modern traveller would go into Exeter and out from the city. A 14th-century vehicle carrying timber would almost certainly have done the same, as consideration of the earliest map of the area which shows the local roads in any detail – a sheet of Donn's map of Devon of 1765 – will show (Fig. App. 5.1).

Chudleigh lies on the main route from Exeter to Plymouth; indeed the town's development in the 14th century was closely linked to the growing importance of this road.[16] Before the turnpikes of the 1760s the road

passed from Chudleigh through the villages of Shillingford and Alphington to Exeter, a journey of 9 miles (14.5 km). The course was first depicted on John Ogilby's road map of 1675.[17] It consisted of a steady climb to the gravel ridge of Haldon Hill, about 250 m above sea level, followed by a steep descent into the hilly area west of Exeter before reaching the crossing over the River Exe at Exe Bridge, just outside the city's West Gate. Celia Fiennes described her journey in 1695: "a continual going uphill and down, some of them pretty steep hills… The lanes are full of stones and dirt for the most part because they are so close [enclosed] the sun and wind cannot come at them".[18]

Once arriving at Exeter from Chudleigh, the wagons would have passed over the stone Exe Bridge (much of which still stands), then into the walled city, departing through its North Gate on the Crediton road – another of the main Devon roads first mapped by Ogilby in 1675.[19] The journey to Norton would have entailed crossing back over the Exe at Cowley, then bearing off the main road around Newton St Cyres – a distance of about 6 miles (9.7 km), bringing the total from Chudleigh to 15 miles (24.1 km). The timbers were of course to be carted back to Exeter before being cut up for use in the throne.

Notes

1 References in the fabric rolls to the carriage of wood from these two places far outnumber records of timber brought from other sources. For the 22 page references to carriage of timber from Chudleigh and 24 from Norton, spanning the period 1299–1332, see Erskine 1983, 328, 335.
2 Parker *et al.* 2006, 193–223.
3 Hingeston-Randolph 1889.
4 Erskine 1981, 106, 159. See also the gifts of wood by Bishop Grandisson, one of which is mentioned below.
5 *Ibid.*, 159.
6 *Ibid.*, 147.
7 *…les ramailles et les braunches de mieismes larbres faites carier a nostre court, pur nostre demoere en yver.* Hingeston-Randolph 1897, 881; Erskine 1983, 320.
8 Erskine 1981, 71.
9 *Ibid.*
10 Erskine 1983, 249, 259, 263.
11 Erskine 1981, 71.
12 *Ibid.*, 41, 93, 100, 131, 159.
13 Erskine 1983, 249.
14 *Ibid.*, 338–9.
15 Marshall 1796, 1, 30–1; Thompson 1932, viii–ix.
16 Hoskins 1992, 366.
17 White 2005, 34.
18 Morris 1947, 249–50.
19 White 2005, 117.

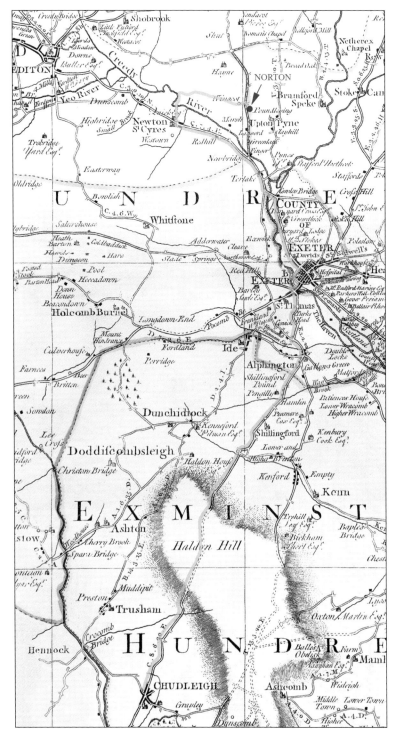

Fig. App. 5.1 Detail of Donn's map of Devon (1765). Courtesy of Devon Record Office.

Abbreviations and select bibliography

Arch. Jnl   Archaeological Journal
BAAJ   British Archaeological Association Journal
BAACT   British Archaeological Association Conference Transactions
BOE   The Buildings of England
BOW   The Buildings of Wales
BL   British Library
Exeter D & C   Exeter Cathedral, Dean and Chapter Acts
NLW   National Library of Wales, Aberystwyth
ODNB   Oxford Dictionary of National Biography
Parl. Paps   Parliamentary Papers Return of the Name of every
                   Member of the Lower House of Parliament, 1213–1874,
                   House of Commons Parliamentary Papers
Pat. Lat.   Patrologia Latina Patrologia Cursus Completus … Series
                   Latina, ed. J. P. Migne, 221 vols (Paris 1844–1864)
RCHME   Royal Commission on the Historical Monuments
                   of England
VCH   Victoria County History of the Counties of England
WCL   Worcester Cathedral Library

Unpublished documentary sources

Society of Antiquaries of London. Coloured drawings by John Carter of plan, elevations, sections, etc. of Exeter Cathedral, 1792–1796.

Budge, A. L. 2011. Episcopal visibility: the extant fourteenth-century bishop's thrones at Exeter, Wells, Hereford, St Davids and Durham. Master of Studies thesis, University of Oxford.

Holton, A. B. 2010. The Archaeology and Conservation of the East Front of York Minster. Unpublished PhD thesis, University of York.

Hope, V. c. 1940. The Bishop's Throne. Exeter Cathedral Archives.

Maddicott, J. 2009. Walter de Stapeldon, Bishop of Exeter and Founder of Exeter College. Transcript of a lecture given at the launch of the Seven Hundredth Anniversary Appeal at Exeter College, Oxford, 26 September.

Morris P. 1940. The Cathedral During the Reformation and the Interregnum. Unpublished Exeter Cathedral Study, 1940.

Paterson, C. 2009. Masons or Managers? Early Fourteenth-century Cathedral Builders in Exeter: the Evidence of the Fabric Accounts 1299–1342. Unpublished PG Cert in Architectural History thesis, Oxford University.

Sinclair, E. 2012. Exeter Cathedral. The Bishop's Throne: Polychromy Report.

Terry, A. 1984. The Architecture and Architectural Sculpture of the Sixth-Century Eufrasius Cathedral at Poreč. Ph. D. dissertation, University of Illinois, Urbana-Champaign.

Wilson, C. 1979. The Origins of the Perpendicular Style and its Development to circa 1360. Ph.D. Thesis, Courtauld Institute of Art, University of London.

Woodworth, M. H. 2011. The Architectural History of Beverley Minster, 721–c. 1370. Unpublished PhD thesis, Duke University.

Published books and articles

Addleshaw P. 1898. The Cathedral Church of Exeter, Bell's Guide (London).

Agnellus, A. 2004. The Book of Pontiffs of Ravenna, trans. D. M. Delyannis (Washington D. C.).

Airlie, S. 2003. Thrones, dominions, powers: some European points of comparison for the stone of destiny. In R. Welander, D. J. Breeze and T. O. Clancy (eds), Stone of Destiny, Artefact and Icon, 123–36. Society of Antiquaries of Scotland Monograph 22 (Edinburgh).

Allan J. and Jupp B. 1981. Recent observations in the South Tower of Exeter Cathedral. Devon Archaeological Society Proceedings 39, 141–54.

Allen. J. 2008. The choir stalls of Lincoln Cathedral, Chester Cathedral and St Mary's Church, Nantwich. BAAJ 161, 104–30.

Appuhn, H. 1978–9. Beiträge zur Geschichte des Herrschersitzen im Mittelelalter. In I. Teil, Gedrechselte Sitze, Aachener Kunstblätte 48, 34–7.

Ashworth, E. 1853. On the woodwork of Exeter Cathedral. Exeter Diocesan Architectural Society Journal 4, 323–31.

Badham, S. and Norris, M. 1999. The brasses and other minor monuments. In G. Aylmer and J. Tiller, Hereford Cathedral. A History, 331–5 (London).

Bannister, A. 1924. The Cathedral Church of Hereford: Its History and Constitution (London).

Barlow, F. 1972. Leofric of Exeter: Essays in Commemoration of the Foundation of Exeter Cathedral Library in A.D. 1072 (Exeter).

Bash, A. (ed.) 2012. Thomas Hatfield Bishop, Soldier, and Politician (Toronto).

Bégule, L. 1920. La Cathédrale de Lyon (Paris).

Belli d'Elia, P. 1974. La cattedra dell'abate Elia. Precisazioni sul romanico Pugliese. Bollettino d'Arte 59, 1–17.

Bennett, N. 2004. Burghersh, Henry (c. 1290–1340), ODNB, http://www.oxforddnb.com/view/article/12598 (Accessed 5 November 2012).

Bertaux, E. 1903. L'art dans l'Italie méridionale (Paris 1903).

Billings, R. W. 1843. *Architectural Illustrations and Description of the Cathedral Church at Durham* (London).

Binski, P. 1995. *Westminster Abbey and the Plantagenets* (New Haven and London).

Binski, P. 2003. A "Sign of Victory": The Coronation Chair, its manufacture, setting and symbolism. In R. Welander, D. J. Breeze and T. O. Clancy (eds), *Stone of Destiny, Artefact and Icon*, 207–20. Society of Antiquaries of Scotland Monograph 22 (Edinburgh).

Binski, P. and Panayotova, S. (eds) 2005. *The Cambridge Illuminations. Ten Centuries of Book Production in the Medieval West* (London and Turnhout).

Bishop, H. E. and Prideaux, E. K. 1922. *The Building of Exeter Cathedral* (Exeter).

Blair, C. H. H. 1922. Medieval seals of the Bishops of Durham. *Archaeologia* 72, 1–24.

Blockley, K., Sparks, M. and Tatton-Brown, T. 1997. *Canterbury Cathedral. Nave Archaeology, History, and Architecture*. The Archaeology of Canterbury NS, 1(2) (Canterbury).

Bond, F. 1905. *Gothic Architecture in England* (London).

Bond, F. 1910. *Wood Carvings in English Churches*. I. *Stalls and Tabernacle Work*, II. *Bishop's Thrones and Chancel Chairs* (London).

Bond, F. 1912. *The Cathedrals of England and Wales* (London).

Bonsanti, G. (ed.) 2002. *La Basilica di San Francesco ad Assisi* (Modena).

Bony, J. 1979. *The English Decorated Style* (Oxford).

Bradshaw, H. and Wordsworth, C. 1892–7. *Statutes of Lincoln Cathedral*, 3 vols (Cambridge).

Brice, A. 1759. *The Grand Gazetteer or Topographical Dictionary both General and Special and Ancient as well as Modern etc.* (Exeter).

Britnell, R. H. 2012. Bishop Hatfield's Legacy. In A. Bash (ed.), *Thomas Hatfield Bishop, Soldier, and Politician*, 47–56 (Toronto).

Britton, J. 1824, 1836, 1847. *The History and Antiquities of the Cathedral Church of Wells* (London).

Britton, J. 1826. *Cathedral Antiquities: Historical and Descriptive Accounts: History and Antiquities of the Cathedral Church of Exeter* (London).

Brooke, J. (ed.) 2001. *The Kalmeter Journal: the Journal of a Visit to Cornwall, Devon and Somerset in 1724–25 of Henric Kalmeter* (Truro).

Brooks, N. 1984. *The Early History of the Church of Canterbury* (Leicester).

Brown, R. A., Colvin, H. M. and Taylor, A. J. 1966. *History of the King's Works* 1–2 (London).

Brown, S. 2003. *Our Magnificent Fabrick. York Minster: An Architectural History c. 1220–1500* (Swindon).

Buck, M. 1983. *Politics, Finance and the Church in the Reign of Edward II. Walter Stapeldon Treasurer of England* (Cambridge).

Buck, M. C. 2004. 'Walter Stapeldon (b. in or before 1265, d. 1326), administrator and bishop of Exeter' in *ODNB*, http://www.oxforddnb.com/view/article/26296?docPos=1 (Accessed 9 October 2012).

Cabrol, F. and Leclercq, H. 1913. *Dictionnaire d'Archéologie Chrétienne et de Liturgie* (Paris). [A compendium of the 19th-century scholarly literature on the Early-Christian form and use of episcopal thrones in the Eastern and Western Churches, some of which has been subsequently superseded. See entries for *Chaire* épiscopale, and *Consécration* épiscopale].

Cameron, J. A. forthcoming. '*Sedilia in choro sunt fracta*': The Medieval Nomenclature of Seating in Churches, *BAAJ* for 2015.

Capes, W. M. 1914. *Registrum Willelmi de Courtenay, episcopi herefordensis, A.D. 1370–1375* (London).

Carter, J. 1797. *Some Account of the Cathedral Church of Exeter: Illustrative of the Plans, Elevations, Sections, of that Building etc.* (eds H. C. Englefield and J. Windham) (London).

Catholic Encyclopedia. http://www.newadvent.org/cathen/03351e.htm [This online publication underlines the need for caution in accepting some of the arguments propounded by 19th-century scholarship. See entries for *Chair of St Peter, Throne, Consecration*.]

Chinnery, V. 1979. *Oak Furniture. The British Tradition* (Woodbridge).

Chope, R. Pearse. 1918. *Early Tours in Devon and Cornwall* (Exeter).

Church, C. M. 1894. *Chapters in the Early History of the Church of Wells* (London).

Church, C. M. 1907. The Prebendal Stalls and Misericords in the Cathedral Church of Wells. *Archaeologia* 55, 319–42.

Clapham, A. W. 1930. *English Romanesque Architecture before the Conquest* (Oxford).

Clapham, A. W. 1950. Stones from Monkwearmouth. *Archaeologia. Aeliana* 4th ser 1–6, pl. 1.

Colchester, L. S. 1956. The Victorian Restoration of Wells Cathedral Church. *Transactions of the Ancient Monuments Society* 4, 79–94.

Colchester, L. S. 1987. *Wells Cathedral* (London).

Coldstream, N. 1994. *The Decorated Style* (London).

Cole, D. 2005. *Glasney College, Penryn, Cornwall*. Cornwall County Council Historic Environment Service Report, 09.58.

Corrigan, K. 1988. *The Witness of John the Baptist on an Early Byzantine Icon in Kiev*. Dumbarton Oaks Papers 42.

Cowley, F. 2007. The Relics of St David: The Historical Evidence. In J. Wyn Evans and J. M. Wooding (eds), *St David of Wales: Cult, Church and Nation*, 276–81 (St Davids).

Crook, J. 1993. St Swithun of Winchester. In J. Crook (ed.), *Winchester Cathedral Nine Hundred Years 1093–1993*, 57–68 (Chichester).

Crook, J. 2010. The Archaeological Report. *Winchester Cathedral Record* 7.

Crook, J. 2011. *English Medieval Shrines* (Woodbridge).

Crook, J. forthcoming. The Bishop's throne platform and relic niche in Norwich Cathedral: a re-examination. *Medieval Art and Architecture at Norwich Cathedral*, (eds), S. Heslop and H. Lunnon.

Crosby, E. U. 1994. *Bishop and Chapter in twelfth-century England: a Study of the Mensa Episcopalis* (Cambridge).

Cross, F. L. 1958. *The Oxford Dictionary of the Christian Church* (Oxford).

Crossley, F. H. and Ridgway, M. H. 1957. Screens, Lofts and Stalls situated in Wales and Monmouthshire, Pt. 8, Section XI: Pembrokeshire. *Archaeologia Cambrensis* 106, 9–45.

Crowfoot, J. W. 1938. The Christian churches. In C. H. Kraeling (ed.), *Gerasa. City of the Decapolis*, 171–262 (New Haven).

Curry, I. 1993. Continuity and Change: Masters, Surveyors and Architects to the Fabric of the Cathedral. In D. Pocock (ed.), *St. Cuthbert and Durham Cathedral: a Celebration*, 36–54 (Durham).

Daly, P. H. 1982. The Process of Canonization in the Thirteenth and Early Fourteenth Centuries. In M. Jancey (ed.), *St Thomas Cantilupe Bishop of Hereford*, 125–35 (Hereford).

Davenport, P. 1996. *The Cathedral Priory Church at Bath*, 19–30. University of Oxford Committee for Archaeology Monograph 42.

Deichmann, F. W. 1969–76. *Ravenna. Haupstadt des spätantiken Abendländes* (Wiesbaden).

Dingley, T. 1867. *History from Marble*. (London).

Dix, G. 1945. *The Shape of the Liturgy* (London).

Dohar, W. J. 1995. *The Black Death and Pastoral Leadership. The Diocese of Hereford in the Fourteenth Century* (Philadelphia).

Draper, P. 1981. The Sequence and Dating of the Decorated Work at Wells. In N. Coldstream and P. Draper (eds), *Medieval Art and Architecture at Wells and Glastonbury*, 18–29, *BAACT* IV.

Draper, P. 1995. Interpreting the Architecture of Wells Cathedral. In V. C. Raguin, K. Brush and P. Draper (eds), *Artistic Integration in Gothic Buildings*, 114–30 (Toronto).

Dugdale, W. 1673. *Monasticon Anglicanum*.

Dugdale, W. 1846. *Monasticon Anglicanum*: or, the history of the ancient abbies, and other monasteries, hospitals, friaries, cathedral and collegiate churches in England and Wales (eds Caley, Ellis, and Bandinel) (London). For Durham, see, I, 219–22, 224, 227, 229; Hereford, VI, 1210–1212; Lincoln, VI, 1266–1269; St Davids, VI, 1301–1302, 1387–1388; Wells, II, 274–6, 279, 283–4.

Duran y Sanpere, A. 1952. *La Catedral de Barcelona* (Barcelona).

Eames, P. 1977. *Medieval Furniture* (London).

Edwards, K. 1949. *English Secular Cathedrals in the Middle Ages* (Manchester).

Edwards, O. T. 2007. The Office of St David in MS lat. 17294. In J. Wyn Evans and J. M. Wooding (eds), *St David of Wales: Cult, Church and Nation* (St Davids).

Emden, A. B. 1958. *A Biographical Register of the University of Oxford to AD 1500* (Oxford).

Erskine, A. M. (ed.) 1981. *The Accounts of the Fabric of Exeter Cathedral, Part 1: 1279–1326. Devon and Cornwall Record Society*, NS 24.

Erskine, A. M. (ed.) 1983. *The Accounts of the Fabric of Exeter Cathedral, Part 2: 1328–1353. Devon and Cornwall Record Society*, NS 26.

Evans, J. W. 2002. *St Davids Cathedral* (Andover).

Evans, J. W. 2007. *The Misericords of St Davids Cathedral* (Much Wenlock).

Evans, J. W. 2009. From Chapel to Cloister. In H. James and P. Moore (eds), *Carmarthenshire & Beyond: Studies in History and Archaeology in Memory of Terry James*, 174–191 (Carmarthen).

Farmer, D. H. 1997. *The Oxford Dictionary of Saints* (Oxford).

Fernie, E. 1993. *An Architectural History of Norwich Cathedral* (Oxford).

Fernie, E. C. 2000. *The Architecture of Norman England* (Oxford).

Finucane, R. C. 1982. Cantilupe as Thaumaturge: Pilgrims and their Miracles. In M. Jancey, *St Thomas Cantilupe Bishop of Hereford*, 137–44 (Hereford).

Fleury, C. R. de. 1883–89. *Messe: Études archéologiques sur les monuments…, continuées par son fils (G. R. de Fleury)* 8 vols (Paris).

Fowler, J. T. 1890. Notes on some grave slabs in the cathedral church at Durham. *Proceedings of the Society of Antiquaries* 13, 34–44.

Fowler, J. T. (ed.) 1903. *Rites of Durham, Being a Description or Brief Declaration of all the Ancient Monuments, Rites, & Customs Belonging or Being Within the Monastical Church of Durham Before the Suppression* [Written 1593] (Durham).

Fraser, C. M. 1959. Prerogative and the Bishops of Durham, 1267–1376. *English Historical Review* 74, 467–76.

Freeman, P. 1873. *The Architectural History of Exeter Cathedral* (Exeter) [2nd edn 1888, with additional notes by E. V. Freeman].

Gaborit-Chopin, D. 1984. Throne-reliquary (the *Sedia di San Marco*). In D. Alcouffe *et al.*, *The Treasury of St Marco, Venice*, 98–105 (London).

Gage, J. 1999. *Colour and Meaning: Art, Science and Symbolism* (London).

Gage, J. 2009. *Colour and Culture: Practice and Meaning from Antiquity to Abstraction* (London).

Gandolfo, F. 1974–5. *Reimpiego di sculture antiche nei troni papali dal XII secolo*. Atti della Pontificia Accademia Romana di Archeologia. Rendiconti (Rome).

Gandolfo, F. 1984. La cattedra 'gregoriana' di Salerno. *Bolletino storico di Salerno e Principato Citra*, 2 (1), 5–29.

Geary, P. J. 1978. *Furta Sacra: Theft of Relics in the Central Middle Ages* (Princeton NJ).

Gibson, M. D. (trans) 1903. *Didascalia Apostolorum* (Cambridge).

Glasscoe, M. and Swanton, M. 1978. *Medieval Woodwork in Exeter Cathedral* (Exeter).

Gloede, G. 1970. *Das Doberaner Münster* (Berlin).

Godwin, F. 1743. *Episcopi Praesulibus Angliae Commentarius* (Cambridge).

Goodall, J. A. A. 2011. *The English Castle, 1066–1650* (New Haven).

Gough, R. 1786. *Sepulchral Monuments in Great Britain*, I (London).

Grabar, A. 1954a. Trones épiscopaux de xiéme et xiième siècle en Italie mériodinale *Wallrauf-Richartz Jahrbuch* 1954, 7–52.

Grabar, A. 1954b. La Sedia de San Marco à Venise. *Cahiers Archéologiques* 7, 19–34.

Greenhaulgh, D. 1982. The Nineteenth Century and After. In L. S. Colchester (ed.), *Wells Cathedral: a History*, 179–203 (Shepton Mallet).

Guidobaldi, F. and Lawlor, P. 1990. *The Basilica and the Archaeological Area of San Clemente in Rome* (Rome).

Haines, R. M. 2004. Hatfield, Thomas (c.1310–1381). *ODNB*, http://www.oxforddnb.com/view/article/12598 (Accessed 5 November 2012).

Harbottle, B. 1958. Bishop Hatfield's Visitation of Durham Priory in 1354. *Archaeologia Aeliana* 36, 81–100.

Harrison, S. A., Morris, R. K. and Robinson, D. M. 1998. A Fourteenth-Century *Pulpitum* Screen at Tintern Abbey *Antiquaries Journal* 78, 177–268.

Harvey, J. H. 1982. The Building of Wells Cathedral, II: 1307–1508. In L. S. Colchester (ed.), *Wells Cathedral: a History*, 76–101 (Shepton Mallet).

Harvey, J. 1984. *English Mediaeval Architects* (Gloucester).

Havergal, F. T. 1869a. *Fasti Herefordenses and other Antiquarian Memorials* (Edinburgh).

Havergal, F. T. 1869b. The visitors' hand-guide to Hereford Cathedral (Hereford).

Heighway, C. and Bryant, C. 2007. *The Tomb of Edward II. A Royal Monument in Gloucester Cathedral* (Stonehouse).

Hingeston-Randolph, F. C. 1889. *The Registers of Walter Bronescombe (AD 1257–1280) and Peter Quivil (AD 1280–1291)* (London).

Hingeston-Randolph, F. C. 1897. *The Register of John de Grandisson, Bishop of Exeter, Part II 1331–1360* (London and Exeter).

Hope, V. 1969a. The Bishop's Throne. *Friends of Exeter Cathedral, 38th Annual Report* (Exeter).

Hope, V. 1969b. The Bishop's Throne during the Commonwealth. *Friends of Exeter Cathedral, 39th Annual Report* (Exeter).

Hope, W. H. S. J. 1917. Quire screens in English churches with special reference to the twelfth century quire screen formerly in the cathedral church of Ely. *Archaeologia* 68, 44–110.

Hope, W. H. S. J. and Atchley, E. G. C. F. 1918. *English Liturgical Colours* (London).

Hoskins, W. G. 1992. *Devon* (reprint of 1954 edn, Tiverton).

Hulbert, A. 1991. An examination of the polychromy of Exeter Cathedral roof bosses, and its documentation. In F. Kelly (ed.), *Medieval Art and Architecture at Exeter Cathedral*, 188–98. *BAACT* XI.

Hulbert, A. 1998. English fourteenth-century interior polychromy: manuscript sources and workshop practice at Exeter Cathedral. In A. Roy and P. Smith (eds), *Painting Techniques: History Materials and Studio Practice, International Institute for Conservation* (Dublin).

Hüller, S. 2009. *The Real Messiah. The Throne of St Mark and the True Origin of Christianity* (London).

Hutchinson, A. 1948. *Selby Abbey Church* (Selby).

Huxley Thompson, A. 1933. *The Story of Exeter Cathedral* (London).

Iles, P. 2000. The Stained Glass. In G. Aylmer and J. Tiller, *Hereford. Cathedral. A History*, 314–21 (London).

James, H. 1993. The cult of St David in the Middle Ages. In M. Carver, *In Search of Cult*, 105–12 (Woodbridge).

Jansen, V. 1991. The design and building sequence of the eastern arm of Exeter Cathedral, c. 1270–1310: a qualified study. In F. Kelly (ed.), *Medieval Art and Architecture at Exeter Cathedral*, 35–56. *BAACT* XI.

Jenkins, A. 1841. *History of the City of Exeter* (1st edn 1806, Exeter).

Jones, W. B. and Freeman, E. A. 1856. *The History and Antiquities of Saint David's* (London).

Kjølbye-Biddle, B. 1993. Old Minster, St Swithun's Day 1093. In J. Crook, *Winchester Cathedral Nine Hundred Years 1093–1993*, 13–20 (Chichester).

Klauser, T. 1969. *A Short History of the Western Liturgy* (Oxford).

Klukas, A. 1981. The Liber Ruber and the rebuilding of the East End at Wells. In N. Coldstream and P. Draper (eds), *Medieval Art and Architecture at Wells and Glastonbury*, 30–5. *BAACT* IV.

Klukas, A. 1995. Durham Cathedral in the Gothic Era: liturgy, design, ornament. In V. C. Raguin, K. Brush and P. Draper (eds), *Artistic Integration in Gothic Buildings*, 69–83 (Toronto).

Knowles, D. and Brooke, C. N. L. 2002. *The Monastic Constitution of Lanfranc* (Oxford).

Krautheimer, R. 1937. *Corpus basilicarum christianarum Romae* Vol. I (Rome).

Lanc, E. 2002. *Die Mittelalterlichen Wandmalereien in Der Steiemark*, 2 vols (Vienna)

Lehmberg, S. E. 1996. *Cathedrals under Siege* (Exeter).

Leland, J. 1910. *The Itinerary of John Leland* (ed. L. Toulmin-Smith) (London).

Lepine, D. N. 2012a. John Trillek (*c.* 1308–1360). *ODNB* http://www.oxforddnb.com/view/article/95146 (Accessed 12 September 2012).

Lepine, D. N. 2012b. Thomas Trillek (b. in or before 1312, d. 1372). *ODNB* http://www.oxforddnb.com/view/article/95196 (Accessed 17 September 2012).

Lepine, D. and Orme. N. 2003. Death and memory in medieval Exeter. *Devon and Cornwall Record Society* NS 47, 317, 320, 324, 328, 333.

Lewes Gee, L. 1979. "Ciborium" tombs in England 1290–1330 *BAAJ* 132, 29–41.

Liddy, C. D. 2012. Hatfield the Bishop. In A. Bash (ed.), *Thomas Hatfield Bishop, Soldier, and Politician*, 35–46 (Toronto).

Lindley, P. 1995. Retrospective effigies, the past and lies. In D. Whitehead (ed.) *Medieval Art and Architecture at Hereford Cathedral,* 111–21, *BAACT* XV.

Lindley, P. 2003. *The Later Medieval Monuments and Chantry Chapels.* Tewkesbury Abbey History, Art & Architecture (Little Logaston).

Lloyd, T. Orbach, J. and Scourfield, R. 2004. *BOW: Pembrokeshire* (London and New Haven).

Loerke, W. 1984. "Real Presence" in Early Christian Art. In T. G. Verdun, *Monasticism and the Arts* (Syracuse, N.Y.).

Lovegrove, E. W. 1951. *The Cathedral Church of St David's* (St Davids).

Lowden, J. 1997. *Early Christian and Byzantine Art* (London).

Lowden, J. 2000. *The Making of the Bibles Moralisées* (Pennsylvania).

Luxford, J. M. 2005. *The Art and Architecture of English Benedictine Monasteries 1300–1540. A Patronage History* (Woodbridge).

Maccarone, M., Ferrua, A., Romanelli, P. and Schramm, P. E. 1971. *La Cathedra Lignea di S. Pietro in Vaticano, Atti Pontificia Accademia Romana di Archeologia*, Ser. III, Memorie X (Vatican City).

Mackenzie, F. 1844. *The Architectural Antiquities of the Collegiate Chapel of St Stephen, Westminster* (London).

Mann, A. 1995–7. Aachens Geschichte und die Geschichten von "Otto von Metz" und dem Karlsthron, von "Aquae Granni" und dem "Grasshaus" neben anderen lokallhistorischen Legendenbeiträgen. *Aachener Kunstblätter* 61, 361–9.

Mango, C. 1986. *The Art of the Byzantine Empire 312–1453. Sources and Documents* (London).

Marchi, G. 1844. *I monumenti delle arte cristiane primitive*, 4 vols (Rome).

Marshall, G. 1951. *Hereford Cathedral: Its Heritage and Growth* (Worcester).

Marshall, W. 1796. *The Rural Economy of the West of England*, 2 vols (Newton Abbot).

McNeill, J. 2011. A Prehistory of the Chantry, *BAAJ* 164, 1–38.

Mitchell, J. 2000. *Painting in East Anglia around 1500: The Continental Connection*. In J. Mitchell assisted by M. Moran, *England and the Continent in the Middle Ages: Studies in Memory of Andrew Martindale* (Stamford).

Morath, G. W. 1940. *Die Maximienskathedra in Ravenna* (Freiburg).

Morgan, F. C. 1979. *Hereford Cathedral Glass*, 3rd edn (Hereford).

Morgan, P. E. 1982. The effect of the pilgrimage cult of St Thomas Cantilupe on Hereford Cathedral. In M. Jancey, *St Thomas Cantilupe Bishop of Hereford*, 145–52 (Hereford).

Morris, C. (ed.). 1947. The Journeys of Celia Fiennes (London).

Morris, P. 1940. Exeter Cathedral: A Conjectural Restoration of the Fourteenth-century Altar-Screen. *Antiquaries Journal* 23, 122–47; 24, 10–21.

Morris, R. K. 1974. The Remodelling of the Hereford Aisles. *BAAJ* 3rd ser. 37, 21–39.

Morris, R. K. 1978. Later Gothic mouldings in England, *c.* 1250–1400, Part I. *Architectural History* 21, 18–57.

Morris, R. K. 1991. Thomas of Witney at Exeter, Winchester and Wells.

In F. Kelly (ed.), *Medieval Art and Architecture at Exeter Cathedral*, 57–84, figs 1–10. *BAACT* XI.

Morris, R. K. 1994. Tewkesbury Abbey. *Medieval Archaeology* 38, 211–12.

Morris, R. K. 2000. The architectural history of the medieval Cathedral church. In G. Aylmer and J. Tiller, *Hereford Cathedral. A History*, 203–40 (London).

Nadolny, J. 2006. *Medieval Painting in Northern Europe etc.* (London).

Neave, D. and Pevsner, N. 1995. *BOE Yorkshire: York and the East Riding* (Harmondsworth).

Nees, L. 1991. *A Tainted Mantle. Hercules and the Classical Tradition at the Carolingian Court* (Philadelphia).

Nees, L. 1993. Audiences and reception of the *Cathedra Petri*. *Gazette des Beaux Arts* 1993, 122.

Nees, L. 1999. Forging monumental memories in the early twelfth century. In W. Reinink and J. Stumpel (eds), *Proceedings of the History of Art, Amsterdam, 1–7 September, 1996*, 773–82 (Dordrecht).

Neville, C. J. 2000. The courts of the prior and the bishop of Durham in the later Middle Ages, *History* 85, 216–31.

Oliver, G. 1861. *Lives of the Bishops of Exeter; History of the Cathedral* (Exeter).

Orme, N. 2009. *Exeter Cathedral. The First Thousand Years, 400–1550* (Exeter).

Orme, N. 2010. *A History of the County of Cornwall*, II, *Religious History to 1560, VCH*.

Ormrod, W. M. 2012. Hatfield the politician. In A. Bash (ed.), *Thomas Hatfield Bishop, Soldier, and Politician*, 21–34 (Toronto).

Park, D. 1993. The interior decoration of the cathedral. In D. Pocock (ed.), *St. Cuthbert and Durham Cathedral: a Celebration*, 57–67 (Durham).

Parker R. W., Allan, J., Fletcher, M., Higham, R. and Laithwaite, M. 2006. The bishop's palace at Chudleigh. *Devon Archaeological Society Proceedings* 64, 193–240.

Parry, J. H. 1916. *Registrum Johannis de Trillek. Episcopi Herefordensis 1344–61* (London).

Pantin, W. A. 1955. *The English Church in the Fourteenth Century* (Cambridge).

Paterson, C. 2011. The master masons of Exeter Cathedral, 1299–1342, based on the evidence of the Exeter Cathedral fabric rolls. *Friends of Exeter Cathedral Annual Report*, 26–33.

Percival-Prescott, W. 1957. *The Coronation Chair. An Investigation into the History and Present Condition of the Chair* (London).

Pevsner, N. 1962. *BOE, North East Norfolk and Norfolk* (Harmondsworth

Pevsner, N. and Williamson, E. 1983. *BOE, County Durham* (Harmondsworth).

Pevsner, N. and Cherry, B. 1989. *BOE, Devon* (Harmondsworth).

Pevsner, N. and Harris, J. 1989. *BOE, Lincolnshire* (Harmondsworth).

Pevsner, N. and Wilson, B. 1997. *BOE, Norfolk I: Norwich and North-East* (New Haven and London).

Pfaff, R. 2009. *The Liturgy in Medieval England* (Cambridge).

Phillips, C. S. 1949. The Archbishop's three seats in Canterbury Cathedral. *Antiquaries Journal* 29, 26–36.

Piper, A. J. 2004. 'Chambre, William', *ODNB*, http://www.oxforddnb.com/view/article/19945 (Accessed 6 November 2012).

Powicke, F. M. and Cheney, C. R. 1964. *Councils and Synods with other documents relating to the English Church*, II, 1265–1313 (Oxford).

Prestwich, M. 2012. Thomas Hatfield at War. In A. Bash (ed.), *Thomas Hatfield Bishop, Soldier, and Politician*, 5–20 (Toronto).

Quiney, A. 1979. *John Loughborough Pearson* (London).

Raine, J. 1839. *Historiæ Dunelmensis scriptores tres, Gaufridus de Coldingham, Robertus de Graystanes, et Willielmus de Chambre* (London).

Radford, C. A. R. 1959. The Bishop's throne in Norwich Cathedral. *Arch. Jnl* 116, 115–32.

Rawlinson, T. 1717. *The History and Antiquities of the City and Cathedral-Church of Hereford* (London).

Reeve, M. W. 2003. A seat of authority: the archbishop's throne at Canterbury Cathedral. *Gesta,* 42(2), 131–42.

Reynolds, H. E. 1880. *Wells Cathedral: its Foundation; Constitutional History and Statutes* (Leeds).

Robson, P. 1901. *The Cathedral Church of St David's* (London).

Rodwell, W. 1982. The Anglo-Saxon and Norman churches at Wells. In L. S. Colchester (ed.), *Wells Cathedral: a History*, 1–23 (Shepton Mallet).

Rodwell, W. 2013. *The Coronation Chair and Stone of Scone* (Oxford).

Russell, T. 1830. *A Short Description of a Portable Shrine*.

Schapiro, M. 1980. *Late Antique, Early Christian and Mediaeval Art* (London).

Scott, G. G. 1873. *St David's Cathedral. Extracts from First and Second Reports* (London).

Scott, G. G. 1879. *Personal and Professional Recollections* (ed. G. Stamp 1995) (London).

Searle, W. (ed.). 1902. *Christ Church Canterbury: The Chronicle of John Stone* (Cambridge).

Sekules, V. 1986. The Tomb of Christ at Lincoln and the development of the sacrament shrine: Easter sepulchres reconsidered. In T. A. Heslop and V. A. Sekules (eds), *Medieval Art and Architecture at Lincoln Cathedral*, 118–31. *BAACT* VIII.

Sekules, V. 1991a. The liturgical furnishings of the choir of Exeter Cathedral. in F. Kelly (ed.), *Medieval Art and Architecture at Exeter Cathedral*, 172–9. *BAACT* XI.

Sekules, V. 1991b. Early 14th-century liturgical furnishings. In M. Swanton, *Exeter Cathedral. A Celebration*, 111–14 (Exeter).

Shinners, J. 1988. The veneration of saints at Norwich Cathedral in the fourteenth century. *Norfolk Archaeology* 40, 133–44.

Simson, O. von. 1948. *Sacred Fortress: Byzantine Art and Statecraft in Ravenna* (Chicago).

Sinclair, E. 1991. The west front polychromy. In F. Kelly (ed.), *Medieval Art and Architecture at Exeter Cathedral*, 116–33. *BAACT* XI.

Smirke, S. 1836. The archiepiscopal throne in the conventual church of Assisi. *Archaeologia* 26, 472–4.

Somner, W. 1640. *The Antiquities of Canterbury* (London).

Spurrell, M. 2002a. *Friends of Wells Cathedral Annual Report*, 35–9.

Spurrell, M. 2002b. *Friends of Wells Cathedral Autumn Journal*, 27–31.

Stiegmann, C. and Wemhoff, M. (eds). 1999. *Kunst und Kultur der Karolingerzeit* (Paderborn).

Stirneman, P. 1999. Note sur la Bible Moralisée en trois volumes conservée à Oxford, Paris et Londres, et sur ces copies. *Scriptorium* 53(1), 120–4.

Stoll, M. 1991. *Symbols as Power. The Papacy following the Investiture Contest* (Leiden).

Stone, L. 1972. *Sculpture in Britain: The Middle Ages* (London).

Stubbs, G. (ed.) 1879–80. *Tractatus de Combustione et Reparatione Cantuariensis Opera Historica Ecclesiae* I (Rolls Series LXXIII).

Swanton, M. 1991. *Exeter Cathedral. A Celebration* (Exeter).

Swanson, R. and Lepine, D. 2000. The later Middle Ages, 1268–1535. In G. Aylmer and J. Tiller, *Hereford Cathedral. A History*, 48–86 (London).

Taylor, H. M. 1969. The Anglo-Saxon Cathedral church at Canterbury. *Arch. Jnl* 137, 101–29.

Terry, A. 1988. *The Sculpture at the Cathedral of Eufrasius in Poreč*. Dumbarton Oaks Papers 42.

Terry, A. and Maguire, H. 2007. Dynamic Splendor. *The Wall Mosaics in the Cathedral of Eufrasius at Poreč*. 2 vols (Pennsylvania).

Thompson, W. H. 1932. *Devon: A Survey* (London).

Thurlby, M. 1991. The Romanesque cathedral of St Mary and St Peter at Exeter. In F. Kelly (ed.), *Medieval Art and Architecture at Exeter Cathedral*, 19–34. *BAACT* XI.

Thurlby, M. 1993. The building of the cathedral: the Romanesque and Early Gothic fabric. In D. Pocock (ed.), *St. Cuthbert and Durham Cathedral: a Celebration*, 15–35 (Durham).

Thurlby, M. 1995. The Romanesque Fabric. In D. Whitehead (ed.), *Medieval Art and Architecture at Hereford Cathedral*, 15–28. *BAACT* XV.

Tracy, C. 1986. The early fourteenth-century choir-stalls at Exeter Cathedral. *Burlington Magazine* (February), 99–102.

Tracy, C. 1987. *English Gothic Choir-Stalls 1200–1400* (Woodbridge).

Tracy, C. 1988. The St David's bishop's throne and its relationship to contemporary fourteenth-century ecclesiastical furniture in England. *Archaeologia Cambrensis* 136, 113–18.

Tracy, C. 2002. A medieval bishop's throne at Lincoln Cathedral. *Apollo* 155, 32–41.

Tracy, C. 2006. The early-thirteenth century choir-stalls and associated furniture at Rochester Cathedral. In T. Ayers and T. Tatton-Brown (eds), *Medieval Art and Architecture at Rochester*, 130–45. *BAACT* XXVIII.

Tracy, C. and Harrison, H. 2011. Thomas Spring's chantry and parclose at Lavenham, Suffolk. *BAAJ* 164, 221–59.

Tracy, C. and Woodfield, P. 2003. The Adisham reredos and its significance in the history of early medieval English furnishings. *BAAJ* 156, 27–78.

Tracy, C., Harrison, H. and Miles, D. 2002. The Choir-stalls at the priory church of St Mary, Abergavenny. *BAAJ* 155, 203–54.

Tuck, A. 2004. 'Neville, John, fifth Baron Neville (c.1330–1388)', *ODNB*, http://www.oxforddnb.com/view/article/19945 (Accessed 6 November 2012).

Turner, R., Coldstream, N., Evans, V., Godbert, J. and Sale, B. 2000. St Davids Bishop's Palace, Pembrokeshire. *Antiquaries Journal* 80, 87–194.

Vallance, A. 1947. *Greater English Church Screens* (London).

Venables, E. 1890. Ancient chair, Lincoln Minster. *Archaeological Institute of Great Britain* 47, 406–7.

Verey, D. 1970. *BOE, Gloucestershire and the Vale of the Forest of Dean* (Harmondsworth).

Walcott, M. E. C. 1868. *Sacred Archaeology* (London).

Watkin, A. 1941. Dean Cosyn and Wells Cathedral Miscellanea. *Somerset Record Society* 56.

White, P. 2005. *The South-West Highway Atlas for 1675* (Launceston).

Whitehead, D. 1995. The mid-nineteenth-century restoration of Hereford Cathedral by Lewis Knockalls Cottingham, 1842–1850. In D. Whitehead (ed.), *Medieval Art and Architecture at Hereford Cathedral*, 176–86. *BAACT* XV.

Whitehead, D. 2000. The architectural history of the cathedral since the Reformation. In G. Aylmer and J. Tiller, *Hereford Cathedral. A History*, 241–85 (London).

Williams, G. 1981. Henry de Gower (1278–1347): Bishop and Builder. *Archaeologia Cambrensis* 130, 1–18.

Williams, G. 2004a. 'Gower, Henry (1277/8-1347)', *ODNB*, http://www.oxforddnb.com/view/article/11174?docPos=1 (Accessed 12 September 2012).

Williams, G. 2004b. 'Houghton, Adam (d. 1389)', *ODNB*, www.oxforddnb.com/view/article/13863?docPos=1 (Accessed 12 September 2012).

Williamson, E. W. 1938. Bishop Marshall and his picture. *Friends of Llandaff Cathedral Annual Report*, 10–20.

Willis, B. 1719. *A Survey of the Cathedral-church of Llandaf* (sic.) (London).

Willis, B. 1724. *Parochiale Anglicanum* (London).

Willis, B. 1727–30. *A Survey of the Cathedrals*, 3 vols (London).

Willis, R. 1845. *The Architectural History of Canterbury Cathedral* (London).

Wilson, C. 1980. The Neville Screen. In N. Coldstream and P. Draper (eds), *Medieval Art and Architecture at Durham Cathedral*, 90–104. *BAACT* III.

Wilson, C. 1990. *The Gothic Cathedral: the Architecture of the Great Church, 1130–1530* (New York).

Wilson, C. 1995. The medieval monuments. In P. Collinson, N. Ramsay and M. Sparks (eds), *A History of Canterbury Cathedral*, 451–510 (Oxford).

Wilson, C. 2011. Gothic metamorphosed: the choir of St Augustine's Abbey in Bristol and the renewal of European architecture around 1300. In J. Cannon and B. Williamson (eds), *The Medieval Art, Architecture and History of Bristol Cathedral*, 69–147 (Woodbridge).

Winnington-Ingram, A. J. 1956. *Monumental Brasses in Hereford Cathedral* (Hereford).

Woisetschläger, K. and Krenn, P. (eds). 1982. *Dehio-Handbuch. Die Kunstdenkmäler* Österreichs. *Steiermark (ohne Graz)* (Vienna).

Woodman, F. 1981. *The Architectural History of Canterbury Cathedral* (London).

Wormald, F. 1934. *English Kalendars before A.D. 1100*, I, Texts (London).

Wormald, F. 1939, 1946. *English Benedictine Kalendars after A.D. 1100*, vols 1 & 2 (London).

Wormald, F. 1988. *The throne of Solomon and St Edward's Chair*, 61–69, *Francis Wormald, Collected Writings* vol ii, *Studies in English and Continental Art of the Later Middle Ages* (London).

Worth, T. B. 1878. *Exeter Cathedral and it Restoration* (Exeter).

Yardley, E. 1927. *Menevia Sacra, Archaeologia Cambrensis* Supplemental Vol. (London).

Index

Numbers in italics denote pages with illustrations